A PRIVATE HISTORY
OF AWE

A PRIVATE HISTORY

OF AWE

Scott Russell Sanders

NORTH POINT PRESS

A division of Farrar, Straus and Giroux

New York

North Point Press
A division of Farrar, Straus and Giroux
19 Union Square West, New York 10003

Portions of this book appeared, in slightly different form, in *Image*,
Maize, *The Missouri Review*, *Orion*, and *Witness Magazine*.

Library of Congress Cataloging-in-Publication Data
Sanders, Scott R. (Scott Russell), 1945–
     A private history of awe / Scott Russell Sanders.— 1st ed.
         p.   cm.
     ISBN-13: 978-0-86547-693-6 (alk. paper)
     ISBN-10: 0-86547-693-4 (alk. paper)
         1. Sanders, Scott R. (Scott Russell), 1945–   2. Sanders, Scott R.
(Scott Russell), 1945– —Family.   3. Authors, American—20th century—
Biography.   4. Awe.   I. Title.

PS3569.A5137Z47 2006
813'.54—dc22

                                                                    2005014236

Designed by Cassandra J. Pappas

www.fsgbooks.com

1   3   5   7   9   10   8   6   4   2

For

Eva Mary Solomon Sanders (b. 1916)

Ruth Ann McClure Sanders (b. 1946)

Eva Rachel Sanders Allen (b. 1973)

Elizabeth Rachel Allen (b. 2003)

who pass the flame of life,

generation to generation

Long enough have you dream'd contemptible dreams,
Now I wash the gum from your eyes,
You must habit yourself to the dazzle of the light and of
    every moment of your life.

                      —WALT WHITMAN

There is no way of telling people they are all walking
around shining like the sun.

                      —THOMAS MERTON

Contents

A PRIVATE HISTORY

OF AWE

PROLOGUE

ON A SPRING DAY in 1950, when I was big enough to run about on my own two legs yet still small enough to ride in my father's arms, he carried me onto the porch of a farmhouse in Tennessee and held me against his chest, humming, while thunder roared and lightning flared and rain sizzled around us. On a spring day just over twenty years later, I carried my own child onto the porch of a house in Indiana to meet a thunderstorm, and then, after thirty more years, I did the same with my first grandchild. Murmuring tunes my father had sung to me, I held each baby close, my daughter, Eva, and then, a generation later, her daughter, Elizabeth, and while I studied the baby's newly opened eyes I wondered if she felt what I had felt as a child cradled on the edge of a storm—the tingle of a power that surges through bone and rain and everything. The search for communion with this power has run like a bright thread through all my days.

In these pages I wish to follow that bright thread, from my earliest inklings to my latest intuitions of the force that animates nature and mind. In the world's religions, the animating power may be called God, Logos, Allah, Brahma, Ch'i, Tao, Creator, Holy Ghost, Great Spirit, Universal Mind, Manitou, Wakan-Tanka, or a host of other names. In physics, it may simply be called energy. In other circles it may be known as wildness. Every such name, I believe, is only a finger pointing toward the prime reality, which eludes all descriptions. Without boundaries or name, this ground of being shapes and sustains everything that exists, surges in every heartbeat, fills every breath, yet it is revealed only in flashes, like a darkened landscape lit by lightning, or in a gradual unveiling, like the contours of a forest laid bare in autumn as the leaves fall.

Saints and bodhisattvas may achieve what Christians call mystical union or Buddhists call satori—a perpetual awareness of the force at the heart of things. For these enlightened few, the world is always lit. For the rest of us, such clarity comes only fitfully, in sudden glimpses or slow revelations. Quakers refer to these insights as "openings." When I first heard the term, from a Friend in England who was counseling me about my resistance to the Vietnam War, I thought of how, on an overcast day, sunlight pours through a break in the clouds. After the clouds drift on, eclipsing the sun, the sun keeps shining behind the veil, and the memory of its light shines on in the mind.

This book is my history of openings, from watching a thunderstorm while riding in my father's arms, to witnessing the birth of my first child while holding my wife's hand. The narrative concludes with my daughter's birth because that event made me feel, for the first time, fully adult, no longer merely a husband, no longer merely a man seeking his own way in the world, but a parent, responsible to my daughter and to all children yet to come, generation after generation.

As sudden as lightning or as slow as pregnancy, these passages of clear vision occur only now and then, yet they give meaning to every hour. There is nothing exotic about such awakenings. They come to me in the midst of family and friends, at work or play, on the street, in the woods, in lighted rooms, under moon and stars. I am convinced they come to each of us, whatever our age or circumstances, whatever our beliefs about ultimate things. The enlightenment I wish to describe is ordinary, earthy, within reach of anyone who pays attention.

I wish to recover, so far as possible, the freshness of apprehension that I behold in my granddaughter, Elizabeth. Since her birth two years ago, I have been looking after her one afternoon a week while Eva goes to work, and I have watched the baby meet the world with a clear, open, wondering quality that Buddhists call beginner's mind. When she sleeps she sleeps, and when she wakes she is utterly awake, undistracted by past or future, living wholly in the present.

On the threshold of sixty, I am no beginner. My mind churns with memories, notions, plans, like froth in a riffle on a creek. But occasionally the waves simmer down, the water clears, and I see pebbles gleaming on the bottom of the stream. Or rather, in these clear moments, the fretful *I* vanishes, and there is only the pure gleaming. Such moments, strung together over six decades, make up my inner history, one hidden behind the facts you could read on a résumé. Those six decades began in October of 1945, two months after the bombing of Hiroshima and Nagasaki. Like others of my generation, I grew up during an era of Red scares and missile threats, A-bomb tests and assassinations, civil rights marches and moon landings, and above all the agony of Vietnam. That outer history enters these pages wherever a public figure, such as Martin Luther King, Jr., or a public event, such as the Cuban missile crisis, helped shape my understanding of what it means to be human, what sort of world we inhabit, and how I ought to lead my life.

A kind of history less easily captured in headlines also figures in this narrative, and that is the grand human effort, now several centuries old, to reconcile the perennial wisdom of religion with the story of the universe as told by science. We live in an era, the first since the Middle Ages, when these two seemingly contrary visions might be reconciled. Today, physicists and biologists no longer describe the universe as a machine but as a pulsing web, a dance of energy, less like a clock ticking than like a mind thinking—the same luminous, animate universe, I believe, as the one described by the great mystics and witnessed by anyone who is sufficiently awake.

In recounting passages from my life, whenever possible I have checked my recollections against those of other people, against the record scrawled in my journals or printed in newspapers or captured in photographs. But for the most part I've had to rely on that notorious trickster, memory. I don't pretend to offer a transcript of long-ago conversations, or to document settings and events as a camera might do, but merely to say how these scenes have stayed with me. Out of respect for the privacy of friends and acquaintances who take part in the story, I have changed several names. Otherwise, I have kept faith with memory.

The trickiness of memory is all the more apparent to me because, while writing these pages, I have been helping to care not only for my young granddaughter, who as yet has scarcely any past to remember, but also for my aged mother, who has lost her grip on the past. Some days I would take baby Elizabeth for a ride in the stroller, telling her the names of the flowers we saw in the park, and then I would take Mother for a ride in her wheelchair, stopping to admire white impatiens, red geraniums, violet petunias, golden coreopsis, or purple asters, rehearsing names that Mother had taught me in my childhood but that she herself could no longer recall.

Until she was eighty-three, Mother lived in her own house near my wife and me in Bloomington, Indiana. She gardened, fed birds, taught ballroom dancing, led aerobics classes for elders, tutored children, volunteered for a dozen good causes, sold china plates and porcelain jewelry she had painted, read Scriptures from the pulpit at church, gadded about town in her red car, traveled overseas. She was a ball of fire, in the words of my father, whose own life ended at sixty-four. Outliving him by decades, Mother carried her memories gaily. Then, as she approached ninety, suffering through surgeries and strokes, she lost hold of what happened yesterday, forgot what happened during her long widowhood, forgot her years of marriage and child rearing and her growing up.

Once a vibrant woman who loved nothing more than talking and dancing, by the time I finished this book Mother was curled in a nursing home bed or hunched in a wheelchair, unable to speak. When she still had a few words, I would show her old snapshots of family and friends, and she would cry, "Oh, those people!" But who the people might be and where the pictures might have been taken she couldn't say. When I reminded her of stories from her own childhood, she would give me a puzzled look and ask, "Where did you hear that?" I heard the stories from her, time and again, and now I carry them after she has let them go.

If I live long enough, I will eventually forget my own stories, which is one reason I write them down. The mind's grip on language and meaning is less secure than the body's grip on life. If you doubt that, visit a nursing home, as I have been doing frequently for more than a decade, first to watch my wife's mother perish from Alzheimer's disease, then to watch my wife's father wither away from congestive heart failure, and now to see my own mother sink into a wordless stupor. Their dying has made me an elder, whether I am ready for the role or not. And elders have a duty to tell the younger generations what they have learned from life, whether the lessons be great or small. So I have been moved to write this book as much by the departure of parents as by the arrival of a grandchild. I have been moved to write by an awareness that the mind's acuity, built up over a lifetime, is precarious and fleeting.

On a wall above the desk where I write hangs an octagonal wooden plaque, the size of a large serving tray, carved with grooves that form concentric rings around a central rosette. It is a miniature replica of a stone labyrinth laid out around 1200 on the floor of Chartres Cathedral in France. Pilgrims who lacked the time or money or gumption to walk all the way to the Holy Land could follow the stone path in their search for God. Unlike a maze, which is designed to get you lost, a labyrinth is designed to lead you home. Home, here, is your true self, the abiding source of all that rises and passes, the sun forever shining behind the clouds.

The wood of my miniature labyrinth is maple, as pale as corn silk, finished with an oil that leaves a satin sheen on the surface and catches light in the fluted rings. If your eye or finger traces the groove from an opening along one edge, it will lead you, after many turns, to the rosette chiseled at the center. The rosette might be a burst or a splash, and the rings might be ripples radiating from a stone dropped in a pool, or sound waves spreading from a struck bell, or photons scattering from a supernova, or quarks seething outward from the Big Bang.

The pattern is that of a mandala, a Sanskrit word meaning "circle." In Hinduism and Buddhism, a mandala is an image of wholeness—of the self, of humankind, of all living creatures, of earth and air and fire and water, of the entire Creation. Tibetan monks draw elaborate mandalas using colored sand, and when they have finished, after days of painstaking work, they ceremonially rub out the pattern and scatter the grains as a reminder that the mandala is only a picture of the sacred unity, not the unity itself.

Even as a child, before I could imagine death, I sensed that the force I thrilled to in thunderstorms could crush me. Now, of course, I know that everything I make, everything I love, everything I am will eventually be scattered like the sand of the mandala. My wonder has always been clouded by fear. The word that comes closest to embracing the dread as well as the reverence, the shadow side as well as the light, is *awe*. The passages in my life that evoke this rapturous, fearful, bewildering emotion seem to me the ones worth recalling.

FIRE

1

WHEN MY FATHER wrapped me in his arms and carried me onto the screened porch of our farmhouse in Tennessee during a thunderstorm, he said nothing about the booming and blowing, merely hummed a tune, a sound I confused with the purr of the rain. It was as though he had swallowed a bit of thunder, which now rumbled in his throat.

Mama thrust her head from the doorway and said, "You'll catch a chill."

"We're doing just fine," Dad answered.

Mama paused, skeptically, for she believed that disaster could strike at any moment, from any direction. She frowned, as if doubting she would ever see us again among the living, and then she withdrew inside.

Dad tucked me closer and pulled his baggy hunting jacket around me. I shivered against him, less from cold than from excitement. Rain drummed on the tin roof of the porch, rattled in the downspouts, hissed on the new grass with the sound of bacon frying in a pan. Wind hurled twigs and last year's leaves across the yard.

This year's leaves, no bigger than the paws on a kitten, were just breaking out on the trees, so it must have been early spring, most likely March. In October I would turn five. I had climbed the smaller trees— pecan and persimmon, sweet gum and tupelo—but the huge oak out by the blacktop road I could only gaze at in wonder, for its lowest branches loomed far beyond my reach. It was the tallest thing I knew, taller than the barn, taller than the windmill in the pasture, taller than the spire on our church.

I was watching that oak sway in the storm, its fat limbs thrashing as if it were a sapling, when suddenly a flash and boom split the air. I lurched in my father's arms, and he jumped, too, but held me tight. My ears rang. Bumps rose on my skin. I felt a heart pounding—whether Dad's or mine I couldn't tell.

He broke off humming to whistle. "Sweet Jesus, will you look at that!"

I blinked but could see only a white glare. I touched my eyes to make sure they were still in place. Gradually shapes thickened in the brightness and I could make out the porch railing, the gravel path stretching away into the yard, the flower bed with petunias bobbing their bedraggled pink heads in the rain, and out by the road, the great oak snapped like a stick, its top shattered on the ground, a charred streak running down the wet gray stub of the trunk.

"What happened, Daddy?" I asked.

"Lightning hit the old guy."

"Will he die?"

"He's done for, buddy. I'll have to cut him up."

His voice shook in a way I'd never heard before. I asked no more questions but only snuggled against his chest, craving his warmth and weight. Soon he began humming again, and I could hear the rain pattering more quietly on the porch roof and thunder grumbling farther and farther away, and I could watch lightning flicker beyond cotton fields at the edge of the world, and I could see the oak scattered across the yard in scraps of bark, broken limbs, and shards of wood the color of bread.

One moment the great tree had stood there by the road, as solid as my father, bigger than anything else I knew, and the next moment it was gone. That erasure haunts me still, over half a century later, long after our Tennessee farm vanished under a subdivision and my father died. I still ring with the astonishment I felt that day when the sky cracked open to reveal a world where even grownups were tiny and houses were toys and wood and skin and everything was made of light.

I learned the words *die* and *dead* that spring of 1950, at the age of four. From a litter of kittens, one quit nursing, quit mewing, quit moving, and the same happened with two runts from a litter of piglets, only the sound the piglets made before they quit squirming was a puny squeal. They lay in their bed of straw like cast-off shoes.

Mama spoke with me about this baffling change from motion to stillness. She had grown up in Chicago as the daughter of a physician who kept an office in the house, and she had met death early in the faces of desperately sick people knocking at the front door. She did not tell me then, would not tell me for years, that when she was eight her mother died of tuberculosis. She would also tell me later how her father sat in the curtained parlor with the black leather doctor's bag in his lap, weeping because he could not heal his own wife. At eight, Mama took on the care of her two younger brothers, and took on the fear that if she relaxed her vigil for an instant, they might come to harm. If her own mother could be snatched away, who around her was safe?

She never had a chance to relax her vigil, for no sooner had her brothers survived childhood than they climbed into planes and flew off to war. The letters they wrote on onionskin paper and mailed home from distant lands were her only assurance that they were still alive. In the meantime, she married a rascal with wavy red hair and a southern drawl, figuring she could cure him of his reckless taste for boxing, gambling, motorcycles, cigarettes, and booze. Then along came my sister, Sandra, and me, and we gave her two reasons for worry that she would never exhaust. As though the sirens she'd heard all those years ago in the streets of Chicago kept blaring in her head, Mama worried that doom could steal up on us through germs on a doorknob, feet wet from rain, a rat drowned in the well, gravel trucks barreling down the county road, milk gone bad.

Dad had grown up on a farm in Mississippi, where he met death frequently in the barn and chicken coop and fields, and twice met it in his own family, when a young sister was taken by diphtheria and a brother was crushed under the wheels of a train. The sister he had scarcely known, and five other sisters remained to fuss over him. But of his four brothers, the one crushed by a train was his favorite, a year older, so much of a look-alike for my father that the two had often been mistaken for twins. At dances, they could switch partners and the girls would never be the wiser. As though to make up for the loss of this brother, afterward Dad lived twice as hard, got in fights, drove the red clay roads in a cloud of dust, tipped the bottles back, kept on dancing at parties until the band packed away their instruments.

Although my father gave me the dead brother's name, Russell, for my own middle name, he rarely spoke of him. The only stories he told about himself were those that made him out to be a tough guy, a daredevil, or a card. He never admitted pain of any sort, past or present. He seemed to think that explaining loss or fear was women's work. And so, when the kitten and piglets died, he left the talking to Mama. Instead of telling me about death, he let me feel the bodies, cold and still, before he buried them in the woods.

We enter the world as warm and squirming bodies, empty of ideas and full of sensation. In her first weeks of life, my granddaughter listens to her stomach and ignores the clock. Elizabeth knows nothing of death, nothing of past or future, knows only the intriguing present. When I carry her outside on a blustery day, she gives herself to the wind and the chatter of leaves. When I sing her a rollicking song and dance her across the room, she bobs in my arms and grins. Every second, neurons are knitting pathways through her brain, and soon enough she will begin sorting the world into categories and concepts. But for now, she still dwells wholly in her body, touching and tasting everything within reach, craning around to see whatever is to be seen, listening to each new sound. Her face reveals a pure astonishment, untainted as yet by fear.

If we live long enough to lose memory and language, as my mother now is losing hers, we leave the world as we entered it, full of sensation and empty of ideas. Eighty-six when Elizabeth is born, Mother cannot tell you her own age, the year, the month, the day, or the hour; she knows only that darkness outside the window means it's time for sleep and brightness means it's time for waking. Nurses bring her medicines; aides invite her to meals; the shuffle of residents past her apartment door alerts her to a video or slide show or gospel sing about to start in the lounge. A woman who always loved to read, Mother can no longer make her way through a novel, because she cannot remember the story from one paragraph to the next. She cannot decipher a newspaper, write a note, or operate a television. By punching the memory button on the telephone, she can still manage to call my wife and me, and this she does five or ten times a day. As often as not when we answer, Mother cannot tell us what she wants; she merely conveys, by her scramble for words, that she is lonely and confused.

The only weekly outing she still makes is to church, where she is comforted by the rituals and hymns, although she cannot follow the sermons. I sense that her mind is no longer spacious enough to accommodate awe. Her wonder at the gift of life has been overwhelmed by anger over what she has lost, and by fear that what remains will soon be snatched away. The knowledge she built up over a long lifetime is collapsing, but she still holds firmly to the discovery of death. She has not forgotten that life eventually comes to an end—not only for oaks and cats and pigs but also for people—a sobering truth that she explained to me when I was a boy, and one that baby Elizabeth, so new to life, has yet to learn.

On our farm in Tennessee, Mama presided over the house and yard. Dad was at ease only in the barn and fields and woods. Indoors, he paced about or sat in his easy chair folding the newspaper with sharp crackling sounds. On weekdays he went off to a factory where men made tires. I had never seen the factory, never would see it, and I could only imagine a room where Dad poured black pudding into big pans shaped like doughnuts, then cooked the pudding until it turned into rubber, then took out the warm tires and put them on cars with a wrench.

At home he never cooked, rarely entered the kitchen except to eat. But he did use wrenches, as well as hammers, screwdrivers, knives, pliers, saws, and other tools he kept on a workbench in the barn. Something we owned was always breaking—the washing machine ground to a halt, a weld broke on the plow, the car's engine sputtered, a door lock jammed, a pipe sprang a leak—and Dad was always fixing it. When the fixing went well, he sang one of his country tunes; when it went poorly, he growled; and when it went badly, he threw down his tools, fetched a dog, and headed for the woods.

I never tagged along with him when he was riled.

"Daddy's got a temper," Mama often said. "It goes with his red hair."

Sandra, four years older than I, also had red hair, wavy like Dad's, and longer. But she never got mad. And even though Mama's hair was brown, sometimes she lost her temper, too, and spanked Sandra and me for being naughty. But her blows were more like pats, meant to shame rather than hurt us. And even at her angriest, Mama never rivaled Dad, who burst with fury now and again the way that oak burst with lightning.

I didn't think it strange that Dad called the oak an old guy. He would introduce me to trees by name—black walnut, shagbark hickory, magnolia, beech—and then to each of them he would say, "This is my son, Scott," as if I were meeting a man on the church steps rather than a tree in the woods. No living creature was ever an *it* to my father, but always *he* or *she*, *him* or *her*. "He's an ornery cuss," he would say of the billy goat. "She's a treasure," he would say of a pear tree when the branches sagged with fruit.

If it was hunting season when Dad stomped off to the woods to cool down, he took a shotgun along. The jacket he wrapped me in during the thunderstorm smelled of gunpowder, tobacco, sweat, and blood. The rusty scent of blood I recognized from watching my father skin and clean rabbits, pheasants, and quail, which he carried home slung in the pouch at the back of his green jacket.

I had blood inside of me. I knew this from cutting my finger and scraping my knee. It flowed beneath my skin, like water in the creek behind our house, where crayfish scuttled backward to hide under rocks and catfish nosed along the bottom fanning their fins. Water, though, was clear, and blood, when it leaked out, was shiny red, as bright as the lipstick Mama wore when she and Dad went dancing. Dried blood turned brown and dark, the color of dirt. Maybe all the dirt in our yard, our garden, the potato patch, the dog run, the cow pasture, the far fields, and the deep woods, maybe all the dirt in the world had come from blood leaking through skin and fur. Maybe that was why Dad said the dirt was alive, because of that spilled blood.

Sandra's red hair came in handy whenever we decided to go to the farm next door and taunt Mr. Jackson's bull. She kept her scarf on until we drew up beside the barbed-wire fence. Then we pulled handfuls of grass and called to the bull, a lumbering black boxy animal that seemed as big as our car. When he quit grazing long enough to lift his muzzle and look in our direction, Sandra untied the scarf and shook out her flaming hair and we tore off running, sure the bull would be charging after us with lowered horns. We didn't wait around to see. We just hoped the fence would hold when he barreled into it.

The fear felt good. It was like a wind blowing through me, cleaning the cobwebs from my head. Sometimes with Sandra or one of the neighbor kids, sometimes alone, I hunted for ways to scare myself. I jumped out of the hayloft. I crept behind the cow's hooves, which could lash out at me. I climbed high into backyard trees until the limbs bent under me. I stole into the billy goat's pen, shouted his name, then clambered out over the gate before he could butt me. I snuck into the windowless room at the back of the house, which Mama called Blue-beard's Closet, and which she filled with boxes, out-of-season clothes, broken-down tables and chairs awaiting repairs, and a papier-mâché dress dummy lacking arms and head. I peered through cracks in the wooden cover on the well, and imagined falling in. I slithered under the porch, where our dogs lay panting on hot days, down among the spiders and snakes. If I crawled back out into the sunlight and stood up quickly while holding my breath, the day would go dark and I would fall. But I soon woke again, which fooled me into thinking I would always wake.

An older neighbor boy named Joe Burns often sat with me inside the screened porch and read aloud G.I. Joe comic books while I studied the pictures. On those inky pages, bombs exploded, tanks flattened buildings, bullets zinged, and bodies went flying. The bodies with slanted eyes were Japs, Joe Burns explained, and the bodies with mean eyes were Nazis. The job of G.I. Joe was to kill as many of them as he could.

As he read the comics, Joe Burns imitated the ka-boom of grenades, the rat-a-tat-tat of machine guns, the snort of engines, the yelling of soldiers as they fought and fell. He knew every kind of airplane and ship by its outline on the page. He knew the names of every battlefield. He knew just where to stick a bayonet and showed me, jabbing a finger under the arch of my ribs. He knew so much about the war, in fact, and he looked so grown-up, with a stubble of beard sprouting on his chin, that I decided he and the famous GI must have been the very same Joe.

When I asked him if this was so, he gave a little nod, almost too slight to see. Then he leaned close and warned me to keep it secret, because he still had a slew of enemies out there. With a jerk of his chin, he sent my gaze through the screen of the porch toward the sheds, trees, bushes, and rows of cotton. There were plenty of places out there to hide enemies, presumably Japs and Nazis left over from the war.

I promised Joe Burns I'd never breathe a word. He rubbed my scalp through its burr of brown hair and opened a new comic. Before he started reading, I asked him what happened to all those dead bodies after the war.

He grunted. "The government buried them with little white crosses on top."

I remembered my father digging a hole in the woods for the kitten and piglets, and I thought about how much bigger it would have to be to hold Joe Burns, or even me.

Now I listened to the adventures of G.I. Joe and pored over the pic-

tures with a new fascination, for I could see in the soldier's bulging
arms and square chin the features of this neighbor from down the road,
a boy who sat right on my porch in T-shirt and jeans and read to me
through the long afternoons while locusts and crickets sawed away in
the grass. And if Joe Burns could go across the sea and fight in wars and
become the hero of comic books, why couldn't I do the same when I
grew up?

On summer afternoons toward dusk, or any time before a storm rolled
in, the trees and grass turned the color of army uniforms. Olive drab,
according to Mama, who knew the name of every color from sewing
and painting. Along the road into Memphis, men wearing olive drab
pants and coats and hats sometimes stood with one hand balled into a
fist and a thumb sticking out. If Mama was driving, she would gesture
at Sandra and me, as if to say she had a carful, and keep on going. But
if Dad was driving, he always stopped to give the men a lift—not because they'd been in the war but because he stopped for every hitch-
hiker. He'd spent too many hours standing in the sun and rain with his
thumb out, he told me, to pass up anybody who needed a ride.

Mama warned him it was dangerous to pick up strangers. Dad
shrugged and said it was dangerous to get out of bed in the morning
because a meteor might smack you, or to eat fish because you might get
a bone caught in your throat. Mama started telling him about a man
who'd come to her father's office with a bone stuck in his throat, but
Dad only laughed, because he didn't believe danger could ever catch up
with him.

The men who climbed into the car wearing uniforms often smelled
of mothballs, a smell I knew from opening a wardrobe in Bluebeard's
Closet where Mama kept our winter coats. Sometimes the hitchhikers
brought in a whiff like vinegar or cough syrup, a smell that I caught
now and again at bedtime on Dad's breath, especially when he and
Mama had been quarreling, and that I would eventually recognize as
whiskey or wine. Poison breath, Mama called it. Dad asked the men
where they were headed, who their people were, what sort of work

they did, where they had spent the war. Some talked a lot; some talked a little; and a few wouldn't say more than the name of the place they wished to go. Dad could usually draw words out of anybody, even shy kids, even old-timers who'd lost their teeth. So the silent riders puzzled me. I learned these men were called veterans, and almost every family had one or more, except for the families whose soldiers had all died.

Mama's two brothers had flown in bombers over the South Seas. She had fretted every minute they were gone, sure they would be shot down. One of the brothers had failed the eye test for flight school when he first applied. So he ate pounds of carrots, took the test again, and passed, but for a while his skin turned orange. When we visited these uncles in Chicago, I was disappointed to find the one with bad eyes was no longer orange. I saw on a mantelpiece a photograph of the two uncles in bathing suits, leaning against a palm tree on a beach of white sand. They showed me bracelets made from seashells washed up on that beach. They showed me a dagger with a pearl handle from Borneo, and coins from China with square holes in the center. They showed me their uniforms, zipped inside nylon bags.

Uncles on my father's side of the family also had uniforms hanging in their closets, but Dad didn't, for he had spent the war at a factory in Mississippi building bombs. Like the tire plant, this was a place I would never see but could only imagine. I knew from G.I. Joe comic books the shape of bombs, like a fat sausage with a point at one end and fins at the other, but I could only guess what my father stuffed them with to make them blow up cities and tanks.

If I was playing outside when a plane flew over our farm, to scare myself I pretended it might be an enemy bomber, flown by men with hard eyes, men who didn't know the war had ended just before I was born. As soon as I heard the buzz, I went running for the house, as fast as ever I ran from Mr. Jackson's bull. If I reached the steps and banged through the screen door before the plane droned overhead, I got to keep on living. If I was too slow, if the plane caught up with me in the open, I had to die and tumble down and count to fifty, breathing dust, before I got to rise again.

2

ONE SUNDAY in the fall, soon after my fifth birthday, Dad set fire to a ditch bank where the dry stalks of weeds rustled in a mild breeze. He made me keep well back, but I could see the tongue of fire licking forward, leaving a trail of black. He carried a shovel for tamping out any sparks that might fly onto the nearby hayfield. I traipsed along behind, enthralled by the flames.

The smoke idled up, twisting in the wind, like smoke from the Pall Mall cigarettes Dad pulled, one after another, from a packet in the bib of his overalls. Coffin nails, Mama called them when she and Dad fought at night after they thought Sandra and I were asleep, and she hissed that his drinking and smoking would land us all in the poorhouse if they didn't kill him first.

Dad never let up on smoking, not even now beside the burning ditch. When he needed both hands for the shovel, he crimped the cigarette in one corner of his mouth and widened the opposite corner to draw in breath. As the breeze picked up, he used the shovel more and more often, running here and there to beat down flames that kept escaping from the ditch. Gasping for air, he finally threw down his cigarette and stomped on it. Then a gust of wind flung a burning stalk into the hayfield, where grass began to smolder. Dad looked from the smoke at his feet to the smoke in the field and yelled at me, "Go ask Mama to call the fire station! Quick, now. Go!"

I set off running toward our house, repeating aloud, "Fire station! Fire station!"

Mama made the call, told Sandra and me to stay in the house, then grabbed two burlap sacks from the barn, dipped them in the cow's water trough, and rushed out to join Dad. After waiting inside for a few heartbeats, Sandra and I hurried to the field, where we found our parents shouting at one another and slapping flames with the gunnysacks. The fire was outracing them, heading for our house, when a red truck pulled up with siren blaring, and men in rubber suits began pumping water from a fat hose.

Our parents stood side by side, watching and panting, the muddy sacks tangled at their feet. After every spark had been drowned and the hose had been folded away, the firemen chided my father for burning ditches on a windy day. I expected him to get mad, as he did whenever Mama scolded him. I expected him to say the day hadn't been all that windy when he lit the fire, and so they could just climb down off their high horses. But instead he looked out over the charred field and said he was sorry to have caused them so much bother, especially on a Sunday.

When the truck pulled away, Mama fussed at Sandra and me for leaving the house. Then she leaned into Dad and he wrapped his arms around her, and she cried into his shoulder, and both of them trembled. I was used to seeing Mama shake. But if even Dad could be afraid, then maybe Mama was right, and the world was a thicket of dangers.

Realizing that my parents did not run the world set me up to welcome news of parents who did. Later on, when I began to absorb the teachings of Bible and church, I would cling to God as the father who could save me from all danger. Had I been reared Catholic or Eastern Orthodox instead of country Protestant, I might have clung to Mary as the all-forgiving, all-healing, infinitely patient mother. Not having learned about those heavenly parents yet, but having glimpsed death, I sought reassurance in the company of anything that breathed.

Mr. Jackson's bull was one of the few animals within reach that I never touched. I wrestled with our dogs and lolled with the cats. I petted the rabbits we kept in cages. I ruffled the feathers of hens as I retrieved their eggs. Poking an arm between the slats of the pigpen, I scratched the sow behind her floppy ears. I even brushed my fingers over the fearsome goat, careful to keep the fence between me and his knobby head. I stroked the taffy-colored flanks of the Guernsey cow my father milked morning and evening. Now and again he let me squat on a stool and tug at her rubbery teats, shooting a white stream into the pail.

I cupped in my palm the toads I found under the porch, running a finger over their bumpy backs, even though Sandra warned me they would give me warts. Frogs were harder to catch, and they leapt away if I eased my grip. The turtles I hoisted from the ground rowed their feet in the air, and the fish I pulled from the pond gulped and jerked. Salamanders wriggled in my hand, snakes writhed, grasshoppers twitched.

Whenever I heard a thump against the picture window in our front room, I ran outside to lift a stunned bird from the grass, and I held it snugly, smoothing the feathers, until it shuddered back to life, and then I let it fly away. One of these birds was black on top, orange on the breast, white on the belly, a pattern I carried in my head for years before discovering its name: American redstart. Long before learning their names, I also carried in my head the shapes and coloring of robins, cedar waxwings, chickadees, goldfinches, juncos, all collected from the grass outside our window, as I carried in my hands the memory of their slight heft and racing hearts. A few of the birds never stirred again after striking the window, and these I buried in a corner of the vegetable garden.

The only pheasants or quail I ever touched were those my father brought back limp from the fields and laid on newspaper spread over his workbench in the barn. Before he cleaned the birds for cooking, he let me study their feathers, which seemed to me as glorious as any gown a king or queen might wear.

The bird dog, Bob, kept to himself inside a fence, unless my father took him out for hunting or training. Bob would laze around, eating and sleeping, until Dad came out the back door and pumped the shot-gun. Then Bob leapt against the fence and whined until Dad let him loose. "Hunt," Dad said, and Bob would crisscross ahead of him over the fields, sniffing for birds. If a flying saucer had landed in front of him, he wouldn't have paid it any mind unless it was loaded with pheas-ants or quail. When Bob smelled a bird, his body stiffened, nose pointed forward and tail stuck out behind as straight as a clothesline. He stayed in that pose until the shotgun boomed or Dad told him to *go*. Then he streaked away to fetch a downed bird or find another one. He obeyed every word Dad said and ignored everybody else.

Bob was a working dog, Dad said, not a playing dog. For play we had a lanky, shaggy, gentle collie named Rusty. Mama wouldn't allow Rusty indoors, wouldn't allow any dog inside the house, not if he was scrubbed as clean as a surgeon. So Rusty waited near the back door on a spot he'd worn down to the bare dirt, or in hot weather he waited underneath the porch, and as soon as I stepped outside he sprang to his feet and trotted beside me wherever I went. When I scared myself more than I had bargained for, I reached down and wove my fingers into Rusty's thick fur, and the fear drained away.

I kept reaching for anything that breathed, even after a snake I found in a backyard apple tree bit my foot and swelled up my leg as fat and red as a ham. Mama washed the bite and wrapped me in blankets. When I couldn't stop shivering, Dad carried me to the car and drove the whole family to the hospital, where the doctor's hand touching my swollen leg felt like an ice cube tray straight out of the freezer. Maybe the doctor gave me a shot, or maybe I fainted, but in any case I went away—not like the slow drifting into sleep but more like the sudden conking out when I would hold my breath and stand up quickly and tumble down in the grass.

When I came back, lying there on the stiff hospital sheets, my leg throbbing, and I saw the ring of grownups gazing down at me, and saw the panic on Mama's face and the crease of concern even on Dad's face, I sensed that one day, after one tumble in the grass, I might not wake up. I thought of the birds that didn't move again after crashing into the window. What if I crashed into some barrier I couldn't see, and fell down like a stone, and never stirred again? No sooner had this awful notion crept into the light than I shoved it back in the shadows.

When Dad borrowed June Bug, one of Mr. Jackson's draft horses, to plow a field too wet for the tractor, he set me onto her broad swaying back, and I balanced there with my legs splayed as on a carpeted floor, while June Bug lumbered on.

Spying me perched up there, Mama ran outside and hollered, "Sandy, you get him down this minute. He'll fall off and break his neck."

Dad only laughed. Leaning close to the ear of the horse, he murmured, "You wouldn't hurt my boy, would you, old beauty?"

June Bug cocked a brown, gleaming, tranquil eye at Dad and plodded on. The huge bunching of muscles beneath me, the slow rocking of the spine, set me thinking what it might be like to ride a boat on the open sea. But the hot, earthy smell of the horse belonged unmistakably to land. The short nap of hair felt dry to my touch when we left for plowing, and wet on our return. During the plowing itself I stood on the ground and watched, because Dad wouldn't make a working horse carry even a slip of a boy like me.

With clicks of his tongue, calls of "Gee!" and "Haw!" when he wanted June Bug to pull right or left, and light flicks of the reins on her shoulders, Dad guided the horse back and forth across the field. For a few paces after turning at the end of a row, having caught his breath, he would croon a line or two from the songs he often sang to me at bedtime. As the soil peeled up like a black wave behind the share, crows hopped over the new furrows, snapping up worms and bugs.

I stood there taking in the sheen on the crows' beaks, the heaving of the horse, the rise and fall of my father's voice, the breeze driving clouds and tousling my hair, and the aroma of freshly turned soil as of something right out of the oven. These sensations went deep into me, along with the shapes and textures of skin, shell, scales, feathers, leaves, bark, and fur. They were the first alphabet I learned, before letters or words. I still don't have words to say what attracted me to the life of woods and fields, except to call it the holy shimmer at the heart of things.

Nothing is quite real for baby Elizabeth until she clamps it between her toothless gums. If I bring within the orbit of her pudgy arms a book, flower, cat, cup, or anything at all, she will latch on with both hands and lean forward, jaws agape, to gnaw and taste.

For me at five, nothing was quite real until I could say its name. *Redstart. Robin. Furrow. Plowshare. Hatchet. Horse.* Instead of tasting the thing itself, I longed to hold its name in my mouth. Although I was learning words at a dizzying speed, I still lacked names for most things in the world. Morning, noon, and night, I asked anyone within earshot: What's it called?

I would ask my father the name of every tool in the barn, every piece of harness, every part in the car. *Drawknife. Martingale. Carburetor.* On our walks, I begged to know the names of garden plants, crops in the fields, trees in the woods, and so I learned peanuts and okra, sorghum and burley, ironwood and sweet gum.

After I wore out my father's patience, I would go ask my mother the names of flowers and spices. *Zinnia. Peony. Oregano. Basil.* I would point at things and ask her to name the color. *Magenta. Chartreuse. Periwinkle.* Rusty's fur, she told me, was cinnamon, so the name of a color could be the name of a spice. The olive drab of army uniforms could also be named khaki, she said, if you weren't particular about how you used words. Mama was particular. Where some people saw merely cloth, she taught me to see linen, muslin, cashmere, denim, calico. Cats, too, could be calico, if they were spotted like the cloth, or they could be tabby if they were striped. Even paper could be called tissue paper, carbon paper, waxed paper, toilet paper, or newsprint.

Mama was the one who taught me that my uncles' wartime letters, which she kept folded in a box in her dresser and took out now and again to show me, were written on a kind of paper called onionskin.

After learning that word, I said it aloud, over and over, to make sure I remembered it. The whispery thin pages of the family Bible, which Dad held in his lap and read a lesson from before Sunday dinner, were also onionskin. At first I imagined that the paper was actually made from onions, like the ones Mama sliced at the kitchen counter, but she said no, it was made from trees and rags. It only looked like the skin of onions. Language is full of words comparing one thing with another, she told me, like Papaw's potbelly, or Sandra's ponytail, or the cowlick on the back of my head.

Once, when Mama was paring apples for pie, I asked her what she would call the shine on a knife, and she thought a moment before answering, "A gleam." How about the shine on the kitchen table? Again she thought a moment: "A glint." And how about the shine in a person's eye? "A sparkle." And how about the shine on the skin of an apple? At that, she shooed me out the door.

When Mama ran out of patience I pestered Sandra, who didn't know as many names, but the ones she did know she would write down on a page or show me in a book. In the afternoons when Sandra came home from second grade and then from third, she played school with me. Sitting on the screened porch where Joe Burns read war comics to me, she taught me the alphabet, like the shapes of so many kinds of birds, and then she taught me whole words, and then sentences. If I worked hard, she promised, before long I would be reading comics to myself.

And sure enough, where the ink marks on a page had once seemed like squashed bugs, now they came alive as letters. Soon I could read the billboards for Coca-Cola and the Burma-Shave signs beside the road. I could lean over Mama's shoulder and sound out the lines in a book, even if I didn't understand most of the words, or I could lean over Dad's shoulder and sound out pieces in the newspaper, until he told me, firmly, to quit. The feel of each distinct word in my mouth was like the taste of so many foods.

Language seemed all the more mysterious to me as a child because the same name could be attached to quite different sorts of things. There was a frog in a horse's hoof, a frog in the pond, and sometimes, when I coughed, a frog in my throat. Some trees were gnarly, according to Dad, and some people were gnarly, like the old men at the feed store with tobacco juice dribbling down their chins, and some of the jobs on the farm were gnarly, like pulling twine out of gears in the hay baler. The metal star I found in the toy box was a jack, but so was the pump Dad used to lift the car when he changed the oil, and so was the young man wearing a mustache and crown in a deck of cards.

At least you could grab hold of all those jacks. But what about things you couldn't touch? What about the feelings that sailed through me the way clouds sailed through the sky? It turned out that even these slippery moods had names. "You're looking glum this morning," Mama might say to me. Or Dad might say, "You're looking as sly as the cat that swallowed the canary." Or Sandra might say, "You tattled because you're jealous." And just like that, my swirling inner weather took on names—jealous, sly, glum. There was a whole universe inside, filled with things I couldn't lay hands on but real nonetheless. They had to be real, because other people could read them in my face, as plain as day.

The dictionary was full of names for things you couldn't touch. Bound in red buckram—Mama gave me the name of the cloth—and as thick as a loaf of bread, the dictionary was one of the few books we kept in our house, aside from Bibles, detective novels, and repair manuals. On the cover was a three followed by five zeros, telling how many definitions could be found inside. When I asked Dad how big that number was, he said it was nearly as many as the number of people in Memphis. I was amazed. There seemed to me more people in Memphis than stars in the sky. When we drove into the city, our car could hardly move along the streets for all the crowds.

If you tried learning all those words, you could dive into the dictionary and never come out. You'd have to be dragged out, like a boy who drowned in a stock pond down the road from us, and when he was pulled onto the shore his body was draped in green weeds. My body, when it was dragged out of the dictionary, would be draped in words. The only way to avoid that fate, I decided, was to set myself a limit—say, ten definitions—and, having reached it, to swim up out of those closely printed pages, shut the red buckram cover, and go paste my new words onto the world.

Although I can remember learning particular words—onionskin, khaki, calico—I can't remember learning to speak. Instead, I recall how, for each of my own children, babbling turned into speech. I recall how Eva would lie in her crib in the early morning and practice making every sound the human voice box can produce, as if she were playing all the keys of a piano. And now, while taking care of Eva's daughter each week, I get to hear the same music, as baby Elizabeth tries out her own brand-new voice.

One day in her sixth month, I'm feeding Elizabeth pureed sweet potatoes, and the taste of them is so intense that she screws up her face with every bite, before gaping for the next spoonful. Eva, a biologist who knows such things, tells me that babies have a hundred times as many taste buds as adults do. That's why, on trying a new food, they sometimes grimace as though in ecstasy. At one point, mouth full, Elizabeth purses her lips and makes them buzz, the way I used to do when I wanted to imitate the motors of airplanes. Flecks of sweet potato spray over her bib, her tray, my face, and the floor. Never having seen her do this before, I'm charmed, so I don't mind cleaning up. Elizabeth is so pleased with herself that she buzzes again and again.

Later, she is sitting on a quilt on the floor, fiddling with wooden blocks, when she mutters, "Buh, buh, buh."

Flopped on the floor beside her, I say, "Hey, bubba! What's up, bubba bubba?"

Elizabeth falls silent and stares at me blankly, as though trying to imagine where I have landed from, before she returns to her blocks.

Minutes pass. I'm on the couch, folding diapers still warm from the dryer, when I hear her pronounce distinctly, "Bubba bubba bubba."

"Tell me about it, kiddo," I say.

Elizabeth fixes her gray eyes on me and repeats once more, but only once more, "Bubba bubba bubba." What she means by it, I have no idea, but I feel certain she is groping for words.

•   •   •

No sooner would I think I had learned the name of everything on our farm than something strange would turn up. I might find that spiky thingamabob called a jack rattling around at the bottom of the toy chest, or I might find a hat called a fedora on a shelf in my father's closet. Wandering the fields, I might scare up some animal I had never seen before—a possum, a mole, a newt. And who could name all the shapes of clouds that sailed over our house?

When salesmen came to the front door, they often peddled outlandish gadgets—a kaleidoscope or a mechanical apple peeler, a back scratcher or a needle threader. My parents would return from the store with strange stuff—cotter pins, a rat-tail file, a pressure cooker, a crochet hook—or Sandra would come home from school with news of colors and countries I had never heard of. I began to suspect that out there in the ever-expanding world, and even right here under my nose, there was an endless supply of unfamiliar items whose names I would have to learn if I was ever going to speak to them.

Even familiar things wriggled free of their names. A horse, it turned out, was not simply a horse. When my father took me to livestock auctions, I learned that horses might be Thoroughbreds, Appaloosas, Arabians, Shetlands, Tennessee Walkers, or dozens of other breeds. The big-shouldered draft horses like the ones Mr. Jackson owned were called Percherons. His were mares, Dad told me, but Percherons could also be stallions or geldings, and the young ones could be fillies or colts. Mr. Jackson's Percherons were a color Dad called dappled gray, like the shadows of leaves on our gravel driveway, but horses came in almost as many colors as breeds—buckskin and bay, sorrel and roan, pinto and palomino, chestnut and dun. Any horse could be divided, like a person, into head, neck, back, and legs. But a horse's hind leg, say, could also be divided into flank, thigh, hock, cannon bone, fetlock, pastern, and hoof.

When the farrier came by in his truck to put new shoes on the Percherons, he showed me that a hoof can be divided into heel, toe, coronet, frog, and wall, and the horny wall can be divided into three layers, and each layer can be divided . . . on and on it went, as if, no matter how thinly you sliced the world, you'd keep uncovering something that needed a name. But what if you kept on dividing things until you reached the very bottom? What would you find there, and what would you call it? What if you came upon something that had no name? What then? Would you have to keep your mouth shut, give up on words, and just point?

Pointing is largely what I am doing now, on the page, when I try to summon from my past these glimpses of the ground of being. Language allows us not merely to experience the world but also to speak about what we've experienced, and to pass on—through books, formulas, recipes, paintings, stories, music, and every other sort of composition— what we've come to understand about our lives and the universe. Just as DNA stores within our bodies a deep evolutionary inheritance, so language stores outside our bodies the cumulative discoveries of our species. At times this legacy might feel like a burden to the child slogging through school. So much knowledge has accumulated, and so much more is accumulating every hour of every day, that no one can hope to grasp more than a tiny fraction of it. We are all, inevitably, ignorant, and yet we are all potentially wizards, because of the power stored in language.

Words dice the world into pieces small enough for the mind to hold, but the world itself is undivided. Every being, from lilac to lover, overflows the boundaries of its name. And this is all the more true of Being itself, that current rippling through all things. The Tao that can be named is not the Tao, Lao-tzu instructs us in the opening verse of the *Tao Te Ching*. When Moses begs to know God's name, God replies, "I am who I am," a phrase that some scholars translate as "I am the One who causes to be." If there is One who causes all things to be, then all beings arise from this One, indeed in their depths they *are* this One, at every moment, whether or not they recognize their true origins. The moments I choose to recount are those in which the shell of my small life has cracked open to reveal this nameless and perennial source.

3

THE MEN WHO LABORED in the cotton fields across the road from our farm were called convicts, I learned, and the men who looked after them wearing cowboy hats and carrying shotguns in the crooks of their arms were called trustees. They trooped into the fields soon after sunup, ate their lunch at noonday in a grove of pecan trees, then worked on through the afternoon until dusk.

When Sandra was home from school and our reading lesson was over, she and I would often stand on our side of the road and watch the men trudge up and down the rows. Sometimes they sang. Sometimes they talked and joked. Most of the time they only grunted as they swung hoes or stooped over to pry stones from the dirt. Their gray coveralls were striped with black, like the tail on a raccoon, and the cloth turned dark under the arms from sweat. As the trustees walked alongside the convicts, the barrels of their shotguns flashed in the sunlight.

Mama said that Sandra and I could watch, but that she'd tan our hides if we ever crossed the road into those fields. So long as Sandra was with me, I never forgot the warning. Then one day, when Sandra was playing at a friend's house, I stood with our dog Rusty by the roadside while the convicts were picking cotton. That day they sang. I couldn't understand the words, but the sound made me sad. The men were tired—I could hear that—tired and hot and sad. I listened as long as I could stand it; then I darted across the road and ran up to the convicts, figuring if I helped them pick, they would finish sooner and be able to go indoors and rest. Seeing Rusty and me approach, they quit their song and straightened their backs. The faces they turned on me shone with sweat, and then with smiles. The trustees squinted at me under their cowboy hats.

"That dog of yours bite?" one of the trustees asked.

"No, sir," I answered, patting Rusty. "He's a good dog."

"You Mr. Sanders's boy?"

"Yes, sir," I answered. "I come to help."

"Help, huh?" The trustee looked me up and down, then waved his gun. "Go on ahead. Maybe y'all can show these lazy mules how to work."

I began plucking white puffs of cotton and stuffing handfuls into the gunnysacks that the men dragged behind them down the rows.

"Son, you a cotton picker for sure," one of the convicts said.

The other men agreed. I grinned at them, and picked faster.

I was still picking a while later when I heard a car door slam. I looked across the road to see my father, back from the tire plant, going inside the house, where he would lift Mama off the floor with a hug and give her a loud kiss. A smooch, he called it. Give Mama a big smooch. Thinking about Mama suddenly brought back her warning, and I got scared. I didn't know whether to beat it for home or to hide among the men in their sweaty gray suits. Before I could decide, my father came back out of the house, moving fast, and his long strides ate up the distance between us. I reached for Rusty, who hunkered down beside me, tail and muzzle lowered, as if to make himself small.

"Scott!" Dad hollered. "Scott Russell, are you out there?"

I kept quiet. It was a bad sign when he used my middle name.

"The boy's here!" one of the trustees yelled back.

I tried to read in Dad's face how much trouble I was in, but he didn't look angry. The look on his face was like when he'd worked all day on the tractor and finally got it fixed.

"Is he a big help?" Dad asked as he drew close and scooped me into his arms.

"Yes, sir," a convict said. "He's a good one."

"You think so?" Dad said. He scrubbed the top of my head with his hard hand. "I was planning on trading him in for a boy who obeys his mama. But if y'all say he's a good one, maybe I'll keep him."

The men laughed and went back to work. As he carried me to the house, stepping over the cotton plants so as not to trample them, Dad told me Mama had been searching high and low for me, worried sick, but she never thought to look over here because she couldn't believe a child of hers would go to the prison farm against her orders, and if I ever did that again, he would jerk a knot in my tail. Did I understand? I nodded. All right, then, he told me, you can get by this time without a spanking. Just don't ever cross the road to the prison farm. You hear? I heard. Mama's warnings I might forget, but not Dad's.

That night I looked up *prison* in the dictionary, which sent me, as usual, hunting for other words, such as *criminal* and *cell*. I figured it would be a mistake, right then, to ask either of my parents to explain what those men across the road had done to wind up wearing striped coveralls and working all day in the hot sun and sleeping at night in rooms with bars over the windows. So I asked Sandra, who told me they'd probably murdered people or robbed banks or fallen down drunk in the street. And why did the trustees carry shotguns? To shoot anybody who tried running away, Sandra explained.

From then on, I didn't wave at the prisoners I saw working in the fields across the road, for fear they might come walking over to see what I wanted, and the trustees might think they were trying to run away. So I stood there in our yard, hands in my pockets, watching the men stoop and sweat, listening to their laughter and sad songs.

Mama sent me on errands sometimes to Mr. and Mrs. Jackson's big white house, past the barbed-wire fence of the bull pasture, past the potato fields, past the barn and tractor shed and pigpen. She might have me deliver a peach pie, or borrow a pound of sugar, or ask after the health of Mrs. Jackson, who lay until noon, many days, in an iron bed set up in the parlor. What else a parlor was for except to hold an iron bed I couldn't guess, because we didn't have such a room in our house.

To thank me for inquiring about her health, Mrs. Jackson would reach out a quavering hand and give me a piece of root beer candy shaped like a barrel.

Heading from our back door in the opposite direction, I would also go on errands to the home of Aunt Minnie and the General. They were the oldest people I'd ever seen, older than my father's parents, Mamaw and Papaw Sanders, who lived on a farm down in Mississippi, surrounded by more grandchildren than you could shake a stick at; older than my mother's father, Grandpa Solomon, who sometimes drove down from Chicago to visit us in a glossy black car with his doctor's bag on the seat beside him.

Aunt Minnie wasn't much taller than Sandra, but she made up in width for what she lacked in height. I never saw but an occasional wisp of her hair, like a curl of cotton, for she always wore a bright scarf wrapped close around her head, and a long skirt that brushed the floor, and an apron as white and spotless as the altar cloth at church. When she smiled, which was often, her face drew into a web of wrinkles and her cheeks all but hid her kindly eyes.

The General was scrawny, not like a kid who'd never had much meat on his bones, but like a large man who'd been whittled down. He could hardly see. His eyes, he told me, were covered with frost. Summer and winter he wore a long-sleeved blue work shirt buttoned up to his chin. He used a cane with a handle carved in the shape of a duck's head, and when he stood up from a chair he leaned on the stick with both knobby hands, gaining his balance before taking a step. His steps were careful and small. Outdoors, he wore a gray felt hat, like my father's fedora, which he kept brushed and creased just so. He touched the brim of this hat when he heard anyone coming, even Sandra or me, and he heard us often, because we liked to walk with him down the dirt lane to his mailbox, where he hoped to find letters from his children. He liked having us along, because we could read any letters he found. Going and coming, he told us stories.

One story he often told was about how he and Aunt Minnie used to live way on the other side of Memphis, until a big wind picked up their house with them and their chickens inside and whirled them around and peeled off all the paint and set them down right here. He would time the story to end just as we climbed onto the front porch, where he tapped his cane on the floor, as if the solid sound proved that every word he said was true. I believed him. The house was barely big enough to swing a cat in, as Dad would say, and without a lick of paint on the boards outside. Clothes were always drying on lines strung between posts in the yard—enough clothes, it seemed, to outfit a town, because Aunt Minnie took in people's laundry. To press the shirts, she heated flatirons on a woodstove, so smoke rose from the chimney in every season. The walls inside were pasted over with pictures from Sears, Roebuck catalogs and lumberyard calendars. Weeds hung from the rafters—herbs and roots drying, Mama told me.

Mama never sent me to the General and Aunt Minnie's place with laundry, for she believed in washing her own clothes, but she would send me over now and again with a casserole or a sack of coffee or a jar of bacon fat. Aunt Minnie used the fat to make lye soap. To thank Mrs. Sanders, as she always called Mama, Aunt Minnie would send home with me a chunk of the brown soap wrapped in a square of newspaper. "Don't want to burn my baby's soft skin," she told me, patting my hands. Her own hands were dry and cracked, like slabs of wood that had been left out in the rain.

Every now and again Dad would cut up a dead tree from our land and haul a load of firewood to the General and Aunt Minnie's house. I rode along, and then helped unload the smaller sticks, laying them in a pile beside the back door. I could see the General wanted to help, too, but he dared not let go of his cane. Instead, he and Dad talked about the best bird dogs they'd ever owned, or the orneriest mules, or the sharpest knives. With his frosty eyes, the General didn't trust himself to whittle anymore, he told my father. He used to do a lot of things he couldn't do anymore. Time was, he could have cut up that tree and unloaded all that firewood without breaking a sweat. Now he was doing good to button his britches. Couldn't dig a garden, couldn't harness a horse. The missus did just about all the man's work, and all the woman's work, too. It was a mighty shame. Trouble was, all their children moved up north to the cities. The children sent a dollar or two in a letter every once in a while, and that was a kindness, but they lived too far away to stop by for a visit or lend a hand.

Gesturing at me, Dad said, "I'm rearing this one to look after me when I get up in years."

"Just don't let him climb in a car and head north," the General said, "unless he taken y'all with him."

When the last of the wood had been stacked, Dad lingered awhile to finish hearing about a son or daughter up in St. Louis, Cleveland, or Detroit. Then he told the General we had to be getting back home, and the old man let go of the cane long enough to shake hands, first Dad's and then mine, saying he and Aunt Minnie were much obliged, much obliged.

If you had asked me back then to describe this neighbor couple, I might have told you about the General's cane and frosty eyes or Aunt Minnie's apron and weathered hands, but most likely I wouldn't have noted the color of their skin. If I mentioned their skin at all, I might only have said it was wrinkled or soft.

Similarly, had you asked me to describe the convicts, I would have told you about their striped suits, their faces glistening with sweat, their sacks of cotton, their sad songs. But I wouldn't have said they were this color or that, because, although their gray-and-black suits were all alike, no two of these men had the same shade of skin. Up to that point in my life, every person I'd met was one of a kind, with a unique shape and voice and smell and way of moving. Although I was puzzled by the signs marked "Colored" and "White" over the doorways of toilets in gas stations, I never had to choose which door to enter, because my parents made sure I used the proper one.

Children notice patterns instinctively. On the day Elizabeth turns six months old, she and I are sitting in the car while my wife, Ruth, goes into a store to buy eyedrops for my mother, who, in her forgetfulness, has squirted her eyes with perfume. The car is warm from the slant of October sun, and Elizabeth, buckled into her seat, drifts toward a nap. As I sing to her about Fox going out on a chilly night to fetch a fat goose for his little ones, this little one gazes fixedly over my shoulder at the sky. She's clearly fighting off sleep to keep staring. What could she be watching up there? Turning to look, I see a gigantic American flag waving from a pole above the store, set against swiftly moving clouds. Never before have the Stars and Stripes appeared so arresting to me. No wonder Elizabeth is mesmerized. Eventually she'll be taught to pledge allegiance to the flag and sing an anthem in its honor; perhaps she'll come to weep or cheer at the sight of it. But for now, it's only a bright cloth rippling against the sky, without history or symbolism, a prospect more seductive than sleep.

Children must be taught, or guess, what meanings to give the patterns they so readily notice. After I learned that husbands and wives go together in pairs, like salt and pepper shakers, for a time I thought that cows were the wives of horses and horses were the husbands of cows. I also imagined that chickens were paired with geese, and cats with dogs. My father straightened out those misconceptions with a laugh. It would have been harder for him, so long as we lived in the South, to straighten out the misconception that people should be divided between "Colored" and "White." My father spent most of his working life in the North, where his Mississippi accent and sunburned neck led some people to assume he was another one of those southern racists. In truth, by some combination of upbringing, religion, and character, he had largely overcome the delusions of racial prejudice. Along with my mother, he did all he could, through his way of treating other people, to spare my sister and me that delusion as well.

My parents weren't saints, on matters of race or anything else; they had their flaws, some of which will appear later in this narrative. But they did impress on me a deep feeling of kinship, first with animals, flowers, and trees, and then with people of every color and class. They lived as though they really believed what I would later hear in church, that we are all children of one God. Indeed, they prepared me to embrace an even broader spiritual vision—one conveyed by the Dineh (Navajo) blessing "All my relations," which acknowledges our kinship with every human tribe, with every other species, with generations past and those to come. My parents' example also prepared me to accept the findings of evolutionary biology, that humans literally *are* kin, not only with one another but also with apes and algae and every living thing.

I realize now that the trustees who carried shotguns on the prison farm would have been called white, and the convicts they watched over would have been called colored. I realize that Aunt Minnie and the General would have suffered all their lives because their skin marked them as descendants of slaves. But when I looked across the road at the prison farm, the convicts and trustees were simply men working in the sun. And when I thought of our elderly neighbors, they were simply Aunt Minnie and the General, two vivid people, as dear to me as any grownups except my own parents.

At first I thought the General was called the General because that was his name, the way mine was Scott. Then one day, when Joe Burns and I were reading war comics on the porch, a more interesting possibility occurred to me.

"Joe," I asked, "was the General a hero in the war? Is that how he got his name?"

"Naw," Joe answered, not looking up from his comic book, "they don't let niggers be generals."

A dismissive note in Joe's voice, as if I were the dumbest kid in Tennessee, kept me from asking him any more questions. Instead, later on that day, I hunted up Sandra and asked her what's a nigger. She clapped a hand over my mouth and whispered, "That's a naughty word! Don't ever say it!"

I started to cry, and Sandra hugged me. But her sympathy didn't stop her from telling Mama that I had said the naughty word for people with dark skin. Without saying the word herself, Mama demanded to know where I had heard it. When I told her, she announced that Joe Burns would never be allowed to set foot in our house again. "I thought he was a nice boy," she said, "but he's only white trash."

Now I was crying in earnest, not understanding what terrible thing I had done. Dad came at the sound of my sobbing, heard a hushed explanation from Mama, and took me outside for a walk.

He rested a hand on my shoulder and waited for me to quit crying before he spoke. Then he told me that Aunt Minnie and the General were a kind of people called Negroes. So were the convicts on the prison farm, and many of the folks we saw on the streets of Memphis, and some of the soldiers we picked up hitchhiking, and the maid who cleaned for Mrs. Jackson, and the men who loaded sacks at the feed store. Didn't I notice how some people had dark skin and others had light skin? I thought about the people he'd mentioned. When I called up their faces, they were just faces. No, sir, I answered, I never noticed. Well, Dad told me, it's so. And the people with dark skin have been hurt by people with light skin. Hurt how? I asked. Dad was quiet for a while before saying, "More ways than I can say."

I could hear the hurt in his own voice, one of the few times I would ever hear him admit pain.

Our walking had brought us to the front steps of the General and Aunt Minnie's house. Dad told me to go inside and ask if they needed anything from the store. "And don't call them General or Aunt Minnie," he added. "Call them Mr. and Mrs. Daniels, and make sure you say yes, sir, and no, ma'am."

I knocked on the screen door. When it opened, I stepped into the smoky, fragrant room and the two ancient people greeted me, and I looked at their kind faces and weathered hands, and for the first time their skin seemed not merely soft and wrinkled and old, but also strange.

4

THE NORTH, I knew, was where Mama had grown up. It was where she'd learned to talk Yankee. When my parents' friends came to play cards at our house, they teased Mama about the way she talked, inviting her to say "buttermilk biscuits" or "way up yonder" or "you all hush up now." The North was where Grandpa Solomon lived, among skyscrapers in Chicago, with a pistol in his doctor's bag and sick people showing up at his doorstep day and night. The North had lured away the General and Aunt Minnie's children, leaving the old folks alone to fend for themselves. It was cold up there, winter nine months long, snow as high as your waist, and the children all dressed like Eskimos.

So when I learned that our family was moving from Tennessee to a place called Ohio, where everybody talked Yankee, I felt excited and afraid. The trip would take three days, and that sounded like a long time to ride in the car. But who knew what surprises we might run into along the way? Maybe there'd be Indians in the North, maybe dinosaurs, maybe wolves.

Neighbors and friends came to wish us well, offering advice about how to deal with those Yankees. The neighbors who couldn't get out and about we went to see. Mrs. Jackson sat propped in her iron bed and gave me a whole bag of root beer candies. In the barn, Mr. Jackson let me sit on June Bug, who slung her muzzle around to snuffle at my pants leg. Mr. and Mrs. Daniels, whom I kept thinking of as the General and Aunt Minnie, leaned down and kissed me on the head, saying I'd likely be all grown up before they laid eyes on me again.

Dad took me around to say goodbye to the trees—the big ones he'd introduced me to by name and the little ones he'd planted. I went by myself to say goodbye to the cow, the goat, the chickens and pigs. I wished I could have said goodbye to Joe Burns, who had read me hundreds of war comics before teaching me the naughty word for Negroes. But Mama put her foot down, saying no son of hers was going to consort with any white trash. I was glad to have the goodbyes over so we could go.

At last, a van the size of our garage pulled into the gravel drive, and two men I had learned to see as Negroes lugged from the house every lamp and chair and box. Mama bustled back and forth to make sure they didn't drop anything. We went inside for a last look around, and the empty rooms echoed to our footsteps. Even Bluebeard's Closet lay bare. Dad put an arm across Mama's shoulders and led her to the car, where the two of them climbed into the front seat. Sandra and I climbed into the back with Rusty.

"Oh, wait," I said. "We forgot Bob."

Bob was staying behind, Dad answered. A bird dog needed room to roam, and there would be no place for him at the new house in Ohio. I pictured Bob all by himself, pointing at birds in the field. Who would set him loose to run? Who would give him water and food? I thought of the cow, the billy goat, the chickens and pigs. The folks who bought the house would move in later that day, Dad explained, and they would take care of all the animals.

As we rolled away, I knelt on the seat and looked out the rear window, watching our house and barn and shade trees dwindle. The last I glimpsed of our place was the white splash of Mama's lilac bushes, like twin fountains on either side of the driveway. Clothes flapped on the line at the General and Aunt Minnie's house, and smoke rose from their chimney. On the prison farm, convicts were bending over the black soil, picking up stones.

•   •   •

When our family left that farm on the outskirts of Memphis in April of 1951, my memory was divided for the first time into *before* and *after*. There is no danger of my confusing memories from return visits to Tennessee with memories from before our move. My mother had been so happy in that place, and she would become so miserable in the place to which we moved, that for years she couldn't bear to go look at the farm during our visits down South. By the time we hunted up the old place one August on our way to see my father's parents in Mississippi, the farm had been turned into a subdivision and had been overrun by Memphis. I saw nothing I recognized.

From the few years of my life before our move to Ohio, I can bring back only a handful of moments, including those I have recounted here; yet I was shaped, as any child is, by every hour of every day. It's often said a young child is like a sponge, but that seems to me the wrong metaphor, because a sponge can be wrung dry, while everything that goes into a child stays there. A child is more like a forest, gathering every drop of rain or flake of snow, every fallen leaf, the slant of sunlight and glint of moonlight, the fluster and song of birds, the paths worn by deer, the litter of bones and nuts and seeds, and whatever the wind delivers, taking it all in, turning everything into new growth.

When my own children were young enough for their ages still to be reckoned in months and half years, I often thought, with a pang, how little of what they were experiencing they would ever be able to remember. I might be standing on a bridge overlooking a waterfall, holding Eva in my arms, feeling the thrum of the current through her body and mine; or I might be lying on a blanket in the park next to my second child, Jesse, the two of us watching clouds by day, stars by night; or I might be playing the guitar and crooning beside the tub while Ruth gave one or the other of them a bath; and I would realize that this moment, so memorable to me, would vanish into Eva or Jesse, beyond recall.

Recently I've been feeling this pang again as I look after my granddaughter. At seven months, Elizabeth gazes boldly at everyone she meets, without caring if they gaze back. She reaches for everything within the span of her arms, feeling it, gumming and licking it. She notices every sound, from a siren in the street to the cluck of a tongue. Her senses are like rivers pouring into her constantly, even in her sleep. When Eva comes back from her job and sits on the couch to nurse the baby, I often stay to visit. Sometimes Elizabeth will suck avidly, but other times she will loll on Eva's lap, distracted by our conversation, and then I put on my shoes and walk home. I must leave the baby in peace to drink in the smell and sound and feel of her mother, along with her mother's milk.

My dearest wish for Elizabeth, as for Eva and Jesse, is that she will never lose touch with the wonder of being alive, that she will never cease to be amazed by the sensations flowing into her. Right now she meets the world without preconceptions, without carving it into categories, without dismissing anything as already known. She has no habits. While her beginner's mind will cloud over as she grows, I pray that she will never forget this clarity of perception. I pray that throughout her life she will find ways of recovering a newborn's freshness. What I wish for Elizabeth, for my own daughter and son, and for all of us blessed with consciousness is not that we remain children forever but that we remain forever awake to the astounding *isness* of things. Why this apple, say, gleaming in sunlight on a pine table carved with lovers' initials, why this sound of a cello and fragrance of lavender filling the air, why this flow of breath, this mind absorbing it all, this planet hurtling through space, this universe unfolding? The moment we begin taking this skein of miracles for granted, we cease to live, no matter if our hearts still beat.

Knowing this, I still sleepwalk through much of my life. But I recognize it as sleepwalking, I keep struggling to wake, and when I do occasionally wake, a rush of awe dissolves the boundaries of this *I*, disclosing the borderless, luminous, abiding ground. Although some of my hunger for awe no doubt derives from genetic inheritance, I suspect that most of it was determined by what poured into me during those years in Tennessee. How my parents held me, spoke to me, sang to me; how my sister played with me or fussed over me; how friends of the family kidded or ignored me; the food I ate and the water I drank; the chance remarks of neighbors; the company of animals and plants;

the skies, the weather, and the lay of the land; the signs and goods in shops; the music or voices on the radio; the scraps of news fed into my ears; the books read aloud to me, and the beginner's books I read to myself; the very air I breathed, spiced with cotton poison and gravel dust and manure—all of these influences, and more, rode along inside of me to Ohio.

Tennessee was abloom when we left. As we drove through Kentucky and into Ohio, crossing the river at Cincinnati, the flowers thinned away and the green faded to brown. We stopped every hour or so to let Rusty run and to stretch our own legs. At the gas stations, I listened for Yankee voices. I watched the roadsides for polar bears. Mama cried off and on most of the way north, quietly, wiping her face with a hankie. Dad sang his country songs—about a preacher who went hunting on Sunday, about possums and rabbits, about train wrecks and bank robberies, about hard work and hard luck.

We were headed to a place called the Ravenna Arsenal, Dad told us, way up in the northeastern corner of Ohio, not far from Lake Erie. Will there be snow up there? Sandra asked. Oh, Lord no, Dad answered. Not this late in the spring.

But the fields turned white and the road turned icy well before we came to the high chain-link fence, topped by strands of barbed wire, surrounding the Arsenal. At the sight of the fence, Mama moaned that it looked like a concentration camp.

"This place helped shut down the camps," Dad said.

I piped up from the backseat. "What are concentration camps?"

"Ask your daddy," Mama said. "He's the one who brought us here."

Dad ignored my question and reminded Mama of the pay raise he would get with his new job, and the big house that she could fill up with knickknacks.

"They aren't knickknacks," Mama said. "They're antiques." She turned away from Dad and glared out at the frozen fields.

We cruised alongside the high fence for miles before we arrived at the main gate, which was flanked by a pair of army tanks covered in snow. I was thrilled by the tanks and thrilled by the snow. The gate swung open, and two soldiers came out of a little house to meet our car, one carrying a rifle, one carrying a clipboard, both of them wearing helmets. These were the first soldiers I'd ever seen except for the ones in comic books and the hitchhikers smelling of mothballs and cough syrup. The soldier with the clipboard looked at some papers Dad handed him through the open window. Then he leaned into the car and stared first at Mama, who turned her face away, then at Sandra and me, then at Rusty.

"You'll need to warn the children of the dangers, sir," the guard said.

"What dangers?" Mama demanded.

"I'll warn them," Dad said.

"And you can't let that dog run, sir."

"We'll keep him indoors," Dad answered.

"We'll do nothing of the sort," Mama insisted.

I could see Dad counting, to keep from getting mad. "We'll keep him tied up," he promised.

After giving Dad directions to our new house, the guard waved us through. The gate swung shut behind us, and we rolled on between ridges of snow.

The movers were just carrying the last of our boxes into a big white house as we pulled up. Mama hurried indoors to see if they had broken anything, and Sandra went along. I stayed outside with Dad, who leaned against the van swapping stories with the movers, the same two husky men who had emptied our house in Tennessee. In spite of the cold air and the snow underfoot, they wiped their foreheads with bandannas. Steam puffed from their mouths as they laughed at something Dad had said. Listening to them, studying their faces, I realized we had seen fewer and fewer of the people called Negroes at our stops on the way north. Maybe they didn't like the cold; maybe they didn't like talking Yankee.

When the movers climbed into their truck and drove away, Dad stood at the curb, his arm lifted, until they were out of sight.

"Are they going back down South?" I asked him.

"They're going back down South," he said.

"It's a long way."

"A mighty long way," Dad agreed. He kept watching where the truck had disappeared, until I began to fidget. Then he turned to me and hoisted me up, saying, "Now let's go in that fancy house and help your mama unpack knickknacks."

Our fancy house was P Quarters, one of fifteen or so identical two-story boxes sided in white clapboard, with green shutters, red brick chimneys, and gray shingled roofs in the form of pyramids. Built during World War II for army officers, the houses were now occupied mostly by civilians like my father, who worked in the Arsenal making bombs for the war in Korea. Because the houses were laid out in a ring, they were known, collectively, as the Circle.

Beyond the ring of houses was a ring of garages, and beyond the garages, I would discover in coming years, lay some 21,000 acres of load lines where bombs were made, bunkers where explosives were stored, dumps where old munitions were detonated, parking lots filled with tanks and howitzers and jeeps, railroad tracks, gravel roads, creeks, ponds, brushy fields, and shadowy woods. There were plenty of dangers out there, which our father duly warned us about, as the guard had instructed him to do.

Scattered through those thousands of acres were hundreds of foundation holes from farmhouses and barns and sheds that had been bulldozed in 1940 for the building of the Arsenal. There were abandoned orchards, beds of asparagus and rhubarb, clumps of perennial flowers that kept pumping out blossoms among the weeds, and family cemeteries growing up in brush. There was an entire Boy Scout camp left to molder, the log cabins tumbling down, the rope bridges rotting, the lake vanishing under a green scum. Muskrats paddled through the scum, leaving black trails. Beavers built dams in the creeks. Foxes hunted mice in the fields. High in the tallest trees, eagles made nests out of sticks. Deer meandered everywhere.

The lawn at the center of the Circle—covered with snow when we first saw it and thronged with kids most of the year—was as tame a place as you could want. Once we had settled into P Quarters, Mama let Sandra and me play out there without checking on us every few minutes to make sure we were still alive. That's how tame it was, inside that ring of white houses. But the land stretching away beyond the Circle was wilder than any place I had known in Tennessee.

Back in Tennessee, Sandra and I had shared a bedroom; here, each of us had a separate room. Mine was in the back of the house, with a window looking out over the garage, past a spinning radar dish, to the woods. I spent many hours dreaming at that window. Wolves or bears might slink from the woods. Enemy planes might fly over and set the radar beeping. Soldiers who came to the Arsenal on weekends to practice war might go clanking by in their tanks. Spies might sneak by in their search for bombs.

I soon learned the sound of bombs from explosions at the ammunition dump, which rattled the china in Mama's corner cupboard and, at suppertime, rattled the fork against my teeth. After supper, I could always run out the front door to the center of the Circle and find kids ready to play kick the can, capture the flag, or hide-and-seek. Or I could run out the back door and set off exploring the Arsenal's wild backcountry, with its bunkers and ruins, its red signs bearing skulls and crossbones, its secret lakes and brushy fields, its dark woods rustling with animals.

5

FOR A WHILE after our move, I wondered if the Arsenal might be like the paradise I heard about when my father read from the Bible at supper or when country preachers expounded on the Good Book. Well before I was able to begin reading that book for myself, I took the Bible in through my ears, in sermons and hymns, in verses proclaimed from lecterns, in psalms muttered by congregations, or in parables invoked by one or another grownup in an effort to straighten out my crooked behavior.

The biblical stories, from Adam and Eve's folly in the garden to the binding of Satan in chains at the last judgment, were the first ones I heard from any source outside our family's history or my father's imagination. So I heard how Cain murdered Abel, Noah built an ark to ferry the world's animals through the flood, a boy named David cut down the giant Goliath with a slingshot and a stone, and Jonah spent three days and three nights in the belly of a great fish for disobeying the word of the Lord. I heard how Solomon offered to settle a quarrel by sawing a baby in half, and for a time I confused that king of Israel with my grandpa Solomon, who had enough knives in his doctor's bag to saw up a dozen babies. And there were Joseph's brothers, driven by jealousy, who stripped away his coat of many colors, dipped it in sheep's blood, persuaded their father that his favorite son had been slain, then dumped Joseph into a well and left him to die, only to have a band of merchants happen by and rescue him and haul him off to Egypt, where he became Pharaoh's right-hand man, and where he wound up bailing out his family when they were starving back in the land of milk and honey. And above all there was Jesus, who was born in a stable, amazed the scholars with his preaching, threw loan sharks out of the temple, healed the sick, gave sight to the blind, fed the poor, died on a cross, and rose up three days later as good as new.

How could you beat stories like that? Compared to such goings-on, even war comics seemed pale and tame.

The first language I ever heard addressed to the heart's deepest fears and longings, the first poetry, the first lessons in what to love and how to behave, were those of the Bible. And not just any version of the Bible, but the one blessed by King James, translated, as the title page announced, "out of the original tongues." Here's how it sounded: "The earth is the Lord's, and the fulness thereof; the world, and they that dwell therein. / For he hath founded it upon the seas, and established it upon the floods." The original tongue, I came to understand, belonged to God, and so did this peculiar way of talking, which I took to be the accent of heaven, as Yankee was the accent of Ohio.

The Bible confirmed what I had suspected from the moment I began learning the names of things—that words have magical power, all the more so when they're uttered by God. When God talked, things happened. Let there be light! And there was light. Let frogs rain down! And frogs rained down. Let the Red Sea part! And the waters drew apart, so the chosen people might walk safely through.

God set in motion everything, from wind in the woods to my own wild thoughts, as I discovered in passage after passage: "For, lo, he that formeth the mountains, and createth the wind, and declareth unto man what is his thought, that maketh the morning darkness, and treadeth upon the high places of the earth, The Lord, The God of hosts, is his name." After making every last thing under the sun, God kept the whole show going, and God alone decided when each bit of the world—each whale and walnut tree and boll weevil—should die: "All flesh is grass, and all the goodliness thereof is as the flower of the field: / The grass withereth, the flower fadeth: because the spirit of the Lord bloweth upon it: surely the people is grass. / The grass withereth, the flower fadeth: but the word of our God shall stand for ever." Such a passage would set me thinking of the grass my father burned on the ditch bank or the lilacs my mother planted in the yard. It would set me wondering if "all flesh" included my own body. I would tingle at hearing such words, not understanding half of them, imagining they came straight from the lips of God.

In my first acquaintance with the Bible, the God I imagined had lips and tongue and every other body part, just like I had, only God's were much bigger. I thought of God as a gigantic and wizardly version of my father, able not only to build things from metal and wood but to make things out of thin air; able not only to calm a horse or ease the birth of a calf but to send whales on errands through the sea; able not only to cradle me during a storm but to crack the sky with thunder and blast an oak tree with lightning. Compared to my father, God was even more tender in his love, more terrible in his anger.

God's anger was a favorite theme of the preachers, who could choose among hundreds of verses to illustrate their point. There was the flood, of course, in which every breathing thing perished, except for the passengers on Noah's ark. There was Lot's wife, hardened into a pillar of salt for turning back to glimpse her home in Sodom before it was consumed by brimstone and fire, just as I turned back to glimpse our Tennessee farmhouse as our car headed north. There was long-suffering Job, heaped with afflictions so that God could win a bet with the devil. There were the plagues of Egypt, from locusts to hail, and the river Nile flowing with blood, and all the firstborn children slaughtered in their beds overnight. There was the whole army of Pharaoh, drowned when the Red Sea closed back up. From one end of the Bible to the other, there were stiff-necked people crushed like bugs under the mighty hand of God.

Preachers intent on scaring the living daylights out of congregations, or at least out of wide-eyed children like me, could also quote any of the prophets, whose watchword seemed to be "Woe!" Isaiah, for example, was always good for a threat: "If ye be willing and obedient, ye shall eat the good of the land: / But if ye refuse and rebel, ye shall be devoured with the sword: for the mouth of the Lord hath spoken it." Or the preachers could cite Jeremiah's vision of a land made desolate: "I beheld, and, lo, there was no man, and all the birds of the heavens were fled. / I beheld, and, lo, the fruitful place was a wilderness, and all the cities thereof were broken down at the presence of the Lord, and by his fierce anger." Or they could quote the indignant Amos: "Woe unto you that desire the day of the Lord! to what end is it for you? the day of the Lord is darkness, and not light. / As if a man did flee from a lion, and a bear met him; or went into the house, and leaned his hand on the wall, and a serpent bit him." Having suffered the bite of a serpent, I would listen to a passage like that as though God were talking straight at me. What wickedness of mine, I wondered, had pushed me onto the fangs of a snake?

The people of God may have dwelt in a land flowing with milk and honey, but they suffered all the same. Many of the psalms give thanks for blessings, but at least as many plead with God to turn aside his anger and stop raining down misery on the singer or the singer's family or the whole tribe of Israel. Psalm 23 famously opens with a promise, "The Lord is my shepherd; I shall not want," but Psalm 22 opens with a lament: "My God, my God, why hast thou forsaken me? why art thou so far from helping me, and from the words of my roaring? / O my God, I cry in the daytime, but thou hearest not; and in the night season, and am not silent." All these pleas for mercy and all of God's threats set me up to welcome the good news of the New Testament the way nightmares make you long for dawn.

Although it would be a long while before I understood how flesh could be grass or the day of the Lord could be a curse, such biblical passages, and hundreds more, soaked into me in childhood, feeding my imagination, tuning my ears and heart. They confirmed my sense of a grand power at work in the world, one that heaves everything into existence and then sucks everything back into oblivion, a power I could now imagine and entreat and name as God.

·   ·   ·

No sooner had Mama unpacked all the boxes in our new house in the Arsenal than she set out to find the right church. She had been reared among Presbyterians, who were a bit too fancy for Dad's taste, and Dad had been reared among Baptists, who were too fiery for Mama's taste. So they compromised by settling on the Methodists, who were plain and calm enough to suit them both. Whatever fire had flared up to inspire the Methodist revival in the early 1800s—making grown men quake with spirit, converting thousands of drinkers from booze to Jesus, scattering churches like sparks over the land—had cooled down to mild embers, at least in our neck of the woods, by the 1950s.

Close by the Arsenal there was a hamlet called Wayland, with a Methodist church presided over by a white-haired minister named the Reverend Mr. Knipe, who spoke without rolling in the aisle or even shouting, which suited Mama, and without wearing a robe or using any words you couldn't hear in a factory, which suited Dad. So we began going to the Wayland church every Sunday, rain or shine.

Although I would worship in dozens of other churches and meetinghouses and cathedrals over the years, that crossroads church in Wayland set the standard by which I measured all the rest. It was small and plain, sided with clapboards, painted white inside and out. The tall windows, filled with clear glass, opened onto cornfields, woods, and sky. The bare wooden benches rested on a bare plank floor surrounded by bare plaster walls. There were no paintings, tapestries, or statues. The sole ornament was a wooden cross above the altar. There were no confessional booths, no side chapels with candles flickering in the shadows, no monuments to benefactors. There were no carvings on the pulpit, where the minister spoke in his naked voice, without the aid of a microphone. Members of the congregation had built the church. When the roof needed new shingles or the clapboards new paint, the worshipers rolled up their sleeves and did the work themselves. The spiky steeple pointed to heaven, but the simple box of the church sat firmly on earth like any house or barn.

To people reared in other religious traditions, such a building might seem to lack mystery. But what I came to appreciate, dimly at first and then more distinctly year by year, was that the unadorned architecture of a country church, a Quaker meetinghouse, a Zen Buddhist zendo, or a Navajo sweat lodge honors the mystery in the world itself, in the crows and clouds visible through the windows, in the breeze blowing through the open doorway, in the grain of wood, in words or song, and in our own depths.

When I began spending Sunday mornings in the Wayland church, soon after our move to the Arsenal, I wasn't allowed to wear my holsters or cap guns or my cowboy jacket with the fringe on the sleeves, but instead had to wear a white shirt and black pants and shiny shoes. It was hard to play in such a getup. Most Sundays, after hearing one of Reverend Knipe's little sermons for the children and being dismissed to our Bible classes, where one or another matron told us stories about Jesus, I stole outside and climbed trees or dug in the dirt and made a wreck of my clothes.

Mama had taught me that cleanliness is next to godliness. What dirtiness is next to, she never said. Still, I couldn't see the point in bathing. Clean skin only gave dirt a new place to stick. Besides, how bad could dirt be if we grew our food in it? Plenty bad, Mama insisted. If I didn't wash my hands before meals, germs would carry sickness into my blood, a sickness as terrible as any of the plagues of Egypt. Mama knew all about germs, she reminded me, because she was the daughter of a physician. She had begun studying to become a doctor herself until Grandpa Solomon, with his Old World views on women, put a stop to her education.

At times Mama seemed to regret that the soul had to ride around in the body, with its bad smells and foul excretions, its unruly appetites and urges. If the body took in and gave out only sweetness—the fragrance of flowers, the melody of song—she would have approved, because she rejoiced in everything artistic and refined. But, alas, the body was prone to ugliness and prey to wickedness.

Mama could overlook ugliness, but she never let wickedness slide by without comment. For people smoking cigarettes—as Dad did every waking hour—and for people stumbling out of bars or kissing in public or getting so fat their bellies sagged over their belts or leaving their hair snarled like a rat's nest, Mama voiced only scorn. Her delicate nose caught the least whiff of unwashed bodies. Her vigilant eye caught any breach in modesty. Once, after church, we trailed a teenage boy and girl on our way to the car, and when the boy's hand slid from the girl's waist to her rump, Mama said, "Disgusting!" loud enough for the neighborhood to hear, and the boy's hand returned to safer territory.

Mama wouldn't let Sandra and me go to the movies because they were filled with such filth from beginning to end, hands and lips wandering everywhere. She knew about movies from having watched Saturday matinees during her own growing-up years. Back then, movies had been chaste and pure; now, in the 1950s, they had become crude.

Long before I heard the word *sex* or had any inkling of what it meant, I gathered from Mama's reproaches that the most dangerous dirt was not outside in the yard or woods, but inside my skin.

Fortunately, the stories about Jesus I heard at the Wayland church offered me an antidote to the Old Testament's warnings about the anger of God and Mama's warnings about the wickedness of the body. I sensed that Jesus loved the body, because he was forever healing people. Lepers came to him poxed and went away clean. The blind regained their sight. The lame lost their limp. A man who couldn't walk at all was lowered on a stretcher into a house where Jesus was speaking, and Jesus told the man to rise up, and the man went dancing away with the stretcher on his shoulder. Or a little girl died, and Jesus came to her house and said, No, she's not dead, she's only sleeping, and he told the girl to get up, and she got right up.

Or there was the time when a man came rushing at Jesus out of the graveyard, a man so crazy that he cut himself with stones and broke every chain and rope the people tied him with. Jesus could see the crazy man was filled with unclean spirits, and the man begged to be healed, so Jesus ordered the unclean spirits to go into a herd of hogs, and the hogs all jumped over a cliff into the sea and were drowned, and the herdsmen who looked after the hogs went and told folks in town what had happened, and a crowd trooped out to see what kind of sorcerer this Jesus was, and when they found him sitting there in his right mind, calm as you please, they were afraid.

I could picture just about everything Jesus did. I could see those hogs. I could see the little girl getting up off her cot after everyone thought she was dead, and her parents looking down on her the way mine looked down on me after I came back from the snakebite. When I heard how Jesus was born in a stable, I thought of our barn in Tennessee. When I heard how he learned carpentry from his father, I thought about sawing wood and hammering nails with my own father. When I heard about the Garden of Gethsemane, I thought of Mama's flowers.

As often as not, if somebody asked Jesus a question, he would answer them with a story. One of the disciples might ask, Who is my neighbor? And Jesus would tell how a man came down the road to Jericho and was set upon by thieves, who took all his clothes and left him half dead in the ditch; and a priest passed by, but he wouldn't help the man who'd been robbed; and a Levite passed by—whatever a Levite was—but he wouldn't help either; then a foreigner came along, a man from Samaria, somebody you wouldn't expect to lend a hand to a Jew, and he patched up the man's wounds, put him on his own donkey, carried him to an inn, and paid the innkeeper to look after the man. "Which now of these three," Jesus asked, "was neighbour unto him that fell among the thieves?" Even the disciples, who at times could be as dense as bricks, realized that the true neighbor was the one who showed mercy to a stranger.

Of course there were still plenty of details in the stories that baffled me. Nobody would explain, for example, what the woman caught in adultery had done wrong. And when I heard how a bunch of men were fixing to throw stones at this woman, and Jesus knelt down and drew in the dust with a stick, and he told the men that whoever was free of sin could go ahead and start throwing, and all the men dropped their stones and turned away and walked home, I could see every last detail of the scene, except for what he scratched in the dirt.

It seemed to me, even as a child, that Jesus was more interested in forgiving people than in blaming them. He ate meals with tax collectors, whom everybody else despised. He laid his hands on lepers, whom nobody else would touch. He died next to a pair of thieves, promising them seats in heaven. He told how a boy ran away from home and spent all his money and slept with pigs like a tramp, then came home again with his tail between his legs, and instead of whipping the boy, his father welcomed him back with open arms and his mother cooked him a feast. Or if a man has a hundred sheep, Jesus taught, and one of them goes astray, the man doesn't say good riddance to the wandering sheep but hunts for it night and day, and shouts for joy when he finds it.

Instead of telling the ragtag crowds who followed him that it was their own fault they didn't have a bite to put in their mouths, Jesus broke up loaves and fishes to feed them. Instead of scorning them for wearing rags, he told them how the poor in spirit and the pure in heart will be blessed, while the rich will have a hard time entering the kingdom of heaven, as hard a time as a camel trying to climb through a needle's eye.

When Reverend Knipe passed the collection plate, he quoted Jesus about the dangers of clinging to money. Be like the poor widow and give generously, however little you may have. And if you have much, sell everything and give it to the needy. You can't serve both God and mammon. Don't lay up treasures on earth, which robbers can steal and rust can devour, but instead lay up your treasure in heaven.

I didn't cling to the coins Mama gave me for the offering—a nickel at first, then a dime, and eventually a quarter—but laid them willingly in the walnut plate.

Jesus himself wasn't going to be kept out of heaven by clinging to money, that was sure. He didn't own a house. He didn't own any clothes except the ones on his back. He didn't own a pot to piss in, as

Dad would have said out of Mama's hearing. Jesus walked everywhere, except for occasional rides in boats and one ride on a borrowed donkey. He ate at other people's tables, or ate sitting on the ground, or didn't eat at all. In fact, son of God or not, he was more or less a beggar.

This occurred to me one night, long after I was supposed to be asleep, as I lay listening to my parents quarrel. Mama was telling Dad as usual that he'd lose his job because of his drinking, and we'd all wind up begging in the streets. It dawned on me that Jesus never had a job. He depended on charity for a square meal or a dry place to sleep. That's why he could tell people not to worry about how they would feed themselves or cover their bones. Look at the birds of the air and the flowers of the field, he said. They don't worry about what they'll eat or what they'll wear, and yet see how God feeds and dresses them? Jesus knew what he was talking about, for he was a creature of the fields and open air himself.

We weren't poor—our new house in the Arsenal had two pots to piss in, and both of them flushed—but we were a long sight from being rich. Whatever else they argued about in the evenings after they thought Sandra and I were asleep, Dad and Mama always got around to money—how little there was of it and how far it had to stretch. Those quarrels were scary, but also oddly reassuring, because they meant I wouldn't be kept from climbing into heaven through the needle's eye by lugging sacks of gold.

I might be kept out of paradise, however, by missing some clues Jesus had dropped in the tiny print of the Bible. I knew there were clues to miss because the disciples kept missing them. There was the time, for instance, when Jesus told about the sower who cast some seeds beside the path, some on stony ground, and some among thorns, but only the seed scattered on fertile soil brought forth grain, thirtyfold and sixtyfold and a hundredfold. After Jesus finished the story, the disciples asked him to explain it. If you don't understand this parable, Jesus replied, how are you going to understand anything I say?

I could hear in his voice the exasperation I provoked in Mama or Dad or my Sunday-school teachers by asking one too many questions. If grownups who followed Jesus everywhere couldn't figure out the meaning of his stories, how was I, a kid who'd never laid eyes on him, to solve the riddles?

The hardest puzzle for me, then and forever after, was how to reconcile what Jesus said about killing and kindness with what I saw going on around me. I would hear Jesus say how we should turn the other cheek if we'd been slapped, we should forgive those who hurt us, we should love our enemies; and then our family would drive home from church into the Arsenal, where men and machines prepared night and day to slaughter our enemies. As I read newspaper headlines about the war going on in a place called Korea, about the testing of A-bombs and H-bombs here in our own country, about the hunt for Communists, about murders in nearby towns, I began to suspect that grownups, no matter how much they talked about loving Jesus, meant to go right on hating their enemies.

Jesus often ended his stories by saying, "He that hath ears to hear, let him hear." I had ears to hear long before I had mind enough to comprehend. I took in the Bible the way I took in air and water and food. The tales, the imagery, the sentence rhythms, and the teachings became a part of my native speech, as much so as the backcountry drawl of Tennessee or the cautious Yankee dialect I acquired in Ohio.

6

SINCE I COULD READ after a fashion, Mama persuaded the principal of Charlestown Elementary to let me skip kindergarten and enroll in first grade, even though I wouldn't turn six until October. The principal, Mr. Hammond, had been a drill sergeant in the Marines. He still wore his black hair cut short all over and flat on top, and he still sucked in his gut and puffed out his chest when he spoke. The school was just outside one of the Arsenal's gates, within sight of the chain-link fence. Sandra and I and other kids from the Circle rode there on a blunt-nosed, khaki-colored bus driven by a GI, a bus like those the soldiers rode when they came to the Arsenal on weekends to play war.

When Mr. Hammond led me to the first-grade classroom, the dozen or so children already in their seats gaped at me as if I were a toad who'd hopped in through the door. The teacher, Mrs. Williams, a plump woman with yellow hair stacked on her head like a bird's nest, asked me to tell everybody my name. I answered with all three parts, including Russell, in memory of Dad's brother who'd been run over by a train. Several kids giggled, and a couple of them repeated my name, as if it were the punch line of a joke. Mrs. Williams shushed them and asked me to say where I was from.

"Memphis, ma'am," I said. "That's in Tennessee."

Again, the kids echoed my words, laughing.

"Don't mind them," the teacher said. "They're not used to your accent."

"Hillbilly," some kid said.

"Now hush," Mrs. Williams scolded. "And Scott, dear, you needn't say 'ma'am' to me. That's not how we talk in Ohio."

"Yes, ma'am."

"Are you sassing me?"

"No, ma'am."

"Then stop saying 'ma'am' or I'll send you to the principal."

I was about to say "Yes, ma'am," as my parents had taught me, but I held my tongue and simply nodded.

"Very well, then," Mrs. Williams said. "Now who can tell me the first letter of the alphabet?"

I knew then that school would be a long row to hoe—not hard, but slow. I'd have to hear over and over again things I already knew. I'd have to obey a slew of rules. I'd have to memorize the multiplication table and the capitals of all forty-eight states and the chief battles of the Civil War. Except for recess, I'd have to stay indoors, sitting in a chair, doing what the teacher told me to do. The only live things within reach would be other kids, who didn't know me from Adam and didn't give a hoot whether I was happy or sad. And just about everything that had ever moved me, from lightning to lightning bugs, would be shut outside the classroom and left out of the rumpled books.

Morning after morning I climbed the high steps of the army bus with Sandra's help, while Mama stood on the sidewalk waving goodbye and reminding me to keep hold of my lunch box, be careful on the playground, use my hankie instead of my sleeve. As soon as I took my seat, the other kids on the bus began repeating Mama's instructions, mimicking her voice. Since I was the youngest, I tried to ignore them, which in any case was what Jesus would have wanted me to do. If they pour scorn into one ear, I figured, turn the other ear. But after a few wisecracks, Sandra threatened to punch anybody who made fun of Mama or me, and some of the older kids threatened to punch her back, and Sandra said just you try it, and the yelling got louder and louder until the GI driver turned around and told us all to simmer down and everybody simmered down.

There were no GIs on the playground, however, to stop kids from taunting one another. Teachers watched over recess from the back steps of the school, far enough from our boisterous play to ignore anything short of bloodshed.

At recess one day the biggest of my classmates, Tommy Thompson, cornered me on the playground and demanded, "How come you ride to school in a square turd?"

I knew better than to say he'd used a naughty word, so I answered, "It's an army bus. Like soldiers use."

"Looks to me like a square turd on wheels."

The first thing Tommy had told me about himself was that his father drove a truck. His father would be on the road for days at a time, hauling tires from Akron or steel from Youngstown, leaving his mother to look after the six children all by herself. She couldn't handle Tommy, who did whatever he pleased until his father came home and pulled out his belt and whipped Tommy black and blue.

"Do y'all like playing war?" I asked, hoping to change the subject.

"How come you talk so funny?" said Tommy.

"What's funny?"

"Saying 'y'all' and such."

"Do *you* like playing war?" I asked again, carefully.

"I like watching war movies on TV."

My family didn't own a television, and I'd never seen a movie, so all I could do was keep asking Tommy questions and keep listening to how he talked. Whenever he or the other kids poked fun at anything I said, I made sure to learn the Yankee way of saying it. Before long, I was sounding pretty much like everybody else. I even talked Yankee at home, to practice, except when I took walks with Dad or fooled around with my dog, Rusty, when I let myself ease back into the speech of Tennessee.

One day when I was loafing with Rusty in a field behind P Quarters, a pack of mean-looking dogs showed up at the edge of the woods. Rusty pricked up his ears and twitched his nose. The other dogs yipped.

Rusty pranced a few steps in their direction, whining, the hair stiffening on the scruff of his neck. I grabbed onto his collar and told him to stay. But he took off running, dragging me along, then tore loose and kept on going until he reached the pack of dogs. They all strutted around him with their legs stiff and their noses pointed at him like he was a quail in a bush. Rusty lowered himself to the ground and rolled onto his back, and the other dogs came up to sniff at him and then they let him get on his feet and the whole crew loped away into the woods.

I feared he was gone for good, but Dad said not to fret. And sure enough, two days later, Rusty came slinking back with his tongue hanging out and his fur matted in cockleburs and blood. I thought he'd been hurt, but Dad looked him over from tail to snout and couldn't find a cut anywhere.

"He's been hunting deer," Dad concluded.

"You mean *biting* them?" I asked, unable to believe this of our gentle collie.

"More than just biting them," Dad said.

Mama wouldn't let Rusty in the house, not even in the basement, where Dad set up his workshop. So Dad tied Rusty with rope to the back porch railing. That worked for a spell, until Rusty chewed through the rope and lit out. Again, I thought he was gone for good. But a few days later a guard car rolled up to our house and a soldier climbed out and opened the trunk and out jumped Rusty wearing a muzzle and a leash. I ran to hug that fleecy neck, only to find it lumpy and wet. My hands came away slick. When the soldier gave the leash to Dad, he told him the pack of dogs had killed several deer, and the next thing you knew they'd be chasing kids, and so the commanding officer had ordered that, from now on, any dog running loose in the Arsenal would be shot on sight.

Later, as Dad washed the lumpy fur with a hose and a brush, I asked if Rusty was sick, and could we take him to a doctor.

"He's not sick," Dad told me. "He's just gone a little wild. When he runs with other dogs and smells those fat deer, the wolf in him rises up."

"Can people go wild?" I asked.

Rusty squirmed to get away from the brush, but Dad smacked him on the rump and told him to lie still. "I suppose they can," Dad said.

"Like how?"

"Oh, maybe you'll be boxing, or maybe arguing with somebody, and you forget yourself and just see red."

"What do you mean, see red?"

"Get mad."

"Like at night, when you and Mama yell?"

Dad kept running the brush through Rusty's cinnamon fur. "Son," he began, "your mother and I—" Then he broke off to say, "Go fetch me some rags from the basement."

"You and Mama what?"

"I sent you to fetch something. Now go do it."

When I returned with an armload of rags, I asked if Rusty and the other dogs really would chase kids. Dad assured me that Rusty wouldn't be chasing anything except maybe squirrels foolish enough to cross the yard, where this ornery mutt would be tied up with a chain.

Rusty had to stay chained to the railing on the back steps even when I played with him, because I wasn't strong enough to keep him from running off. Every now and again he would prick up his ears and twitch his nose, as if sensing the dogs running free in the woods. At night, even with my bedroom window closed, I could hear the chain scrape against the railing. I remembered the crazy man in the graveyard who broke every rope and chain, until Jesus sent the man's unclean spirits into a herd of pigs. Maybe Rusty had been filled with an unclean spirit. Maybe that was what it meant to go wild.

Sometimes at night the wild dogs would howl from the darkness, making my skin tingle, and Rusty would howl back until Dad stormed outside and swatted him, and then Rusty whimpered and went back to dragging his chain.

The morning after the first snowfall, when I went to give Rusty a pat before climbing onto the army bus, the chain lay slack, broken off where it had rubbed against the concrete steps. In the fresh snow, a trail of paw prints headed straight for the woods.

After school I put on my boots and went looking, the way the shep-

herd in the Bible looked high and low for his lost sheep. I found lots of
tracks but never laid eyes on Rusty, even though I called his name until
I was hoarse. I skirted the woods but dared not go in, for fear the dogs
would chase me and pull me down and rip open my belly.

That night at supper and every night for a week, Sandra and I asked
Dad if Rusty was going to come back, and Dad said yes, more than
likely, as soon as he gets tired of eating venison. Then one night Dad
said no, Rusty wasn't coming back.

When he gave no explanation, I asked, "Did the guards shoot him?"

"Of course not," Mama said, giving Dad a look.

Dad reached across the table and took hold of Sandra's hand and
mine, the way he did when he offered grace. Only he'd already said
grace before we started eating. "They shot the whole pack," he said.
"They had to."

Sandra burst out crying, but I just sat there and shook, thinking
about unclean spirits and a herd of pigs jumping from a cliff.

The upsurge of wildness that doomed my first dog, and the implacable
logic that forced the guards to shoot him, left a deeper imprint on me
than anything I learned at Charlestown Elementary School or Wayland
Methodist Church. I couldn't have explained, back then, what the
shooting meant. I merely felt the blow of a force beyond my parents'
control, like the force that sundered the world into "colored" and
"white," built A-bombs, hunted Communists, and sent armies to Korea. I wondered why God let such things go on, unless maybe the angry side of God had a hand in them. No matter what the preachers said
on Sunday mornings, no matter what I prayed at night, the men with
guns would decide who was a friend and who an enemy, who lived and
who died.

Nothing lived inside the Arsenal fence without permission from the
commanding officer—not people, not deer or dogs. What Rusty and
the other dogs had done wrong was to act like wolves. They had left
the Circle, with its barbered lawns and white clapboard houses, to run
with bloodied jaws and panting tongues through the deep woods and

far fields. For all the Arsenal's 21,000 acres, however, no woods were deep enough, no fields were far enough, to leave much room for wildness.

Soon after the pack was killed, the army hired a man named Albert Fritz to come trap the coyotes, who were riling up the dogs; the foxes, who were eating the cats; the beavers, who were flooding the creeks with their dams; as well as the muskrats and minks, whose skins would help pay him for his trouble. In less than a year, Mr. Fritz had cleaned out everything except the coyotes, who stepped neatly around his traps and shat on his poisoned bait.

"Coyotes are too damn smart," he told my father once. "If they were Communists, they'd be running the country."

Because he played poker with my father, Mr. Fritz came by our house now and again to swap stories. Once, near the end of the trapping, he drove up in his muddy Jeep to show my father a stack of fox skins piled in the backseat. Dad ran his fingers through the ruddy fur and asked if Mr. Fritz had seen any sign of bears. None at all, Mr. Fritz answered. Any sign of mountain lion? Not a hair, said Mr. Fritz. The old-timers got every last lion and bear and buffalo before we ever came along. And where would he go next, Dad asked, now that the Arsenal was empty? Up to Alaska, Mr. Fritz answered. They'll never run out of skins in Alaska.

A child begins learning about this world as she draws her first breath, and she will go on learning until she draws her last one. Knowledge flows into us swiftly in the beginning, more and more slowly as the years roll on. If we live long enough, eventually the rate of our forgetting exceeds the rate of our learning, and each day we know—or at least remember—less. Mother, who tried in vain to shield me from life's ugliest lessons, passed over that threshold of forgetfulness some years ago, and now she slides down the slope toward ignorance, where all of us began.

Unlike baby Elizabeth, for whom ignorance is still bliss, Mother grieves over what she has lost. It's as if her arms and legs had been lopped off, and yet she can still feel the ache of phantom limbs, still remember when she danced and gardened and painted. She has forgotten nearly everything she learned in classrooms, nearly everything she read in books, nearly everything she saw on journeys overseas. What she can't forget is the fact of her forgetting.

"Things get so muggled up," Mother says to me when I take Elizabeth for a visit. She's sitting in her easy chair by the window, where a Christmas cactus has begun to drop scarlet blossoms on the sill. A patchwork afghan covers her shoulders, but at her throat I can see three layers of blouses, their gaudy patterns clashing.

"So confused?" I say.

"Yes." Mother gives a vague wave of her hand. "Twisted . . . bed."

She has telephoned me several times lately to ask would I come over right away to make her bed, which is all a mess. Now I guess at her meaning: "Things are twisted up like the blankets on your bed?"

Again Mother says yes. She reaches for the baby, so I put Elizabeth on her lap. At eight months and twenty pounds, Elizabeth is too heavy and wriggly for Mother to hold for long. While Mother strokes the baby's cheek, I quickly make the bed, empty the wastebaskets, check the toilet paper in the bathroom, check the fruit in the refrigerator, check the phone messages and the mail. By the time I return to Mother, she is struggling to keep Elizabeth from slipping to the floor, so I gather up the baby and the three of us go for a stroll down the hallway.

Mother is walking again, having mostly recovered from yet another knee surgery. She leans on a cane, clutches my elbow with her free hand, and shuffles cautiously over the carpet. The other assisted-living apartments are mostly shut up tight, TVs blaring through the doors, but here and there a neighbor peeks out to smile at the baby, and nurses interrupt their errands to make over her. Mother beams. Although she can't remember Elizabeth's name, can't even recall that Elizabeth is a girl, Mother summons everyone to come have a look, as if she were escorting the world's original child.

Elizabeth studies each face with care. We stop at a birdcage in the hall, and she listens closely to the chatter of the parakeets. She sniffs as

we pass the kitchen. She brushes her fingers over wallpaper and uphol-
stery and wood. Taking a rest on a couch in the lounge, Mother and I
loop round and round the small circle of conversation we can still manage. For a while Elizabeth watches the gas logs flicker in the fireplace.
When she grows restless, I pull a miniature flashlight from my pocket
and show her how to turn it on and off. She pushes the button to make
it glow, shining the light onto the walls, onto the carpet, into her gray
eyes. Mother, who can no longer work a television or a thermostat, declares that the baby is a genie.

"You mean a genius?" I ask.

"A mecko," Mother says.

"A mechanical genius?"

Mother nods. "Like your daddy."

"She could do worse than take after Dad," I say.

As we talk, Elizabeth studies the flashlight beam intently, as if she
were discovering from scratch the laws of physics.

My teachers did their best with an impossible task, which was to civi-
lize a roomful of restless, mischievous, curious animals while teaching
us the rudiments of knowledge that human beings had accumulated
over the previous five or ten thousand years, from counting to cooking,
from farming to physics.

Instead of being shot, like Rusty and the roving dogs, children who
didn't tame easily were made to stand in the corner of the classroom, or
were paddled in the principal's office, and as often as not were paddled
again when they got home. By and by even the most wayward children
settled down, including me.

In second grade, the classroom windows faced the Arsenal. Every
few hours, a guard car cruised along the gravel road inside the fence, on
the lookout for wild dogs and Communists and spies. When I saw the
cruiser's olive drab tail fins and long radio antenna slicing the air, sometimes I couldn't resist leaping up and rushing to the window. At first the
teacher asked me to sit down, then she led me to my seat by the hand,
then she tugged me by the ear, and then one day she made me stay in-

side over the lunch hour and scrub the piano bench and repeat aloud, "I will sit still, I will sit still, I will sit still."

By the end of recess, when the teacher came to check on me, I had scoured my way through the varnish on the bench. She marched me to the principal's office, where Mr. Hammond smacked me twice with his long wooden paddle. Then he telephoned Mama and made me tell her what I had done. I sobbed into the phone that I had only done what the teacher told me to do, whereupon Mr. Hammond paddled me again for not being sorry and sent me back bawling to the classroom.

I kept itching to gaze out the window, make jokes, pass notes, do anything to break up the tedious days at school, but I learned to bite my tongue. I kept hankering to be outdoors, to flop down on the floor to read, to color outside the lines, but eventually I figured out how to behave so the teacher would ignore me, just as I figured out how to talk so the other kids would quit mocking my hillbilly drawl.

Like the draft horses that stood still while Mr. Jackson put on their harness, like the convicts who kept their heads down all day chopping weeds, I learned to stay in my seat, raise my hand before talking, and fill in the blanks on page after workbook page. At recess I faithfully obeyed the rules of baseball, marbles, and tag. I wanted to slide by without calling attention to myself. I wanted to go my own way, like a coyote that steals through the woods, sniffing and snooping, pondering things, howling now and again in the safety of darkness, evading all traps.

7

I MIGHT HAVE DREAMED of howling at night like a coyote, but after losing Rusty, and after nearly dying from surgery when I was eight, I dreaded the actual darkness.

The surgery, Mama explained, was to remove my tonsils, useless lumps in my throat that made me get sick every winter. The doctor would put me to sleep, and when I woke up the operation would be over and I wouldn't remember a thing. I'd go home the next morning. My throat would be sore for a few days, but we'd soothe it with milk shakes and crushed ice soaked in Coca-Cola syrup.

If tonsils were useless, I wondered, why had God put them in my throat? And if they made me sick, why didn't God reach down and pluck them out?

God wasn't answering, and all Mama would say was that sometimes God gave us troubles to test our faith. Faith in what? I asked. Faith in God's love, she answered.

At the hospital, I clung to the hope of God's love as I rolled on a cart into the operating room, where a circle of strangers in blue masks gazed down on me. Can you count backwards from twenty? someone asked. I nodded, thinking maybe if I passed the test they'd let me go. Before I reached fifteen, a rubber cup settled onto my nose and mouth, a smell like a spilled bottle of perfume washed over me, and I never counted as far as ten.

What happened next would give me nightmares for years, well into high school, and it still occasionally snatches me from sleep. A steel I-beam, glowing red-hot, writhed against a black sky, while a sledgehammer pounded it over and over, sending sparks shooting in all directions, and each blow of the hammer pounded through me as if my bones were being smashed.

When I opened my eyes, a nurse was studying me from one side of the bed, Mama from the other. They gave me pinched smiles. I tried explaining my nightmare and why it had been so terrifying, but my throat burned and I kept sliding back into sleep.

"He wasn't supposed to remember," Mama whispered.

"Ether does that sometimes," the nurse replied.

Instead of going home the next day, I stayed in the hospital most of a week. Overhearing snatches of conversation between the doctor and my parents as I drowsed, I learned that I had bled so much they'd had to fill me up with new blood, and then they'd had to give me a second dose of ether, to keep me under long enough for the stitches.

At one point I heard Mama say, "He could have died."

"There's always a risk with surgery," the doctor said.

"He's tough," Dad said. "He'll be up running around before you know it."

I kept my eyes closed, my ears open. I didn't feel tough. I felt as flimsy as a moth. When I slipped back into sleep, the red-hot steel snaked through the blackness and throbbed under the beat of the hammer, and I woke up screaming.

After the surgery, the prayer I recited at bedtime took on a new urgency:

> Now I lay me down to sleep,
> I pray the Lord my soul to keep.
> If I should die before I wake,
> I pray the Lord my soul to take.

Before the surgery, nightfall had simply made me eager for the coming of daylight, when I could resume playing. But now it was as if the dark set loose a pack of dogs to gnaw on me until morning. I came to dread sunset, when the shadows of trees lengthened in the yard. I went to bed earlier and earlier, in hopes of falling asleep before the last light drained from the sky. But fear kept me awake, as I felt darkness pooling at the bottom of the stairs and then rising, step by step, to my room, where it spread across the floor like a black flood.

At first Mama thought leaving a light on in the hall would be enough to soothe me. When I kept shivering, she put a night-light in my room. Then she put on the light in my closet and left the door open. Then she asked Dad to come up and shine a flashlight under the bed and into all the corners.

"You see," he'd say, "nothing hiding. Now go to sleep."

Because he didn't hold with boys being afraid, Dad would make only one trip with his flashlight, except on nights when he began snoring in his chair right after supper, his breath smelling of booze, and then he wouldn't come upstairs at all. But Mama would come up time and again, staying for a while to sing me a song or read me a story, until even she grew weary and told me to just close my eyes and think about pleasant things and for goodness' sake not to call her again.

The pleasant things I thought about in the awful darkness were mostly creeks and trees and skies full of stars. Usually one or another of these pictures would lull me to sleep. But some nights I would hear Mama shouting at Dad, and Dad shouting back, and then Mama weeping, and a door slamming, and the car's engine starting. Then I knew Dad would be going to the Bachelor Officers' Quarters, where men smoked and drank while they gambled at poker and pool, and Dad wouldn't be home for a day or two, maybe not for a week. On those nights, the creek I tried to ride into sleep turned black and overflowed its banks, the trees pulled up their roots and charged about, lashing their limbs, and a hand holding a chalkboard eraser wiped out the stars.

In search of a remedy for my fear, Mama consulted with Reverend Knipe, who invited me to come by for a chat, just the two of us. He and I sat in rocking chairs on the front porch of the parsonage, a frame house next door to the Wayland church. Since the church, the parsonage, and Reverend Knipe's hair were all white, they seemed to go together, like a matched set. I couldn't imagine any other minister living in that house or preaching in that church. His face made me think of the General and Aunt Minnie—he was that old, and that kindly.

He asked me to describe my bad dream. Even in broad daylight I shuddered as I told about the fiery steel, the sledgehammer, the inky sky. In the telling, it never sounded all that scary. Then I told him how I lost nearly all my blood, how I never knew when I fell asleep whether I'd wake again, how the darkness seemed to swallow me.

After hearing me out, Reverend Knipe said, "Remember, the Lord is your shepherd. Would he let anything bad happen to his lamb?"

"I don't know, sir. Would he?"

"No, no, of course not. God loves children. Jesus loves children. Jesus said suffer the little children to come unto me, for of such is the kingdom of God."

If the kingdom of God was filled with children, I wanted to ask, did they all have to die to get there? But I remembered my manners and simply nodded.

Reverend Knipe went on to speak of Moses plucked from the bulrushes, Daniel rescued from the lions' den, Jonah saved from the belly of the whale, the Hebrew children hauled out of the fiery furnace. What I kept thinking was that no matter how many times God saved those Bible folks, by now the Hebrew children and Jonah and Daniel and Moses were all *gone*, wiped clean away. They had run out of rescues.

All the while, men were baling hay in a field across the road from the parsonage, stirring up the sweet smell of cut grass. Swallows carved the sky. Every now and again a laugh or shout from the men would reach my ears above the creaking of the rockers and the murmur of the minister's voice. I wanted to go over there and help those men stack bales of hay, the way I'd helped convicts on the prison farm pick cotton; but I knew it would be rude to run away, so I rocked and listened.

When Mama came to collect me, Reverend Knipe gave her a list of Bible verses to read aloud on the nights I couldn't sleep, and he told me to remember that Jesus would be keeping watch over my bed.

Not long after my conversation with Reverend Knipe, he finished preaching one Sunday morning, walked next door to the parsonage, and sat in one of those rocking chairs on the porch while Mrs. Knipe finished cooking dinner. By and by he fell asleep, and he never woke up.

This news did not encourage me to close my eyes at night. Here was a holy man, who knew the Bible forward and backward, who most likely never hurt a fly, and still the darkness swallowed him, from his polished leather shoes to his crown of white hair.

"He lived a long life and just wore out," Dad remarked.

"Reverend Knipe was old," Mama said, "and you're young."

Still, my nights got worse. When I cried, Mama came to sit beside my bed, looking pale and weary but also looking swollen. She'd never been fat. Now, as I lay in bed those long evenings, struggling to keep my eyes open, I noticed she was getting rounder. She had to catch her breath after climbing the stairs. Often she fell asleep before I did, her head tilted against the chair back, her mouth sagging open.

One night, when I called for Mama a third or fourth time, I could hear Dad telling her she wasn't going up those stairs again tonight except to her own bed. I tried keeping quiet, but the pressure of darkness squeezed one more cry out of me.

This time Dad charged up the stairs, flung open my door, and loomed over me. "I don't want to hear any more blubbering out of you," he said. "Not a peep. When you go to bed, you shut your eyes and shut your mouth and go to sleep. No more bothering Mama. I won't have you wearing her out. She's expecting a baby and needs her rest. You hear me?"

The weight of his anger and word of the baby stifled my sobs. "Yes, Daddy."

He softened then, leaning down to punch me lightly in the chest.

"You're going to have a little brother or sister, so you need to start acting like a big boy."

From that moment I started acting like a bigger boy than I was. What jolted me into the future was the realization that Mama could be worn out from carrying a baby in her belly and climbing stairs, and if we didn't take care of her she could die, just like Reverend Knipe. So I cured myself of crying. I was still terrified of darkness, but pretended not to be. Instead of asking Mama for comfort, I helped her all I could, drying the dishes without complaint, carrying bags of groceries in from the car, vacuuming rugs, running errands.

Mama kept swelling. She would sit at the kitchen table calling out girls' names and boys' names from a book, while Sandra fixed supper and I set the table. "What do you think of Audrey?" she might say. "How about Zane?" Sometimes, while Sandra and I cleaned up after a meal, Dad would fall asleep in his chair and Mama would fall asleep in her chair. If they kept on snoozing, I would put myself to bed and lie there in silence, choking back my fear.

As if to make up for not keeping me company while I slid toward sleep, Mama came home one day from a farm auction with a picture to hang beside my bed. It showed a lady angel with big wings and a little girl angel with nubbin wings, both of them wearing pink gowns and looking into a cradle where a baby slept. The little angel could barely see over the side of the cradle, even standing on tiptoe.

"God sent them to protect the baby through the night," Mother said. "You've got your own angels looking after you, only you can't see them."

The light from my closet shone on the picture, so I often studied it as I lay there battling the darkness. I couldn't decide whether angels were like Santa Claus and the Easter Bunny and the Tooth Fairy—made-up characters you had to pretend you believed in, to humor grownups—or whether they might really come down from heaven, like aliens from outer space. If angels did fly down to watch over children, I hoped mine was like the lady in the pink gown and the big white wings. I would just as soon not have a little girl angel watching me at night—or a little boy angel, for that matter. Then I wondered if there even *were* boy angels, or if God made all of them girls, since everybody knew that girls were nicer than boys. But Jesus started out as a boy, and he was about the nicest person who'd ever lived.

And so thoughts of angels and Jesus and God kept the darkness at bay some nights; other nights the darkness won.

In college during the 1960s, reading about the antics of my generation, I would conclude that my ether nightmare was a drug trip gone bad. In childhood, I had imagined the nightmare to be a glimpse of God's terrible workshop, where our bodies were hammered into shape. By my late teens, when I believed that science could explain away every mystery, I decided the pounding hammer was my own pulse, the red-hot filaments were my overwrought nerves, and the terror was a side effect of neurochemistry.

Now I think the nightmare was only a cover for the real bugaboo, which was oblivion—the chalkboard erased, the sky emptied of stars. The surgery brought home to me the fact that one day I would cease to be, as the deaths of kittens and piglets on our farm in Memphis, and the bodies of birds lying stiff in the grass below a picture window, and the shock from snakebite, and the withering of elderly neighbors, and even the shooting of my dog had failed to do. Ether gave me images of dread to fill my dreams. But the source of the dread was the nothingness between dreams.

Sooner or later, every child makes this discovery. What occasions the discovery—the sight of a grandparent laid out in a casket, news of a friend mangled in a car wreck, minor surgery that goes awry—is less important than the discovery itself, which is one of life's few lessons you never unlearn. The knowledge sinks into your bones and stays there. You may go long spells without thinking of your own death, but then suddenly the inescapable fact of it will rise like a fever and shake you.

What you do with this knowledge will, to a large extent, determine the shape of your life. You can salve the ache with religion, drown it with drink or drugs, numb it with a frenzy of shopping or hobbies or good works, deny it with philosophy, or defy it with science; but there the knowledge remains, coiled in your marrow. It led the Buddha to declare that to live is to suffer. It moved the Psalmist to sing, "Though I walk through the valley of the shadow of death, I will fear no evil: for thou art with me; thy rod and thy staff they comfort me." It inspired Newton to discern God's handiwork in the circling of planets through the void. In every age, in every land, awareness of death has given rise to rituals and prayers, elixirs of youth and miracle cures, crackpots and saints, priests who claim to know the secret of immortality, and guardian spirits with or without wings.

The picture of the two angels peeping into a cradle now hangs over my mother's bed in her assisted living apartment. After having nursed me through my nightly tussle with oblivion during those childhood years, now she's the one who needs comforting. "I'm lost," she says, holding my hand. "I'm so afraid."

The religion she has faithfully practiced since her own childhood assures her of a place in heaven, where her decrepit body will be restored and her departed loved ones will be gathered. Several times in recent months she has asked me if I believe in heaven, and I have lied and said yes. I hide my doubts from her as she hid hers from me when I was a boy. For all her Bible study and churchgoing, doubt still assails her. Otherwise, as age whittles away her body and mind, she'd welcome death. Instead, she fights every downward lurch into darkness.

The first time Dad went slamming out the door with his suitcase to the Bachelor Officers' Quarters after a shouting match with Mama, I asked her what *bachelor* meant.

"It means a man without a wife," Mama answered grimly.

"But Dad's got you," I said.

"He does for now," said Mama, still seething from their latest fight, "but he might not have me for long."

I could see she regretted the words as soon as she let them loose. Dad would count under his breath to keep from boiling over when he got mad, and the higher he counted the madder he was trying not to be. But Mama would always blurt out whatever she was feeling, from delight to rage, as soon as she felt it.

What she mainly felt, in those months after nightmares began swirling in me and the baby started swelling in her, was misery. She was sick of pinching pennies. She was fed up with working her fingers to the bone while Dad played poker and guzzled beer at the BOQ. She was tired of driving in and out through gates, tired of barbed wire, tanks, and guns. She didn't care if she never saw another soldier or their silly salutes. She didn't care if she never heard another scrap of gossip from those military wives, with their painted faces and cigarette breath. She was sick of bombs exploding at the ammunition dump during supper, sick of fighter planes zooming overhead, sick of every last thing to do with the Arsenal. Mark her words, she wasn't going to raise a baby in this godforsaken place.

"It's hormones," Sandra informed me, drawing on the wisdom of sixth-grade health class.

Sandra and I were usually the main audience for Mama's tirades. Dad heard enough of them evenings and weekends, however, to decide that he and Mama should go looking for a house outside the chain-link fence. There was still enough of Chicago in Mama to make her hanker for a place in town. But Dad reminded her how happy she had been on the farm in Tennessee, and besides, there were no towns nearby. So they looked for a place in the country.

While they drove the back roads, Sandra and I stayed with one of Mama's friends on the Circle, Mrs. Kurtz, whose house was so jammed with china figurines that I was afraid a sneeze would cost me a lifetime's allowance. Her face had more lines than a road map, so I was puzzled by her mop of curly blond hair, until Sandra told me it was a wig. Nobody who lived in a house jammed with figurines would have kids, of course, nor any toys for us to play with. To entertain us, Mrs. Kurtz taught us how to shuffle cards and play roulette while she told us stories about being abducted by aliens. The aliens were polite but firm as they dragged her out of bed and carried her up into a flying saucer that hovered over her house. They were studying human beings, to find out how we ticked, and they'd chosen Mrs. Kurtz as the ideal specimen. If she cooperated with them, they would take her for a visit to their home planet, where jewels grew on trees.

Since all the kids on the Circle were convinced that UFOs kept buzzing the Arsenal, these tales of Mrs. Kurtz hobnobbing with aliens seemed reasonable to me. The stories were so riveting that I almost felt disappointed when Mama and Dad returned from one of their drives to announce they'd found a one-story house—no more stairs for Mama to climb—on a small farm surrounded by woods, with a pasture, a pigpen, a stable, and a pony. The pony was the clincher for me. It drove out of my head all thought of aliens, soldiers, and war machines. From the moment I heard about the pony, I couldn't wait to move.

In the race between our moving to the new house and the coming of the baby, the baby won. Soon after school was out for the year, Sandra and I woke up one morning to the sound of Mrs. Kurtz bellowing hymns in the kitchen as she fixed breakfast. "Rise up, rise up, you sleepyheads!" she called to us. "While you two were sawing logs, your mother gave birth to a bouncing boy."

Over scrambled eggs, Sandra begged for more details about our new brother. I begged for another installment in the alien saga, which Mrs. Kurtz readily supplied. Because she had cooperated with them, the aliens not only took her for a tour of their home planet, where jewels really did grow on trees and streams flowed with liquid gold, but also decided not to invade Earth, which had been their plan all along. A fleet of spaceships had been lurking behind the moon, just waiting for the word, but now they were zipping away to attack some other planet. Mrs. Kurtz didn't want people fussing over her for saving us from an alien invasion, so she asked Sandra and me to keep this news to ourselves.

Naturally, as soon as Dad and Mama cruised up to our house on the Circle in our white Pontiac, I stuck my head through Mama's open window, glanced at the bundle in her lap, and began rattling on about Mrs. Kurtz and the aliens.

Sandra laughed. "It's a story, silly."

"It's the gospel truth," I insisted.

"His name is Glenn Craig," Mama said, unwrapping the bundle enough to reveal a swatch of black hair and two squinched-up eyes. "Isn't he adorable?"

Sight of my brother's face halted me in midsentence. He had ears, a nose and mouth, a rosy chin, and there peeping from the blanket a curled fistful of tiny fingers, everything just like a real person, like somebody you could play with when he got bigger.

AIR

8

ON THE DAY Glenn came home from the hospital, President Eisenhower signed a law to combat "godless Communism" by amending the Pledge of Allegiance, so in school that fall of 1954 we learned to add the words "under God" as we spoke to the flag each morning with hands over our hearts. The coins I collected into folders, hunting for examples from every U.S. mint and every year, already proclaimed "In God We Trust," all the way back to my earliest find, a quarter from 1898 with an eagle on one side and the head of Liberty on the other, both sides worn as smooth as a baby's bottom.

I formed my impression of a baby's bottom from watching Mama change Glenn's diaper. The trouble with kid brothers, I soon decided, was that they started out as babies. In the beginning, all Glenn did was eat, sleep, cry, and wet himself. Sandra got to cradle him in her lap, but Mama didn't trust me to hold him, I was so fidgety. About the only thing I could do with him was tickle his chin and try to get a peep at his eyes. At this rate, it would be a long while before he and I could climb trees, build boats, or play war.

So the novelty of having a kid brother had worn pretty thin by the time we moved to our new place outside the Arsenal a few months after his birth. The farm was on a blacktop road called Esworthy, which curved and kinked for about five miles from the Charlestown cemetery to a branch of the Mahoning River, where in coming years I would fish and trap and, on two clumsy occasions, nearly drown. Between the river and the cemetery was a scattering of shacks, trailers, run-down houses, and overgrown fields.

"My kind of road," Dad noted.

"Leading from nowhere to nowhere," Mama said with a laugh.

Mama called our new place a ranch house, although there wasn't any ranch in sight, just a weedy lawn and a scruffy pasture surrounded by woods. It was a failed farm, Dad said, which made it cheap enough for us to buy. The fences were mostly down. Plows, a harrow, a manure spreader, an iron-wheeled tractor, and other old equipment rusted in a ravine at the edge of the woods. The pigpen was a warped box on skids. The low-slung house needed paint and new shingles. The barn had burned, leaving only a cracked foundation, and you could see daylight through the walls of the stable.

One end of the stable was piled with bales of hay and sacks of oats, while a stall in the other end held what I had imagined would be the prize of the place—a pony named Belle. Her coat was the roasted red of brick, a color horse people call sorrel, and in summer, when I first laid eyes on her, it was shiny and sleek. In winter her coat grew shaggy, for she was a cross between the long-haired Shetland breed and the big-shouldered Hackney. Another hand higher and she would have been a horse.

It was a blessing for my bones that Belle wasn't any higher, because I would have had farther to fall when she bucked me off. She could be counted on to buck me off almost every time I climbed into the saddle. For variety, she would scrape me off by trotting beneath a low branch, or she would break into a gallop, lulling me into thinking she had finally accepted my weight, and then she would skid to a halt, lower her head, and fling me over the saddle horn. As often as I tumbled, Dad told me to climb back on. And I did climb back on, more determined to satisfy my father than to defy the pony.

When Belle was especially mean, Dad would seize hold of the bridle straps, pull her face close to his, and tell her sternly how he expected her to behave. She gazed at him with glistening eyes, for all the world as if she were paying attention; then she nuzzled his pocket until he drew out a cigarette and fed it to her in his open palm.

"You see," he'd say, "you've got to show her who's boss."

So far as I could see, Belle was the boss, even of Dad. He talked a tough line, about how he was going to train her to wear a harness and pull a wagon in summer and a sleigh in winter, how he'd break her to be such a gentle pony that even Glenn could ride. But Belle wouldn't break. She fought the bridle, the saddle, the harness. When Dad managed to hitch her to a wagon, she wouldn't budge, no matter if he slapped her rump until the dust flew. When I managed to saddle her, she would bloat up her belly until I had the girth cinched, and then as soon as I put my foot in the stirrup she would let out her breath, the cinch would loosen, and down I would tumble.

So long as you curried her red coat with a steel comb or scratched her neck or forked hay into her stall or fed her oats—in other words, so long as you did exactly what she wanted you to do—Belle would be all sweetness and light. But try getting her to do what *you* wanted, and she would kick your shins or bite any part of you within reach.

Dad tried talking to her, petting her, bribing her with apples and sugar cubes. But Belle had too much dignity to be coaxed into good behavior. Sooner or later, therefore, Dad would boil over with rage and hit her with his fist or a coiled rope. Belle shied away, eyes rolling, hooves clattering on the oak planks of the stall or gouging up dust in the yard, but she wouldn't give in. When his arm grew tired, Dad quit beating her and pretended he'd won. Belle went back to grazing on grass or munching oats, as if nothing had happened, except that her skin would twitch where he had pounded her.

Watching these battles, I decided never to do anything, if I could help it, to make Dad furious with me, and never to force my will on another living thing. I succeeded more or less on the first count. During my teen years, Dad and I would have run-ins over chores, church, girls, cars, politics, and his penchant for booze, yet we never escalated our quarrels beyond shouts and slammed doors. The second vow, never to force my will on another living thing, didn't keep me from trapping muskrats and hunting squirrels in a haphazard sort of way, nor until recently did it discourage me from eating meat, but it gave me a guilty conscience for doing so, and it combined with the teachings of Jesus and the examples of Mohandas Gandhi and Martin Luther King, Jr., to make me a pacifist during the Vietnam War and an advocate of nonviolence ever afterward.

Without saying so, Dad eventually gave up on training Belle. By the time we acquired her along with the farm, she was too settled into bad habits ever to be reformed. Although I hated her for bucking me off, I admired her for refusing to be broken to our ways, a fierce quality I came to understand as wildness. If Mama had accepted that our gambling smoking drinking Dad was also beyond reforming by the time she married him, our house would have been a more peaceful place. But until his dying day at the age of sixty-four, she never gave up believing she could improve him, if only he'd listen to her instruction. He listened just long enough to do the opposite of whatever she told him, all the while counting out loud as a measure of how mad he was trying not to be.

Nearly a quarter century after my father's death, until her mind began to fail, my mother still rarely met a person she didn't feel could benefit from her instruction. As she did throughout my childhood, she would tell wailing children to hush up, tell slouching teenagers to straighten up, tell grown women to brush the hair out of their eyes, warn men to avoid drinking beer lest they wind up in the gutter, prod the residents of her assisted living community to get off the couch and stir their limbs. And her sharp tongue still made me cringe.

"I had two little brothers to look after when my mother died," she used to remind me. "If I hadn't bossed them around, Chicago would have gobbled them up. I learned early on to take care of people who don't have the sense to take care of themselves."

Mother can no longer say anything that complex, but she can still embarrass me. When Ruth and I take Elizabeth to visit her, the four of us make our way slowly down the halls, Mother pushing her walker and the baby riding in my arms. When we meet other residents, Mother exhorts them to admire the baby, whose name she can't remember and whom she calls a little boy. Most of the residents have met Elizabeth before, and they have settled into one of two responses. Some of them glow at sight of the baby, while others glance at her reluctantly, as if she were too painful a reminder of their own babies long since grown, or of their own lost youth. If Mother detects anything short of adulation for her great-granddaughter, she exhorts all the harder, and I try to nudge our crew into motion down the hall before she can get really cranked up.

Pretty soon, Elizabeth will be able to toddle down the hall on her own legs. At nine months, she has now lived in the open air as long as she lived inside Eva's womb. She has learned to crawl, to stand up by tugging on the lip of a coffee table or the rung of a chair, to stagger along while holding on to a grownup's hand. I'm always happy to supply the hand, because I never cease to wonder at her drive for movement. It's a force of nature, as insistent as the current in a creek.

I also wonder at the baby's drive for speech. She yodels when you're spooning peas into her mouth, mutters when you're lounging on the floor with her, sings when you're changing her diaper. Nowadays when she wakes from a nap, instead of crying to be rescued from her crib, she lies there for a few minutes babbling. I steal up to the door of her nursery and listen. Whole sentences flow out of her, some of them marked with the rising intonation of questions, some with the certainty of declarations, none of them burdened by words you'd find in the dictionary. Soon enough she'll learn which of those sounds make sense to the people around her, and she'll begin speaking our language. Already she says "mama," naming the most important person in her life, and she says "bye-bye" while waving her hand when anybody leaves. Using a sign language Eva has taught her, Elizabeth also gestures with her hands to say "milk," "daddy," "cat," "sleep."

If this headlong flow into motion and speech weren't the birthright of every healthy child, we would more easily recognize it for the miracle it is. The urge to crawl, stand, and walk; the urge to utter sounds, learn language, and speak; the urge to explore the world with body and mind is universal among children, ferocious, irrepressible. Most of what a child learns is the product of culture—how to say a word, drink from a cup, eat from a spoon, tie a shoe—but the impulse for learning is utterly wild, as wild as the hunting instinct in Rusty and the pack of dogs, as wild as a stubborn pony's urge to buck, as wild as the rising of an oak from an acorn or the beating of a heart.

My mother's heart is weakening, the doctor says, which is why she can't get enough oxygen to her brain, which is why she's losing her grip on words. On our strolls through the hallway, Mother stops every now and then to say, "Oh, here's something," or "Listen to me, now." Then she stands there with a stricken look in her hazel eyes, her mouth working but silent. Ruth and I cue her with questions: Is it something about your apartment? The nurses? The food? The other residents? Did somebody call on the phone? Do you hurt anywhere? Mother shakes her head no, in more and more frustration, then shrugs and says, "Well, *any*how," and we resume our stroll. Mother's steps are shorter and more cautious than those Elizabeth already takes.

As Elizabeth gains her faculties of motion and speech, Mother loses hers. And so they maintain a sort of balance, one coming and one going, the infant climbing up a steep slope, the old woman sliding down.

After our move from the Arsenal to the Esworthy place, my kid brother, Glenn, went through the same wild stages that I observe with fascination in Elizabeth now, but back then I was too busy being a kid myself to take much notice. Nor did I notice the changes in my parents, who seemed to me, like God in heaven, immortal and omnipotent.

Mama could paint, draw, cook, can, grow vegetables and flowers, find a bargain, refinish a chest of drawers, furnish the house from auctions, and outfit everybody in the family except Dad with clothes she sewed herself. Until I rebelled at the beginning of high school, I wore shirts she had made. Although finely tailored, they favored large collars and bold prints, the sort of getup that would have looked good on the matrons in Mama's Bible study but that looked, in the opinion of my schoolmates, ridiculous on a scrawny boy. From working with fabrics and paints, Mama knew a name for every shade in the rainbow. She remarked on the play of light and the texture of shadows, the shape of petals or buckles, the drift of clouds or conversation. She taught me to love color and design, in nature as well as in things humans had made.

While Mama could help with homework involving pictures or stories, Dad helped with anything involving numbers or equations. He was as rational, as logical, as clear-thinking as she was emotional and fuzzy-minded. When one of her brothers, considering Mama deprived, gave her a mixer or vacuum cleaner for her birthday, she would ask Dad or Sandra or me to show her how to run it, because she couldn't follow a set of written directions to save her life.

"I have an artistic temperament," she'd say with a sniff.

Artists, I gathered, didn't need to understand how anything worked; they needed only to appreciate how it looked or sounded or felt.

Mama's artistic temperament was also the reason she gave for filling our house with antiques—chairs and love seats too frail for sitting on, cut glass and porcelain dishes too fragile for table use, pendulum clocks that wouldn't run, Victrolas that wouldn't play. From rummage sales, bargain barns, and auctions, she brought home broken items for Dad to fix. "It only needs a little glue," she might say of a bundle of sticks that had once been a stool, or "It's only missing a few parts," she might say of a wooden radio.

More often than not, what time and hard knocks had rent asunder Dad could put back together. If Mama's temperament was that of an artist, Dad's was that of a mechanic. Had he grown up in different circumstances, he might have become a first-rate scientist. Once Mama held an opinion on any subject, she held on tight, immune to reason or evidence. But Dad held his opinions provisionally, experimentally, testing them against experience. While she read mysteries, he read repair manuals. While she took drawing classes, he studied electronics. He didn't much care how anything looked, but he would puzzle for hours to figure out how it was put together and how it worked. He could do carpentry, masonry, plumbing, wiring, and welding; he was an expert hunter and fisherman; he could fell trees, tune engines, run fencing, grow crops, and doctor livestock. Belle was the only animal I ever saw him fail to gentle, and even she feigned obedience so long as Dad was looking at her.

Like many another odd couple who stay together against all expectations, my parents maintained a kind of truce by staking out their separate territories, the way hostile tribes preserve the peace by honoring boundaries. Mama ruled the house and yard; she determined what we ate, how we dressed, where and how we worshiped; she administered first aid; she dealt with doctors, teachers, preachers, and merchants. Dad ruled the garage and barn and woods; he brought home the paycheck and kept track of money, insurance, bills, and taxes; he dealt with bankers, policemen, lawyers, and strangers. Mama hauled us to the library, the grocery store, and the houses of friends. Dad hauled us to Lake Erie, to Scout camp, to baseball games, and back into the Arsenal to drive among the munitions bunkers and count deer. Mama shouted and spanked to make us behave; Dad raised an eyebrow. Except for clothes, which belonged to Mama's domain, Dad fixed everything we owned.

What appealed to Dad about the farm on Esworthy Road, I suspect, was that it was so in need of fixing up. Everywhere he looked, he saw gullies to be plugged, crooked buildings to straighten, bare siding to paint, gimpy machines to mend. Snakes lurked in the wet basement. The well pump wheezed. The chimney wouldn't draw. The electrical circuits were so overloaded they burned out fuse after fuse. Dad rewired the house, rebuilt the chimney, oiled the pump, dried up the basement, and rooted out the snakes. It wasn't that he welcomed trouble; he liked proving he could deal with trouble when it arrived. He kept a shotgun behind the door of his bedroom for the same reason. I think he also hoped to show, by healing the house and land, that he was a strong man in spite of his weakness for drink and a rich man in spite of his meager paycheck—altogether a better man than Mama made him out to be.

What appealed to Mama about the new place, as she often said, was that it would provide our family with a fresh start. No more bombs rattling the supper dishes, no more carousing at the Bachelor Officers' Quarters, no more soldiers brandishing guns at the gate, no more gossip from busybodies on the Circle, no more nightmares for her elder son.

I have never entirely shaken loose from those nightmares of oblivion, not even to this day, when I'm the one who offers reassurance at bed-time and Mother is the one who needs comforting. She often calls after she has returned to her room from supper, just as Ruth and I are sitting down to our own meal. As the food cools on my plate, I tease words out of her, asking questions, guessing at her meaning. Before these calls end, I often feel impatient. I want to visit with my wife, eat our meal, rest between the labors of the day and the labors of the evening. I want to be relieved from having to play the parent to my mother. And then I feel ashamed of my impatience, for I understand Mother's need. What-ever she might say on the phone, what she really wants is to hear, be-fore she closes her eyes, the voice of someone who loves her. Love is, at last, our only rejoinder to darkness.

If I had not suffered hallucinations under the influence of ether, if I had not nearly died in a routine surgery, if I had not lived several of my childhood years surrounded by the machinery of war, the timing and furnishing of my nightmares might have been different; yet sooner or later I would have had to face the fact of extinction, my own and that of everything that breathes. Once I crossed that threshold of awareness, there was no crossing back.

I had learned to wrestle with fear in silence by the time Glenn moved from his crib into the bottom bunk in my bedroom. Henceforth it was *our* bedroom, and I rarely had a moment to myself in the house or yard so long as Glenn was awake. Once he could toddle, he clung to me like a tick to a dog.

Sometimes when he napped I would sneak away to the woods, just to be alone. My favorite place to go when I needed privacy was a grassy meadow I had discovered deep in the woods soon after our move to the farm on Esworthy. Whatever kept the meadow clear of trees—maybe fire, maybe browsing deer—I was grateful for the grass, which rose in the heat of summer as high as my chest. I would flatten a circle in the grass and lie there staring up at the clouds. Birds swooped by, as name-less to me as the clouds, intent on their errands, intensely alive. In sum-mer and early fall, butterflies lolled about on the Queen Anne's lace and purple asters and other gangly wildflowers. Later in the fall, the seed heads of poison sumac turned red, like glimmering torches.

Hidden there in my nest of grass, I felt both happy and afraid. It pleased me to have this secret place, and it also scared me to think that no one on earth knew where I was. If I broke my leg in a groundhog hole or passed out from snakebite or bee stings, would I be lost in that meadow forever, my bones bleaching in the sun? No, I decided. Dad and Mama would call out the neighbors, the people from church, the kids and parents from school, and they would scour the woods. And if they still couldn't find me, if days and weeks passed and the other folks got tired and gave up, Dad and Mama would never quit. That was what it meant to be loved—there were people who would never give up looking and longing for you, no matter how far you wandered lost.

The very differences that set my parents at odds made our household a nourishing place for me. I moved back and forth between my mother's realm and my father's realm like an ambassador or a spy. In the house and garden, I learned from Mama to love books, to revel in flowers, to honor my feelings, to appreciate the shape and texture and tone of things, to confess amazement. In the garage and barn and woods, work-ing alongside Dad, I learned to love animals, to delight in the use of tools, to admire good work and the skill required to do it, to laugh at myself and the whole quirky human race, to rejoice in the wild energy flowing through my body and the earth.

What I learned from Dad I learned mainly by watching him. While he loved to joke and tell stories, unlike Mama he never lectured. Ser-mons were for churches, he would say, and lectures were for schools, and he wasn't running either sort of enterprise. With a few words or maybe no words at all, he would show me how to make a square cut with a handsaw by steadying the blade against my thumb, how to swing a hammer with my whole arm instead of only my wrist, how to judge if an ear of corn was ripe, how to pull cockleburs out of Belle's tail without hurting her, how to sharpen a knife, how to dig a posthole or tighten a fence, how to change a fan belt or a light switch, how to find enough worms to fill a coffee can and how to use those worms to catch a fish.

Although Dad worked hard on the Esworthy place, he never hurried, partly because he enjoyed working and partly, I came to realize, because he wanted his children to be able to help. Judging by the clock, our help was more of a hindrance; but he never judged by the clock. If he didn't finish a job one day, well, there would be other days, and no end of jobs.

Mama was impatient. She wanted that old wreck of a house fixed up, as Dad had fixed up the place in Memphis, and she wanted it done right away. But Dad wouldn't rush. When he came to a new problem—and his life on that run-down farm was a string of problems—he would consider it carefully, telling whichever child was handy how he thought it might be solved, and asking our opinions, as if we might think up a solution that hadn't occurred to him. Because he believed in us, sometimes we actually did come up with a workable idea, which would make him slap his leg and say, "Why, I wouldn't have thought of that in a blue moon." Then he would gather the necessary tools, decide what parts of the job a child could do, and we would set to work.

One day in my tenth summer, Dad was patching the foundation of the barn that had burned, thinking he might build a shop on the site if he ever laid by enough money. While he smoothed mortar into cracks with a trowel, I mixed a fresh batch of mortar in a wheelbarrow, and Glenn hunted for bugs in the grass near my feet. Dad was humming, which meant he was happy, as clear a sign as the purring of a cat.

For the pleasure of hearing that hum, I kept on dragging the hoe through the slurry of sand and cement long after my arms were tired. When Dad came over to look, he declared my batch of mortar to be mixed about as well as any he'd ever seen. He asked me if I thought I could push the wheelbarrow over to the wall, and I told him yes, and I did push it all the way without spilling a drop, although just barely. As usual, Glenn toddled along beside me, as if tied to my leg by a string. Dad scraped the mortar onto a board, picked up a dab on his trowel, and began filling a wide crack. Suddenly he leapt back, swatting the air around his head. "Bees!" he yelled. "Run, Scott! Grab the baby and run to the house!"

I dropped the handles of the wheelbarrow, scooped up Glenn in my arms, and lit out, legs pounding, heart pounding, and I never slowed until I burst into the kitchen and butted the door shut behind me and plumped Glenn down onto the linoleum floor. Until that moment he'd been too surprised to cry, but now, seeing Mama and Sandra slicing tomatoes at the counter, he let out a wail.

"What in heaven's name is going on?" Mama asked, picking up Glenn and looking him over for damage.

Between gasps I told her about the bees. Now it was Mama's turn to gasp, because she knew I was deathly allergic to stings. One bite on the cheek and my eyes would swell shut. One bite on the wrist, and my hands would grow so thick I couldn't bend my fingers. Half a dozen bites might have killed me. More than likely, Glenn was vulnerable as well, because the allergy came straight from Mama.

"Did they sting you?" Mama demanded. "Did they sting the baby?"

"I don't believe so," I answered. "But they swarmed all over Daddy."

We rushed to the kitchen window then and looked out to see Dad slapping the bees from his face and doing a kind of jitterbug with his feet while he pushed a flaming wand of straw into that crack in the foundation. Mama yelled for him to come away from there, but you could see he wasn't going to stop until he'd killed or scattered every last bee. Ordinarily he liked bees, because they pollinated his crops, and they were hardworking and smart; but these ones had got him riled up. By and by he quit slapping, quit jitterbugging, and mashed out the smoldering straw beneath his boot. Then he came on up to the house with a worried look on his face that didn't relax until he found out Glenn and I had escaped without a sting. Only then did he take off his shirt and sit down at the kitchen table and let Mama draw out with tweezers the dozens of stingers from pretty much every quarter of his body above the waist.

"You look like a pincushion," Mama said, her voice shivery with relief.

Dad laughed. She told him they ought to go see the doctor, but he said no, he had a first-rate batch of mortar to use before it set up. Besides, we had more need for our money than the doctor did.

"You saved the boys," Mama said.

"Did I? Well, then," Dad said, making a frown at Glenn and me, "I reckon they'll just keep eating me out of house and home."

I had often seen my father without his shirt, because he liked to work that way in hot weather, but seeing him now, upright at the table, with welts rising all over his ruddy skin, and seeing Mama bent over him, pulling out the stingers and then tenderly dabbing the spots with cotton soaked in ammonia, the two of them oblivious for the moment of Glenn or Sandra or me, their fights forgotten, it came over me how beautiful they were, and how much they loved one another. The love seemed larger than my parents, larger than all five of us in the kitchen, larger than our ragged farm, larger than the Arsenal laced with bombs, large enough to hold every creature and river and stone on earth.

Right there was a taste of heaven, I decided. If Dad could have just kept sitting at the kitchen table and Mama could have kept tweezing out those stingers and dabbing the welts gingerly, while we three kids stood by watching like a little chorus, all of us caught up in a force brighter and bigger than sunshine, we might have been happy forever.

But the clock ticked on. Glenn tugged at Mama's dress and said, "I'm hungry." Mama said she'd fix supper just as soon as she finished doctoring Daddy. Sandra told me it was my turn to set the table, and I said no it wasn't, and she said it was too, and I said not on your life. Mama told us to quit squabbling, but we kept on, back and forth, neither willing to yield, until Dad rose abruptly.

"Sandra," he said, "you'll set the table, and Scott, you'll clean out the wheelbarrow while I finish up that mortar."

"But the bees—" Mama protested.

"The bees are dead or gone," he said.

"You ought to rest," she said. "You could go into shock."

"I'm right as rain." Giving me a hard look, he demanded, "Son, did you grow roots?"

"No, sir."

"Then why are you standing there like a stump?"

I picked up my feet and ran down to the old foundation, where I scraped and hosed out the wheelbarrow until it was clean, all the while remembering the taste of heaven, like a tiny seed lodged in my teeth that I kept touching with my tongue.

9

THE KINGDOM OF HEAVEN is like to a grain of mustard seed," I read in my pocket-sized New Testament, a copy of which had been presented to each member of my fifth-grade class in the spring of 1956 by two earnest, burly men from the Gideons: "The kingdom of heaven is like to a grain of mustard seed, which a man took, and sowed in his field: / Which indeed is the least of all seeds: but when it is grown, it is the greatest among herbs, and becometh a tree, so that the birds of the air come and lodge in the branches thereof." In the Gospels I also read that if you have faith even as small as a mustard seed, you can tell a sycamore tree to pluck itself up by the roots and go plant itself in the sea, and it will go, or you can tell a mountain to move, and it will obey. With only a tiny seed of faith, nothing would be impossible for you.

But faith in what? Faith in the Father, Son, and Holy Ghost, said the minister at the Charlestown Methodist Church, where our family started going after Reverend Knipe died on the porch of the parsonage in Wayland and after we bought the run-down farm on Esworthy Road. The Father, I knew, was God, a moody, mighty king who lived in the sky and punished sinners; the Son was Jesus, a kind man who walked barefoot down here on earth and forgave sinners; but what the Holy Ghost might be, I had no idea. Ghosts, in general, weren't holy. They were spooky and mischievous, haunting the places where they'd been mistreated or killed.

In those days I took as proof of my belief in God that I feared him almost constantly. The proof of my belief in Jesus was that I wanted to be like him when I grew up, except without dying on a cross. The gap in my faith, I decided, fell in the region of the Holy Ghost. As nearly as I could tell from asking the minister and Sunday-school teachers, the Holy Ghost was a kind of energy, like gravity or electricity, only it came down from heaven into people's hearts, and it bent the laws of nature to suit God's will.

I was learning about the laws of nature in school, and even more from reading science books I borrowed at the library in Ravenna, the county seat. None of those books made mention of God's will or the Holy Ghost. They didn't seem to allow any way for the laws of nature to be bent.

I tried a few experiments to see what faith could do. If a mustard seed's worth of faith could pluck up a tree or move a mountain, surely I had enough faith to shove a coin. On the windowsill in the bedroom I shared with Glenn, I drew a line with a pencil. Next to the line I placed my 1898 Liberty quarter, the one worn smooth as a baby's bottom, and then I shut my eyes and prayed for the quarter to slide. It didn't budge. Glenn was watching, because he tagged after me everywhere. I thought maybe Glenn interfered with the operation of the Holy Ghost, so I told him to run outside and play, but he only sidled up closer. Then I decided the Holy Ghost wouldn't begrudge an innocent child. Maybe the problem was that a quarter weighed more than my faith could handle. So I repeated the experiment with a nickel, a penny, and a dime, but got the same results. At last I pulled a feather from my pillow and laid it on the sill, shut my eyes, thought about everything holy, and willed it to move. When I opened my eyes, the feather was afloat in the air, swooping back and forth as it settled to the floor.

"Wind," said Glenn, watching the feather.

"Out of the mouths of babes," I said.

What I understood about religion told me I should credit faith for lifting the feather, but what I was beginning to understand about science told me Glenn was right, and I should credit the wind. After all, if faith really could move mountains, there were enough true believers in my church alone to revise the whole geography of Ohio. But the hills just sat there. Now, a glacier could move a mountain, and so could rain and wind, if you allowed enough time. When I came to think about it, ice and rain and wind seemed at least as amazing as the Holy Ghost.

It would be a long while before I could admit even to myself that what I was reading in library books about the Big Bang, nuclear fusion, and evolution made a lot more sense of the universe than what I read in the Bible. The story told by science was also just more *interesting*, more chock-full of curious details, more in keeping with the astonishment I felt about every scrap of the wild world, from a pill bug in the palm of my hand to a galaxy in the deeps of space.

The turning of water into wine didn't seem to me half as much a miracle as the turning of tadpoles into frogs, and that happened every spring in every puddle without any help from Jesus. I wasn't ready to say that Jesus or God or the Holy Ghost *couldn't* turn tadpoles into tigers, say, if they took a mind to. I just didn't see any evidence that they were fiddling with the rules of nature. I still believed God had created the universe and made up all the rules. But I was beginning to suspect that ever since the Creation, the universe had run pretty much on its own, and I wanted to learn every detail about how it ran. I wanted to know about magnetism, migration, geology, subatomic particles, the periodic table of the elements, and a host of other fascinating things, not one of which appeared anywhere in the Bible. If reading the Bible and going to church and praying hadn't built up my faith enough to budge even a thin dime, there didn't seem to be much future for me in that line. By studying science, however, one day I might travel to the bottom of the sea or away to other planets, I might discover a new species or a new element, I might help unlock the secrets of the universe.

Still, I loved the old-time poetry and comforting stories of the Bible. So every night before giving in to the fearful darkness, I pored over the little volume from the Gideons. The Psalms assured me that God had named and numbered every star. I read again and again the Psalmist's cry: "When I consider thy heavens, the work of thy fingers, the moon and the stars, which thou hast ordained; / What is man, that thou art mindful of him? and the son of man, that thou visitest him? / For thou hast made him a little lower than the angels, and hast crowned him with glory and honour." At this point in my history of awe, I couldn't decide which prospect was more frightening—facing a God who is mindful of every human act, facing a God who takes no notice of our puny lives, or facing a universe entirely empty of God.

In a book that fit into the palm of my hand, the Gideons had crammed the Psalms and Proverbs as well as the whole New Testament. I didn't know how small a mustard seed was, but I doubted it was any smaller than the letters in these pages. The print was so small neither Mama nor Dad could read it without squinting, but I made it out just fine. Yet the teacher's writing on the blackboard at school appeared fuzzy to me. How could tiny letters look clear and big ones look blurry?

One July noonday in the summer after fifth grade, the answer to that riddle came hurtling down at me out of a clear sky. I was in center field of the baseball diamond at Charlestown School, warming up for a game. The coach was hitting fly balls, some of them carrying nearly to the fence, which separated the outfield from a pasture belonging to the school janitor. Three cows chewing their cuds were gathered at the fence to watch. Leaping grasshoppers thwacked against my legs.

The surest way of getting hit by a baseball, I'd learned from Dad, was to shy away from it. Keep your eyes on the ball and keep your glove ready, he'd taught me. So when the coach hit a high fly toward me, I raced to the spot where I thought it would come down, lifted my glove, and waited. The waiting was a scary pleasure when I had judged the flight of the ball accurately, as I had this time, taking into account the crack of the bat, the push of wind, and the tug of gravity. At the last moment I lost the ball in the sun—but it found me, nicking my glove and smacking me in the left eye.

The first person I saw when I looked up from the grass was Dad, and I didn't see him too well.

"That's not what I meant by keeping your eye on the ball," he said, trying to josh me through the pain, but then, pulling my hand away from my face, he sobered up, lifted me in his arms, and began trotting toward the car.

We'd gone only a few paces before we met Mama, who told him to slow down and not jounce me so, and for once he did what she told him, and then we met the coach, who brought a wet towel wrapped around some ice, and by the time I was laid across the backseat of the car with the cold pack over my face, I could hear, above the crunching of our tires on the cinders of the school parking lot, my teammates wishing me good luck.

My good luck was in having deep-set eyes, according to the emergency-room doctor who shaved my eyebrow and put in six or eight stitches. The bone of my cheek and brow had taken the blow, and the eye itself, so far as he could tell, hadn't been harmed. But he recommended that an optometrist have a look at me, just to make sure.

Instead of feeling like a pirate because of the patch I got to wear over my banged-up eye, I felt like a fool for losing that fly ball in the sun. Dad showed me scars from the stitches he'd collected during his career as a Golden Gloves boxer, minor-league baseball player, weekend farmer, and weeklong bomb maker, which was his way of telling me you couldn't play hard or work hard without picking up a few dings.

Soon after the mishap, Mama took me to Ravenna, where I climbed into the black leather chair of an optometrist, who peeled away the patch and studied my bloodshot eye. Then he projected a light onto the wall across the darkened room from me and asked what letters I saw there. I couldn't see any letters, only a squarish blob. Covering by turns my left eye and then my right, twirling knobs, making me peer through little glass disks, asking me over and over again what I could see, the optometrist finally announced to Mama, as though I weren't in the room, "The boy's eye is fine, Mrs. Sanders, but he's quite nearsighted. It's a wonder he can manage in school."

"How can he need glasses?" Mama asked indignantly. "My husband and I have perfect vision."

"Unfortunately, he doesn't have your eyes."

If I hadn't cured myself of crying, I would have cried right then. The few kids I knew who wore glasses were teased relentlessly. Sensing my alarm, the optometrist cheerfully assured me that being able to see better would raise my batting average. And because of my nearsightedness, when I grew old I'd still be able to open the Bible across my lap and read, even without glasses. The prospect of reading the Bible without glasses in old age didn't console me. I couldn't imagine being old, but I could imagine arriving at baseball practice and hearing the other players yell, "Here comes four-eyes!" I had yelled those words myself at more than one bespectacled kid.

A week or so later I sat once more in the leather chair while the optometrist fitted the new glasses on my face. Blinking through the lenses, I could see that his forehead was creased and cratered in a way I hadn't perceived before, as if the weather had got to him since I'd been here last. I could also make out row after row of letters in the square of light across the room, even the ones as small as mustard seeds. What really startled me, though, was going outside with Mama onto the main street of Ravenna and looking across at a big elm on the courthouse lawn and seeing branches covered with millions of leaves, each one distinct and aflutter in a brisk wind.

I hadn't forgotten, of course, that trees in summer are covered with leaves. But it had been a long while since I had actually *seen* them, each separate leaf with its frail stem and saw-toothed border. I stood gazing at that elm as if it were the apple tree in the Garden of Eden, made fresh that morning. As I gazed, a robin lit on a branch, lifted its head and whistled, and I could see the bobbing of its beak. I looked and looked.

My parents let me stay up late enough that night for the sky to get good and dark. Belle heard me go out the back door, for she gave a soft whinny from her stall. The dew in the grass wet my bare feet. I kept walking until I left behind the rhomboids of light cast from the house windows, and then I looked up and saw the stars, each one a fierce, individual fire.

"If the doors of perception were cleansed," William Blake famously wrote, "every thing would appear to man as it is, infinite. For man has closed himself up, till he sees all things thro' narrow chinks of his cavern." When I first read these lines, I remembered the fiery stars, the elm's fluttering leaves, the robin's bobbing beak.

Now I am reminded of this clarity by keeping company with baby Elizabeth. When she isn't asleep, she is utterly awake. The expression on her face ranges from curiosity to astonishment as she watches a white pine sway in the wind, listens to a cricket sing, feels a pebble in her palm, smells the peel of an orange, tastes a blueberry. The five rivers of sensation flow into her without dams or diversions. While I can see how open she is, how mindful, how *present*, Elizabeth herself cannot see. Her mind is not yet split between her feelings and what she thinks about her feelings. By the time she grows old enough not merely to experience the world but to reflect on her experience, she will have lost the infant's unsullied vision, and she will be able to appreciate what she has lost only when some form of grace restores the clarity for a moment.

My vision was renewed by optics known to Galileo and formulated by Newton and refined by generations of optometrists. Much as I hated wearing them, my new glasses woke me again to the dazzle and depths of the world. As I grew accustomed to my sharper sight, however, the film of habit began to cloud my doors of perception. I stopped seeing infinity in grains of sand. I stopped seeing infinity even in the night sky. At the same time, I was becoming more and more aware of my seemingly separate self, an "I" struggling to disentangle from everything else. This self-consciousness would eventually become a new kind of sleep from which I would have to rouse all over again, and from which I am still, I confess, only fitfully awake.

•   •   •

Clear skies were rare in that corner of Ohio, which lay much of the year under a pall of moisture blown from Lake Erie. According to Dad, the location for the Arsenal was chosen because there was more cloud cover thereabouts than anywhere else between the Allegheny Mountains and the Mississippi River. All those clouds would keep enemy pilots from getting a good look at the munitions load lines, the lots filled with tanks, and the bunkers filled with bombs.

Whether because of those overcast skies or because money was so tight in our household, I never thought of asking for a telescope. Instead I dreamed of riding on a rocket ship and having a look at stars and planets close-up, the way aliens in UFOs, I supposed, were having a look at Earth. I read every book on astronomy and rocketry in the children's section of the Ravenna library, and then Mama persuaded the librarians to let me work my way through the section for grownups. I wrote SPACESHIPS on the cover of a notebook and filled the pages with diagrams. On my bedroom wall, I pasted photographs of German V-2s from World War II, the latest Russian and American rockets, and artists' renderings of space stations and moon bases. From talking with older boys at school, I knew what a pinup was, although I wouldn't actually see one until my first day of college. But on the brink of adolescence, I couldn't feature why anybody would rather look at pictures of naked girls than look at pictures of the Redstone, Vanguard, Jupiter, or Juno straining on the launch pad or streaking through the air.

I longed to make my own rockets go streaking through the air, in preparation for the day when President Eisenhower would invite me to head up the American space program. Fortunately, since moving to Esworthy Road, I had made a new friend who was also nuts about rocketry. Marty Sanford lived in a hollow beside a stony creek a couple of miles from us, within biking distance. He was in Sandra's class, a football player, three years older than I was and far better versed in the mysterious ways of girls, who draped themselves all over him in the hallways at school. Yet he treated me as an equal when we hunched over the lathe in his father's shop and turned out nose cones and hulls and combustion chambers for our model rockets.

Our fuel was mostly gunpowder, because the ingredients were easy to come by and cheap. The carbon we got by grinding up charcoal. The sulfur we bought at one drugstore in Ravenna, the saltpeter at another, hoping the druggists wouldn't guess what we were mixing up. We did the mixing in the basement of our house until one winter night, when I dropped a screwdriver while stirring a pan of gunpowder. The blade struck a spark from the concrete floor, lighting the powder, which burned up in a flash and filled the air with choking black smoke.

"Nice move," said Marty out of the murk.

"It slipped. Okay?" I couldn't see Marty. I couldn't see myself.

We both coughed, as quietly as we could because my parents and Sandra were directly above us in the living room, watching a comedy on our brand-new television. We could hear the canned laughter sifting down through the floor. As we took shallow breaths, the darkness thinned. I saw first the lightbulb glowing over Dad's workbench, then Marty's sooty face looming a few inches from mine.

"Maybe the smoke will clear out before they smell it," I suggested.

"Fat chance," Marty said.

Just then the oil furnace kicked in, and then the blower. I knew what was coming. Within seconds Dad yelled, "What in tarnation!" He came roaring down the stairs while Mama stood at the top wailing that we'd kill ourselves and Sandra tried to calm her down and Glenn, wakened from sleep, began to howl. Even before Dad lost his way in the smoke and barged into the canning shelves and upset a clatter of jars onto the floor, I knew that we'd made our last batch of gunpowder indoors.

After we lay low for a few days, to let my parents simmer down, Marty and I moved our operation to the old pigpen at the back of our property. A roofed-over hutch in one corner served as our laboratory. The walls were sheathed with oak boards stout enough to restrain a thrashing hog, so we figured they would protect us from the occasional exploding rocket. From inside the hutch we could gaze out through knotholes at our launching stand in the open area of the pigpen, where sows and piglets used to lounge about. Some rockets fizzled; some burst. But as we perfected our craft, more and more of the rockets went shooting off on an arrow of flame. Even though we aimed them at

Belle's pasture, they didn't always go where they were aimed, and some of them soared away beyond the range of my new glasses.

Because each rocket required so many hours of painstaking labor, Marty and I decided to rig spring-loaded parachutes in the nose cones, to slow the descent and, by using colorful cloth, to make them more visible and thus increase the chances of recovering our handiwork. In spite of her conviction that we were bound to maim or kill ourselves, Mama dug out a remnant of pink taffeta from a prom dress she'd made for Sandra, and she stitched up a supply of parachutes on her sewing machine. Newly outfitted, our rockets blossomed at the peaks of their trajectories like pink flowers, easy to spy as they drifted down onto the nibbled grass of the pasture or into the branches of nearby trees. Now and again a parachute would fail to open, and a rocket would soar out of sight, giving us the thrill of watching something we'd made with our own hands vanish into the wild blue yonder, as if our fingers and minds were reaching into space.

When the Soviets launched a silvery, whiskery satellite called *Sputnik I* in October 1957, the month I turned twelve, I cheered the news. But in the newspaper, beneath a headline proclaiming REDS ORBIT ARTIFICIAL MOON, a subhead warned RUSSIAN ROCKETS THREATEN USA. Commentators on the round, grainy screen of the television blamed our schools for failing to produce enough scientists, blamed our scientists for lagging behind the Soviets, blamed the Soviets for stealing our secrets, and blamed our government for the whole fiasco. Somebody, somewhere, must have betrayed us. Otherwise, how could godless Communists have outstripped and outwitted God-fearing Americans?

I didn't see what believing or disbelieving in God had to do with applying the laws of physics. Scientists ever since Newton had understood the principles involved. I was convinced that Marty and I, given enough time, enough gunpowder, and a large enough pigpen to launch from, could eventually have sent our own satellite into orbit.

Sputnik I weighed just under 190 pounds, about as much as Dad's all-time favorite boxer, Joe Louis, weighed in his prime. *Sputnik II*, launched a month later and carrying a dog named Laika, weighed over half a ton. I thought surely the Russians meant to bring Laika back down, a four-legged hero, the first creature to circle the earth. Maybe they would send her on tour, even here to America, and schoolchildren could curl their fingers into her fur and dream of space. But within days her oxygen ran out and Laika died up there in the chilly dark. The scientists had never planned to bring her down, for she was only a dog. I thought of Rusty, shot by the guards.

A rocket capable of hurling half a ton into orbit could hurl a nuclear warhead across the North Pole onto American soil. And what likelier target for Russian missiles than the Arsenal? From our seats in the seventh-grade classroom at Charlestown School, we could watch guards cruising in their big-finned Chevrolets inside the chain-link fence. Ever since first grade, we had been rehearsing for an A-bomb attack. If you see a bright flash, our teachers warned us, dive to the floor and cover your head with your arms. Keep away from windows. Crawl under a table or hide in the coat closet.

And that will keep us safe? we asked.

Our teachers didn't seem to hear the question.

Once a month or so the bells would go off in the middle of the day and we would all troop down to the school's basement, lining up in the corridor between the smelly locker room and the banging furnace room. Mr. Hammond, the principal, would march past us, counting heads, to make sure no child had dillydallied upstairs, and to quiet us down. The school board had known what they were doing when they hired a former Marine drill sergeant to keep order in our school. If, as he passed by, we put our nervous question to him about surviving a nuclear blast, he, too, seemed not to hear.

By the fall of 1957 I had read enough books, including John Hersey's *Hiroshima*, to know that any reassurance our teachers might have given us would have been a lie. If a Soviet warhead had struck the Arsenal, any flash of light we happened to see would have turned our eyes to jelly; the concussion following at the speed of sound would have burst our eardrums; the shock wave from the blast would have leveled our school and buried everyone in the basement under rubble; and any creature within hundreds of square miles not killed outright would have sickened or died from radiation.

Living in the Arsenal had filled me with a dread of bombs early on, but the full horror of nuclear weapons came home to me only in those days following the Sputnik launches. No school, no house, no plot of ground would ever again be safe from missiles. In any place, at any hour, something humans had made could come hurtling down and wipe away everything humans love.

I didn't know whether to blame God for allowing us to fall into such peril—if God really was running the show—or to blame scientists for pursuing their cleverness to this dead end. Could the curiosity and excitement Marty Sanford and I felt while launching our model rockets lead, step by fascinating step, to annihilation? Could our sweet tinkering and passionate questioning be harnessed to hatred? This worry would stick with me and eventually turn me away from the study of physics, throwing me off the path I had felt sure would lead to the stars.

10

A COUPLE OF WEEKS after *Sputnik II* curved into orbit, my grandma Reita, Mama's stepmother, swept through our place like a queen checking up on the yokels. She arrived, as usual, in a long, white, gleaming Cadillac, which looked as improbable on our country road as a bejeweled carriage. She climbed out of the car wearing high heels, a mink coat, and a quail-feather hat. The hat she had made herself, for she had opened a millinery shop after divorcing Grandpa Solomon back in the 1930s. She had promptly sued him for all he was worth, but he had withdrawn his money from the bank and stuffed it into a grocery sack, which he kept forever after in the trunk of his car, to prevent Reita from laying hands on it. To protect his grocery sack and himself in the tough immigrant neighborhoods of Chicago where he made house calls, Grandpa Solomon carried a revolver in his doctor's bag. Reita, meanwhile, had gone on to marry a richer and more pliable man, who had obligingly died, leaving her enough money to close the millinery shop, buy the latest, longest Cadillac, and once every couple of years or so, descend on our farmhouse with a clutch of pious gifts.

Reita visited so rarely, and when she did visit she hovered at such a haughty altitude above us, that I never warmed to her. She didn't approve a thing about Dad except his pizzazz on the dance floor. She considered him a poor provider, a man lacking ambition, who'd rather run his bird dog on weekends than work a second job to lift his family out of a ramshackle house. Dad never spoke ill of her, or of anyone else, but he did find reasons to stay outdoors so long as Reita was holding court. "Take a deep breath," he advised me once, "before your grandma uses up all the air."

Mama, however, looked on her stylish stepmother as a fount of wisdom. Mama would ask Reita for advice on fixing whatever was currently wrong with one or another member of the family, the way a peasant might ask a visiting queen to lay a healing hand on the sick livestock. How could she stop Sandy from drinking and smoking and gambling? How could she get Sandra to lose weight? What could she do about Glenn's rash? What could she do about Scott's smelly feet? Mama routinely posed her questions in the presence of the troublesome husband or child, so we could benefit from hearing Reita's answer.

In my case, Reita prescribed a thorough scrubbing between the toes, and not merely with water but with soap, and not just any soap but a brand fortified with deodorant, a bar of which she withdrew from her suitcase and solemnly gave to me.

The more I saw of Reita, the more I recognized one source for Mama's enlargements on the Ten Commandments: Thou shalt not smell. Thou shalt not burp or fart. Thou shalt not refer to the body's wastes. Thou shalt not chew with thy mouth open. Thou shalt not let others see thy nakedness or look upon anyone else's. Above all, thou shalt not think or learn about sex.

Although I was feverishly curious, I did not in fact learn much about sex for some years, and the little I learned, especially in high school, was largely mythological. Nor did I see or touch or make love to a naked female until I married one. As for the lesser commandments, I broke one or more of them every day.

The pious gift that Reita had brought for me on this occasion, to mark my twelfth birthday, was a zippered Bible bound in fake leather. The edges of the onionskin pages were dyed a startling red, the color of lipstick worn by racy girls at school. I couldn't help thinking of those girls when I drew the zipper and the Bible sprang open like a mouth. Inside

I found not just the New Testament and Psalms and Proverbs, as in the Gideon volume, but the whole saga, from Genesis to Revelation.

"Read this faithfully, my boy," Reita told me in her imperious way, "and you'll find answers to every question."

I did read my new Bible, diligently if not faithfully. I read it as I would any other book, from first page to last, a couple of chapters each night before sleep. By the end of eighth grade I had plowed straight through from "In the beginning" to the final "Amen."

What I discovered was that a great deal of this perplexing book never made its way into the sermons I'd heard or the hymns I'd sung. Much of the Old Testament was about slaughtering enemies with God's help, stoning bad women, taking slaves and concubines, begging for favors, jostling for thrones, and wiping out rival religions. Much of the New Testament was about settling fights among followers of the Prince of Peace. The more I read, the more confused I became. Instead of answering my questions, the Bible deepened them.

As hair began to sprout and smells began to seep from the crevices of my skin, and cravings I had never felt before began to stir inside me, the puzzle that intrigued me the most was what to do with my rebellious body, especially if, as St. Paul maintained—and Mama and Reita appeared to agree—the flesh is the prime source of sin.

By the time of my graduation from eighth grade, I had accumulated enough flesh on my bones to weigh a hundred pounds, which meant I could pass on to Glenn, a wiry five-year-old, the duty of riding Belle. When she bucks you off, I told him, climb back on. Show her who's boss.

As a graduation present, my parents gave me a wristwatch with hands that glowed in the dark. The glow came from a streak of radioactive paint, which made me think of Hiroshima and Nagasaki. Radiation was nothing to be afraid of, our leaders assured us. According to the head of the Atomic Energy Commission, the waste from nuclear power plants was so harmless you could eat it by the spoonful. Fallout from bomb blasts in the western deserts wouldn't hurt so much as a lizard.

Shoe stores featured X-ray machines you could stand on to behold the green, shimmering bones of your feet. When I strained my right elbow pitching curveballs, the doctor casually prescribed radiation treatments.

Eventually I would learn that many of the people who painted those luminous streaks onto the hands of watches, after years of licking tiny brushes to smooth the bristles, had died from cancer of the mouth. I would learn that fallout from A-bomb tests had killed not only lizards but also sheep and cattle and people. I would learn that, by the time doctors quit irradiating sore joints and shoe stores quit X-raying feet, the children of my generation had absorbed potentially lethal doses of radiation.

But in June of 1959, at the eighth-grade dance, the glow on my wrist was still a wonder of science. We called our graduation party a dance, although boys clumped on one side of the gym and girls on the other, while a scattering of parents, including my own vigilant mother, watched from the bleachers. Music poured from a record player set up on the stage. Mr. Hammond, acting as DJ, mixed in with the waltzes a few military marches, to recall his time in the Marines, and enough rock-and-roll to pacify us kids. Whenever anything fast came on, the girls paired off to jitterbug. Standing there in our white shirts and ties, we boys pretended not to be interested in the twirling of those frilly dresses or the flash of stockinged legs.

The legs that most interested me belonged to Vicki May Langston. Actually, I wasn't so much drawn to her legs as I was wary of looking higher up, at her swiveling hips or swelling chest or shining face. Daring and smart, she had burst upon our Podunk school the year before, when her father, an Army colonel, took up a post in the Arsenal. For most of that year I'd been staring at her whenever I could do so without getting caught. At first I'd merely noticed the way she lifted her long black hair with both hands and then let it fan out over her shoulders like a shawl. Soon I was riveted by her every gesture—the way she put a hand to her mouth when she laughed, the way she leaned down to tie the rainbow laces on her sneakers, the way she dotted the *i*'s in her name with little stars. Because they flowed out of her fingers, those little stars became more bewitching to me than the ones in the sky.

In hopes of actually holding Vicki May's fingers in mine at the graduation dance, I had asked Mama to give me waltzing lessons. Dancing was one thing Mama did that made it clear she enjoyed being made out of muscle and bone. By her own account, she was a dancing fool. When she and Dad were courting in Chicago before the war, they had given lessons in everything from tango to fox-trot at the Aragon Ballroom, in exchange for free passes to hear the big bands—Guy Lombardo, Count Basie, Benny Goodman. Now she put on records by one or another of those bands and waltzed me around the living room, teaching me to slide my clumsy, smelly feet without stumbling. When Mama was away, Sandra brought out her stash of rock-and-roll records and taught me to jitterbug. We had to wait for Mama to leave because she thought rock-and-roll was devil music and the jitterbug was lewd.

If lewd meant moving the way Vicki May Langston did, over there among the gyrating girls, while Bill Haley and the Comets sang "Rock Around the Clock" or Elvis Presley moaned "All Shook Up," then I was wholly in favor of it. She flung out her arms and spun like a leaf caught in a whirlwind. Why didn't I go over there and whirl with her? Why had I taken all those dance lessons, only to stand here in this clump of boys? As song after song played, I kept longing to break away from the boys and walk across that void in the middle of the gym and ask her politely for the next dance, as Mama had taught me to do. But shyness pinned me in place.

Eventually Mr. Hammond announced the last tune, and all of us kids groaned. Out of the scratchy speakers poured "The Tennessee Waltz," which I thought of as my song, on account of my birth in Memphis. Now was the moment. I saw myself striding up to Vicki May, taking her by the hand and leading her to the jump-ball circle at the middle of the gym, and then gliding with her over the polished floor while I told her she was the prettiest girl in the whole school, maybe the prettiest girl in Ohio, and all the parents looked on admiringly, even Mama, who would see nothing nasty in her son spinning with this girl in his arms. Although I imagined every step of the dance, every whispered word, the song ended before I could stir.

Then a miracle happened, on a par with anything in my zippered

Bible—right up there with walking on water, say, or multiplying the loaves and fishes. Mama had been sitting beside Mrs. Langston, Vicki May's mom. When the two mothers climbed down from the bleachers, naturally Vicki May and I sidled up to meet them, and so I found myself within arm's reach of this girl. It was like drawing close to a cat I wanted to pick up and stroke. I put my hands behind my back, to keep them under control. Not sure where else to look, I studied Vicki May's black patent leather shoes.

Mrs. Langston bailed me out by saying, "Your mother tells me you're a wonderful dancer, Scott."

"He is," Mama insisted. "And he just stood there like a stick."

All I could think to say was that I'd sprained my ankle playing basketball. While classmates straggled by, wishing us a happy summer, the two mothers moseyed outside to the parking lot, where they paused to gnaw on a bone of gossip. Vicki May and I stood far enough away from them to show our independence. It was another of those rare, clear nights, the June air mild and the stars intense.

"Does it hurt much?" Vicki May asked, breaking our shy silence.

"Does what hurt?" I answered.

"Your ankle."

"Oh, that. Not too bad." I realized I'd forgotten to limp. In the darkness, I dared a look at her face, which flared briefly in the headlights of a departing car. I swallowed. "I'm sorry I never asked you to dance."

"Me, too," Vicki May said. "It's no fun just dancing with girls." She thought a moment. "Unless you're a boy, I guess."

Racking my brains to think of anything to say that wouldn't seem rude or stupid, I remembered my watch. "Take a look at this," I said, pulling up the sleeve of my shirt, which gleamed like snow in the starlight.

"Cool," she said. Bending close, she placed a warm and almost weightless hand on my wrist, and her hair tumbled across my outstretched arm. She smelled of lilacs, and suddenly I recalled the twin white fountains of Mama's lilac bushes beside our driveway in Memphis. "It's like a dish of fireflies," Vicki May said.

"The paint's radioactive."

"Better living through chemistry," she said, quoting a slogan from TV.

We both laughed. She let go of my wrist and we stood primly apart once more. Roused by our laughter, the two mothers began herding us toward the cars.

"And when do you move?" Mama was asking Mrs. Langston.

"In three weeks," Mrs. Langston replied. "Can you imagine? The colonel's already over there, leaving me to supervise the packing by myself."

"You're moving?" I said abruptly to Vicki May.

"My dad's been transferred to Berlin."

"You never said you were moving."

She looked down at the cinders of the parking lot. "It's too sad."

"Oh, I'm sure it will be exciting to live in Germany," Mama said.

"Vicki May is used to starting over, aren't you, sweetie?" said Mrs. Langston. "Poor thing's never lived anywhere more than three years."

"Well," I said. "Goodbye, I guess."

"Have a good life," Vicki May said, forcing a laugh that broke apart.

The last I saw of her was the glisten of long black hair in the dome light as she and her mother climbed into their car. I turned back to watch their taillights disappear through the Charlestown gate into the Arsenal, while Mama drove us down the crumbling, curving blacktop of Esworthy Road.

I had thought I would love Vicki May Langston for the rest of my life. I suppose I have, after a fashion. Without raising her voice, merely by moving to her own beat, she woke my body from its childhood trance.

When my latest watch gave up the ghost, I replaced it with the same cheap brand as the one my parents had given me for eighth-grade graduation. The hands on this model also glow in the dark, although without benefit of radiation, the box assured me.

With a magpie's eye for anything that shines, ten-month-old Elizabeth pulls back my sleeve to uncover the watch, then paws at the buttons or chews on the chrome case. Afterward, I sometimes discover that the alarm has been triggered or the calendar has been changed and then I have to figure out how to reset the controls. It does little good to consult the instructions, which are printed in four languages on a scrap of paper the size of a playing card, with minuscule illustrations that bear scant resemblance to the watch. So I fiddle with the buttons until I've undone Elizabeth's accidental mischief.

All our devices keep sprouting more controls and more options, as if machines, like organisms, were evolving toward higher and higher levels of complexity. For old people, the gizmos that surround us must seem ever more inscrutable. Even in her prime, Mother declared herself to be unmechanical. "So long as there's a man around, a woman shouldn't have to bother with machines," she'd say, in a tone reminiscent of Grandma Reita. And Mother has always had a man around—first her brothers, then her husband, then her sons. After my father died, whenever she felt the oil in her car needed changing or an odd sound in the engine needed checking, she'd pull up to my front door and honk the horn. Whenever a storm cut off her electricity, she summoned me to reset her clocks. I changed the filter in her furnace, the batteries in her smoke detectors, the lightbulbs in her lamps. I relit the pilot light on her water heater, restrung the cord on her weed trimmer, sharpened the blade on her mower and cut the grass. And all of that, remember, was in her prime.

Since turning eighty, Mother has lost one by one her few mechanical skills. After playing a favorite tape of Strauss waltzes, she couldn't rewind the tape to hear it again. When she began leaving burners alight on her stove, we persuaded her to cook in the microwave oven. Then she forgot how to work the microwave. A time came when she couldn't find a station on the radio in her car; then, emerging from a store, she couldn't find her car; then, out driving, she couldn't find her way home. After a long battle, and much grieving on our part and hers, we took away the keys. Soon the lock to her apartment began to baffle her, then the television, then the telephone.

Now she goes to the nurses' station and asks them to call me. When

I answer, she might say that she's cold. So I remind her about the thermostat, but she claims never to have seen such a gadget. I remind her to turn on the electric blanket, and she says, "What electric blanket?" It's on your bed, I tell her. No, she can't see it, can't find it. I must come and fix things. If I loved her, I would come right now and save her from the cold.

Or she might say over the phone, "Do you want to hear about a murder?" What murder? I ask. The girls tried to drown her, she tells me. I figure she's talking about the whirlpool bath, which we've arranged for the aides to give her twice a week because she can no longer operate the shower. Ah, I say, they gave you a bath? Yes, with suds up to her chin, a motor whirring, one of those girls fussing over her. What if her hair got wet? She'd lose all her curl. And worst of all, they made her undress, and the nurse was looking. The nurse was trying to help, I explain, to keep you safe, to make sure you had soap and towel and things. "You don't understand," Mother says. "You're not a girl."

Or she'll call in the morning to complain she didn't sleep a wink all night. When I ask why, she says the sky was too bright. Eventually I guess that the light over her bed must have been left on. I ask why she didn't turn it off. Oh, she says, how do you do that? I remind her of the switch on the wall, and she claims, with an exasperated sigh, that nobody explains these things. "I'm no good with metal," she confesses. And that one word, *metal*, sums up all the contrivances that balk and betray her.

One day when I carry Elizabeth into Mother's apartment, the baby lunges for the light switch beside the bed, and I let her toggle it back and forth, which only confirms Mother's sense that her great-granddaughter is a genius.

"Can he tell time?" Mother asks, still seeing short-haired Elizabeth as a boy.

"Not yet," I answer.

Mother herself has come adrift in time. Every now and again she glances at her watch, or at one of the clocks in her apartment, but the numbers no longer mean anything to her. Less and less able to imagine the future or recall the past, Mother settles into the here and now—

which is where the mystics urge us all to dwell. Unlike the mystics, though, having shed both memory and expectation, she seems to feel no closer to the Holy One. Out of old habit she still invokes the name of God, but no longer as an intimate presence. Instead, the name sounds on her lips like that of her dead husband, a companion who has withdrawn, leaving her to age and die alone.

Elizabeth will learn soon enough how to read calendars and clocks, but for now she, too, is adrift in time. The only rhythms she obeys are those of her body, which is not yet a source of confusion or shame. Except when she's hungry or tired, she's happy, and never more so than when her clothes come off for a bath. Squealing with joy, she flails her arms and legs, as if freed from shackles. The skin she was born with still seems wholly good to her. Nobody has yet told her that anything she feels or desires is wrong.

Once I awakened to girls, thanks to Vicki May Langston, I stayed awake. By the time I started high school in the fall of 1959, I was less interested in the stars than in the way light from the sun tangled in the long blond hair of the girl who sat beside me in homeroom, the way rounded shadows formed on the front of her blouse, the way her legs rubbed against one another when she shifted in her seat.

I now understood those mysterious lines from the Song of Solomon, which I read again and again in Grandma Reita's Bible: "O prince's daughter! the joints of thy thighs are like jewels, the work of the hands of a cunning workman. / Thy navel is like a round goblet, which wanteth not liquor: thy belly is like an heap of wheat set about with lilies. / Thy two breasts are like two young roes that are twins." Once I had looked up *roe* to find out it meant "deer," I could see how the jostling of breasts might seem like the stirring of two fawns, dainty and secret. I took it for granted that the author of these voluptuous lines was the same Solomon who settled a quarrel by threatening to saw a baby in half, a shrewd king who, like my grandpa Solomon, turned out to have an eye for the girls.

Reading on, I discovered that King Solomon had come by his lust honestly, as it were, for he was the son of Bathsheba, whom his father, King David, had spied upon while she bathed. Liking what he saw, David summoned Bathsheba to his bed and got her with child, as the old translation decorously puts it, and then he got rid of her husband, a soldier, by ordering him to the front lines of battle, where the husband was duly slain. After Solomon ascended to the throne, he made sure he stayed there by ordering the execution of his half brother, using as a pretense the half brother's request to take one of David's mistresses as his own. That mistress belonged now to Solomon, for she was part of the harem passed down to him from his father.

If even God-appointed rulers of Israel burned with such fierce desire, how could I keep from yearning? David and Solomon had prophets on hand to denounce them. I had St. Paul, who wrote in his letters, "Flee also youthful lusts: but follow righteousness, faith, charity, peace, with them that call on the Lord out of a pure heart." It was as though Paul could see into the depths of my impure heart the way those shoe store X-ray machines disclosed the bones of my feet. "For the flesh lusteth against the Spirit, and the Spirit against the flesh: and these are contrary the one to the other," he warned. "And they that are Christ's have crucified the flesh with the affections and lusts." Night after night I read these cruel exhortations, along with the scandals of kings and concubines, in the pages of my grandmother's Bible, their edges stained lipstick red.

11

THE NEAREST I CAME to hearing, from outside my skin, the
sound of my own fierce desire was when hounds ran through our
woods, baying ardently and mournfully on the trail of raccoons. Several
times a year, men gathered across the road from our place, down along
the West Branch of the Mahoning River, to see whose coon dog had
the best nose. The day before the race, one of the men would lead a
raccoon on a leash up and down creeks, through brush piles and bram-
bles, over ledges and along fallen trees, laying a devious path to confuse
the dogs.

Since my father never had a hound in the contest—he was a bird
dog man, not a coon dog man—he was often the one who led the raccoon on its tortuous path. I went along with him one Saturday morning; it must have been March, for the snow had melted away to patches
and the ground had begun to thaw, yet there was still enough nip in the
air to make our breath bloom. The raccoon on the leash was a tame
one, a veteran of these jaunts, fat and spoiled, but the scent she left behind was wild enough, Dad assured me, to drag the dogs in her wake.
"Like a bunch of teenage boys chasing a twitchy skirt," he observed.

This was about as close as he ever got to expounding on the birds
and the bees. I guess he figured a boy who'd watched a mare get bred
by a stallion and then give birth to a foal, as Belle had done the previous summer, knew all he needed to know on the subject. Unlike
Mama, Dad held no grudge against the flesh. On the contrary, you

could see from the way he walked, the way he ate, the way he played softball or stroked a dog or swung an ax that he relished the body and all its gifts. He just didn't hold with talking about what comes naturally.

As he led the raccoon up hill and down holler that March morning, I asked him what he thought of St. Paul's doctrine that the flesh and spirit are at war.

"You've got to take Paul with a pinch of salt," he answered.

"How about where he says a follower of Christ has to crucify the flesh?"

"If everybody followed Paul's advice," Dad said, "pretty soon we'd run out of babies and the pews would empty and all the preachers would be laid off. That's why you don't hear more about it in church."

The raccoon waddled on, pausing now and again to rake a tidbit from a rotten log. Whenever we crossed a creek, she stopped to lick her paws. She picked her way through briars unscathed. Dad and I were scratched and muddy by the time we reached our destination at the riverbank, while the raccoon looked as though she had just stepped from a bath. Dad put her in a wooden cage, with a dish of water and a dish of food, and she curled up for a snooze as we hoisted the cage above our heads by a rope slung over the branch of a sycamore tree.

The next morning, men released their dogs all in one whining pack up near our house at the beginning of the trail, then drove down to the river, where they opened card tables under the dangling cage and began laying bets. Profaning the Sabbath twice over, they also began drinking, which was why Mama let me skip church to tag along. I was to keep an eye on Dad and report back to her if he so much as sniffed at a bottle.

Every now and again the raccoon thrust her head between the bars and gazed down on the drinkers and gamblers. She didn't seem the least bit flustered by the baying of the hounds, who sang out as they followed her zigzag trail. If they'd had any sense, they would have run straight to this giant sycamore beside the river, where the raccoon invariably waited in her cage like a princess in her tower. But these dogs were captives of smell; they couldn't lift their noses from the ground long enough to think. I sat on a pillow of moss with my back against the tree's broad trunk, listening to their cries.

Each dog's voice was known not only to its owner but also to most of the other men, and so as the yelping drew closer, the men called out the names of the leaders, their own voices as frenzied as those of the hounds. The betting intensified. The men slapped greenbacks onto the card tables as they passed the bottles. Caught up in the excitement, Dad pulled bills from his wallet, and when a bottle reached him he took a couple of swigs before passing it on. As he dried his lips on the back of a wrist, he suddenly remembered me. Shooting a glance my way, he caught me watching—his son the spy. We both looked away.

By and by the first of the dogs came loping into the clearing, and the men who'd picked this one to win gave a cheer while the others groaned. Dad was one of those who groaned. How much had he lost? The cost of a week's groceries? A mortgage payment? Seconds later another dog came scrambling up, then a third and a fourth, and soon there was a scrum of hounds leaping and yapping at the cage suspended in the air. The raccoon surveyed them from on high, her eyes gleaming in the bandit's mask of her face, as if she accepted all this hullabaloo as a tribute rather than a threat. Had she been on the ground, the dogs would have torn her to pieces. But she had survived enough of these trials to know she was safe.

The winners and losers divvied up their dollars. The owner of the raccoon put her cage in the back of his pickup, shooing away the dogs that tried to shove their snapping jaws between the bars. The other men folded the tables, collected their dogs, exchanged a few final boasts, and drove away. Dad and I stayed behind to scour the riverbank one more time, making sure no trash had been overlooked, for the land belonged to our neighbor, a Swedish farmer whom we both admired. While Dad searched upriver, I searched down. I found nothing, but as I turned back I saw Dad pick up a small bottle, hold it to the light, and then stuff it into his pocket.

In the car on our way home, he said, "Having you along makes a good time even better. You enjoy yourself, buddy?"

"I sure did."

"Sometimes I have such a good time I get carried away." He looked across at me, then back at the road. "You hear what I'm saying?"

"Yes, sir, I hear you."

"Mama doesn't understand a man's need to unwind."

"She's not much for cutting loose."

He laughed, and reached over to slap my thigh. "So if you don't say anything to her about our coon dog party, you'll save us both a whole lot of misunderstanding."

When we came to our place, he pulled into the head of the driveway and told me to hop out. He had to go on up to Sly's store to buy some oil for the tractor. When I reminded him there was a case of oil in the barn, he said it wasn't the right weight. When I asked if I could ride along to the store, he set his jaw and told me to go on now and do my chores, and he'd be back in two shakes of a lamb's tail.

The two shakes took over an hour, as I had feared. Meanwhile, Mama grilled me, and I clamped my lips, like those comic book GIs who refused to betray their comrades. Putting the question every way she could, Mama kept asking me if Daddy had gambled and guzzled with the other men, and I kept saying, No, ma'am, not that I could see.

When Dad finally came home from Sly's—or wherever he had gone—his eyes were bleary and his voice was slurred. Mama lit into him right away. After a few shouts, he reeled back outside. I later found him in one of his favorite sleeping spots, stretched out on bales of hay in the barn. From the neighboring stall, Belle's foal nickered softly.

I'd been playing the role of spy for Mama and chaperone for Dad almost since I'd learned to walk—accompanying him to town, to gas stations, to roadhouses, anywhere he could buy booze—and when I was younger I had obediently tattled whenever I'd seen him drink. He couldn't help knowing of these betrayals, yet he never seemed to hold them against me. With each passing year, however, I found them more painful, and eventually I found them impossible. By that March morning when the baying dogs, boasting men, flying bets, and handy bottles distracted him into lowering his guard, I could no longer squeal on him to Mama, even though I worried myself sick that the drinking would kill him.

If Dad worried, he never admitted it. No matter how many times I surprised him in the garage or barn, sucking on a flat green bottle of Gallo wine or a brown cylinder of rotgut whiskey, he always pretended I hadn't seen, and well up into high school I pretended the same. I found full bottles under the seat of his car, in his fishing tackle box, in the drawers of his workbench, between sacks of oats, and I found heaps of empty or shattered bottles in the ravine at the back of our yard amidst the rusted farm machinery. I rarely found a bottle partially filled, for when he opened one he usually drank it down.

I couldn't help feeling a kinship between Dad's craving for drink and mine for girls. Mama condemned both impulses, and so did the Bible. In fact, Mama took a harder line than the Bible, which often praised wine and occasionally winked at lust, as in the story of David and Bathsheba. I sensed that Dad no more chose to thirst for alcohol than I chose to hanker after girls. The desire came unbidden. The crucial difference, of course, was that I never acted on my craving except to follow the girls' least movements and trace their tempting curves with my eyes, while Dad in those years stopped on his way home from work several nights a week and drank himself into a stupor.

On those nights he would slouch in the door after the rest of us had eaten our supper. His face would appear bloated, the features blurred, the skin ruddy as if a fire were burning inside his skull. He glared at us with drooping, bloodshot eyes, daring us to say what we all so plainly saw. He gave off such an air of menace that even Mama held her tongue, serving his meal in silence. After he'd eaten, he would sag into his easy chair and promptly fall asleep. As he snored, he filled the cramped house with the reek of booze. We tiptoed around his chair all evening, as if he were a sleeping dragon.

After Sandra, Glenn, and I had gone to bed, Mama would dare to wake the dragon. Sometimes he merely got up and stumbled along to their bedroom in silence. Other times he growled at her, she snapped back, and then their voices clashed like swords, a clatter of accusations and denials that might continue for an hour or more, the pitch of anger rising and rising until Mama collapsed in sobs. On those nights, I often climbed from bed and stood outside their door. I meant to fling it open and rush in to grab Dad if Mama called for help. She never called and I never opened the door, although a few times I heard what I took to be the smack of skin on skin. I told myself the sound was most likely Mama slapping Dad, for she slapped us children when we misbehaved, though never hard enough to hurt. The truth was, I feared my father— the Golden Gloves boxer, the tamer of horses, the master of machines. So I stood outside the door shaking, bewildered by his illness, or madness, which nobody would name.

The drinking was a shameful secret, his and ours. I couldn't speak of it to anyone outside or inside the family, least of all to Mama, who treated his drinking as a sin, on a par with stealing or adultery. So I closed myself around the secret the way bark grows over fence wire nailed to a tree.

Today when I ask Mother what she can remember of her own mother, she says, "I was little when she died."

"You were young," I agree. "But do you have any pictures of her in your head?"

Mother's hazel eyes drift out of focus. Eighty years after that loss, her memory has become like the March landscape on the day of the coon dog trial, when the remnants of snow were swiftly melting.

"She was pale," Mother recalls. "She had a soft voice. She loved the crusts of bread." Mother pauses. Her face, tender a moment ago, suddenly wrenches with pain. As though against her will, she blurts out, "And my pappy beat her when she was sick."

"Sick with tuberculosis?" I say, appalled.

"Yes."

"Why did he beat her?"

"She was weak."

"Too weak to look after you and your brothers?"

Mother nods. Her lip is trembling. She has never told me this before, and only the helpless candor of old age tears the confession from her now. To spare her further pain, I shift into the sunlight on her windowsill the vase of burgundy mums I've brought. "How do you like your bouquet?" I ask.

"Oh," she says, the pain in her face just as quickly replaced with a smile, "it's lovely, lovely."

Shame runs in our family. Much of it may be traced to St. Paul's cleaving of human wholeness into warring fragments of spirit and flesh, a division exaggerated in the Protestant churches where my father and mother, and then we three children, absorbed our religion. Time in the wilds and nearly forty years in a good marriage have largely healed that split in me. I no longer believe in opposing earth to heaven or body to soul. I now accept what moments of illumination have been teaching me all along—that the lightning and the oak are one, and so are the flame and the grass, the current and the river, the music and the vibrating string. *Flesh* and *spirit* are names for the outward and inward faces of one reality.

The occasions for our family shame were ordinary: no incest, no suicide, no crime or madness; merely drink, sexual desire, family fights, patched clothes, pinched circumstances. For me, at least, there was—and is—another prime cause for shame, which comes of my being a man with pale skin born in the South, the son of a man with pale skin born in the South.

As a boy, I breathed in racial guilt along with the cotton poison spread on those prison fields in Memphis, where black men in the striped suits of convicts labored under the cold eyes of white men carrying shotguns. I swallowed guilt as I sipped from drinking fountains labeled "White" and avoided ones labeled "Colored." I took in guilt as I swam in pools, ate in cafes, dawdled in stores, sat in churches, and walked in Memphis neighborhoods where nobody had dark skin. No one explained to me why light skin brought membership in a privileged club, yet I couldn't help sensing the gulf between those of us who belonged and those who were kept outside.

Way back in Memphis, I learned from Joe Burns the scornful name for people with dark skin, including our beloved neighbors Aunt Minnie and the General. After Dad explained the history of hurt that lay coiled in this bitter word, I never spoke it again, yet I couldn't wash the taste from my mouth. Although I couldn't begin to understand the legacy of slavery, Jim Crow laws, and segregation, it was my inheritance all the same, as inescapable as the color of my skin. The cleaving of black from white cut me as deeply as St. Paul's cleaving of body from soul, and the wound it left in me has been just as slow to heal.

Every summer after our move to Ohio, we took our vacations in the South, visiting Dad's relatives in Mississippi, Alabama, Georgia, Tennessee, and the Carolinas. For their time and place, those relatives were remarkably free of racial bias, speaking politely of "Negroes," counting black people among their neighbors and workmates, if not their friends. Yet even though they mixed with blacks more frequently and amiably than did most white people in the North, my southern relatives didn't challenge the division that ran from the church pew to the jail cell, from the mansions in town to the weather-beaten shacks in the countryside. They obeyed an unspoken code, which even as a child I could sense in the averted eyes and cautious words of those who met across the color line. Black people made their deliveries to the back door; they sat in the rear of the bus and in the balcony at the cinema; they visited the library on a day set aside for them alone. If a white family had a nanny, maid, cook, chauffeur, gardener, or handyman, that servant was invariably black; the poles of master and servant were never reversed. Though rarely mentioned, this racial barrier was as firm as the Arsenal's chain-link fence, and it was just as militantly patrolled.

In Montgomery, Alabama, when a woman named Rosa Parks refused to move to the back of a bus and yield her seat to a white man, black people boycotted all the buses, demanding the right to sit anywhere whites could sit. When they marched peacefully in the streets, white crowds heckled them, politicians denounced them, and police harassed them. The story of Rosa Parks caught my attention because I had walked the streets of Montgomery myself, on visits to Sanders kin. I had also visited kinfolk in Birmingham, Jackson, Memphis, and other southern cities where blacks were now marching for the right to attend school with whites, to vote without hindrance, to eat at lunch counters and sleep in hotels, and whites were answering with violence. The governor of Arkansas called out the National Guard to prevent black students from enrolling in Little Rock Central High School. The troops did little to control the white mobs. Instead, across the South, police used truncheons, dogs, tear gas, and fire hoses to disperse the marchers. White thugs hurled stones through windows and burned crosses outside the homes of black leaders. They murdered volunteers who dared to register black voters. They bombed black churches.

Night after night I watched in bewilderment as these images of hatred poured into our living room through the television. I didn't yet recognize the depth of racism in the North, and so I thought it was a sickness peculiar to the South. Because of my birth in Tennessee, because of my father's birth and upbringing in Mississippi, because of our annual visits with southern relatives, and because of my pale skin, I felt implicated in this cruel history—implicated and ashamed.

One evening in February a nurse calls to ask if we could look in on Mother, who is greatly upset. The staff have tried everything they can think of to calm her. Ruth and I find Mother limping back and forth in her apartment, face blanched, jaw quivering, white cloud of hair awry.

"Oh," she cries on seeing us, "thank God you've come. I kept praying and praying." She squeezes her palms together to demonstrate.

We coax her into a chair. She's panting. Ruth sits on one side, holding her hand, and I sit holding the other. Mother's bones feel as fragile as a bird's.

"Everything's all right," I say. "Now tell us what's the matter."

She stammers awhile, searching for words. By asking questions and filling in blanks, Ruth and I gradually piece together an implausible story. Mother claims she was mugged by two black men who came into her apartment, grabbed her by the arms, and shook her, all the while gruffly telling her to stay in her room and leave the other residents alone. The men were dressed like nurses, all in white, and very large and strong. Mother shows us where they squeezed her arms.

Ruth and I look at one another. There is one black woman on the staff, but there are no black men. Nor could anyone have entered the home from outside without the staff's knowledge, because someone must unlock the door for visitors coming or going.

"Mother," I say, "whatever happened, I don't think you were mugged by two black men."

"You never believe me!" She yanks her hand from mine and bangs the chair with her fist.

"It's not a question of believing you. I just think maybe you're confused."

She stiffens with fury, and I half expect her to slap me, as she would have done when I was a boy. "You think I'm crazy!" she cries.

"I don't think you're crazy."

"I'm not crazy!"

Knowing how raw my nerves are, how ready I am to feel guilt over Mother's misery, Ruth signals for me to leave the room, and I do. When I glance back, she's murmuring to Mother and stroking her arm.

I close the door behind me and lean against it until my heart steadies. Then I seek out the supervisor, who tells me that after supper one of the nurses found Mother in the lounge denouncing another resident for sitting in the wrong chair. The nurse tried to convince Mother that residents may sit wherever they choose, but Mother only grew more and more angry, until the nurse had to lead her firmly back to her apartment and ask her to stay there until she calmed down.

"Was it Laura who dealt with her?" I ask, naming the one black nurse, a large, mild, gentle woman, the mother of seven.

The supervisor consults a paper on her desk. "Yes. Why? Are you suggesting she did anything wrong?"

"No, no. I'm just trying to understand my mother's fear."

By the time I return to the apartment, Mother is in bed asleep, a quilt pulled up to her chin. The color has returned to her face and her hair has been brushed. Stirring from the chair where she has kept watch, Ruth whispers that we can go.

"What if she's frightened when she wakes?" I whisper back.

"We can't always be on hand when she wakes."

We can't, not without buying a different house, moving Mother in with us, and giving up one of our jobs. Like millions of other sons and daughters, we've chosen to continue our own lives while paying others to look after an aging parent. Our phone calls, visits, cards, and bouquets, our paying of her bills and taxes, our outings with her to restaurants and doctors and stores, all of these efforts assuage our conscience and ease her life. But what she wants is to be looked after day and night by someone she loves.

On our drive home, Ruth and I speculate about why Mother's imagination turned one black woman, the easygoing Laura, into a pair of violent black men. We've never known Mother to speak or act in a racist way. And yet she grew up in Chicago, one of the most thoroughly segregated cities in America. Her father had acquired from his own upbringing in an Assyrian village in what is now northern Iran a range of prejudices encompassing not only blacks and Jews but also Babylonians, Chaldeans, Hittites, and other biblical tribes. And Mother lived for nine years in the South, breathing in the same racial poison I breathed as a child. So it's not surprising that fear dredges up from her unconscious the hulking, vengeful shapes of black men.

"I wish we could take care of her," I say.

"We are taking care of her," Ruth says.

"Not very well."

"As well as we can."

We ride in silence. I stare at the ridges of dirty snow along the sides of the road. As we near home, Ruth asks me when I think Elizabeth will begin to walk. The question is a transparent effort to relieve my gloom, but I'm grateful to her for asking, and I allow myself to slide into cheerful talk about the baby.

When we reach the house, the red light is blinking on the message machine. Ruth urges me to go on upstairs while she listens to it. But I insist on staying, and so we both hear Mother's voice pleading, "Help me, Scotty. Help me, please, please, please help me. I'm all alone. Help me. In Jesus' name I pray. Amen."

Her phone messages often end in prayers, as if I were God's ambassador, her only source of safety or consolation. The sound of her voice abrades away all joyful thoughts of my granddaughter. I'm plunged back into childhood, helpless to relieve my mother's grief, because I can't mend our old house, can't pay our debts, can't settle the nightly quarrels, can't cure my father of drink.

12

THE SPELLBINDING VOICE of Martin Luther King, Jr., rang out from our television set like the voice of a Hebrew prophet. Other dark-skinned people showed up on the screen, often dressed in Sunday clothes, marching or preaching. But we had no black neighbors on Esworthy Road. I never met a black child during my eight years of elementary school. On our return visits to the Arsenal I saw black soldiers, and I saw a few black people on our trips to the library or stores in Ravenna, but they were as opaque to me as any other strangers. In the rural high school where I spent the years between 1959 and 1963 devouring books about science, playing basketball, acting in plays, and yearning after girls, there were a few black kids, maybe ten or fifteen in a student body of nearly four hundred. I knew them all superficially, as one knows everybody in a small school.

The only black student I knew well enough to call a friend was a boy in my grade named Jeremiah Pond, a tall, stringy, shrewd galoot who played forward on the basketball team. He had to be shrewd in order to pick his way through the minefield of our nearly all-white school. It was basketball that gave us a chance to talk, for no matter how many times I invited him to our house, he always found a reason not to come, and he never invited me to his place. In the locker room after practice, though, or on bus rides to and from away games, Jeremiah and I often discussed books, for he, too, loved reading. We talked about our weekend and summer jobs—mine loading hay and framing houses, his mowing lawns and pumping gas—or we talked about our families, classes, teachers, and tests. Sometimes we mulled over the Bible, for Jeremiah was another churchy boy.

Riding home on the bus one night after a game our team had lost to a Catholic school, we puzzled over the way players from the other team would cross themselves before taking a shot at the foul line. I told Jeremiah I couldn't believe God would tweak the flight of a basketball to make it fall through a hoop. In fact, I wondered if God, with a whole universe to look after, really cared about anything that happened on our two-bit planet. Wasn't it just human pride to claim we mattered so much? Not pride, said Jeremiah, but faith in the Good Book, which tells us that God watches over every sparrow. God counts the hairs on your head. You can't lift a finger without him knowing, Jeremiah insisted, and right now God must be so disgusted with the way things are going, he's liable to burn up all the sinners with fire and start over.

"The way what things are going?" I asked, thinking of our stockpiles of weapons, the scientists working around the clock here and in Russia to build more accurate missiles, more powerful bombs.

Jeremiah shrugged. "You heard of Birmingham? You heard of Selma?"

Television images flashed in my mind. "It's ugly down South," I agreed.

"You think it'd be any prettier up north if we crossed the line?"

"What line?"

"The color line, man. You been living under a haystack?"

Fearing I might say the wrong thing, I said nothing. Jeremiah also fell silent. Tongue-tied, we sat there gazing out the bus window, past our twin reflections, at the dim countryside flowing past.

Our silences were as eloquent as our speech. Although we speculated about God, we couldn't really discuss religion, for there were no white faces in the church he attended and no black faces in mine. We never spoke of girls, for I wouldn't dare venture an opinion about the few black girls in our school and he wouldn't venture an opinion about the white ones. Nor did we talk about 4-H or Boy Scouts—clubs that were unofficially but effectively closed, in our neighborhood, to kids with dark skin.

Jeremiah's dream was to win a basketball scholarship, become the first member of his family to earn a college degree, go on to play in the NBA, and when his playing days were done, study for the ministry and become a preacher. His hero was Reverend King. My dream was to earn a Ph.D. in physics and uncover the secrets of the universe. My hero was Einstein. Jeremiah and I both wanted to get married, have children, build a house in the country, raise a few chickens and pigs. Once I asked him where he hoped to do all of that, and he answered, "I don't ever want to live more than walking distance from my parents and my brothers and sisters."

"You all must be close," I said.

"As close as that," he said, holding up a hand and squeezing his fingers together. His palm was the color of peaches.

Jeremiah and I were the last players in the shower after practice one day in December of our sophomore year. His long, sinewy body gleamed like the wet trunk of an ironwood tree. By comparison, mine seemed as raw and slack as bread dough.

I was rinsing off when I heard my kid brother's piping voice, telling me to hurry up. I wasn't surprised, for Mama often sent Glenn to fetch me when I was slow. As a first grader, he thought it was a big deal to enter the high school locker room.

"Hurry up, Scott," he called again.

"Hold your horses," I called back.

"Come right away! Daddy's in the hospital."

I shut off the water to hear him better. "What's Dad doing in the hospital?"

"He's really, really sick. So come on."

I toweled off hurriedly and threw on my clothes. As I was leaving, Jeremiah said, "Hey, I hope Mr. Sanders is okay."

I wanted to say it was probably only too much booze, but I couldn't bring myself to confess the family secret, not even to Jeremiah. So I

merely grunted thanks and followed Glenn out to the car, where Mama
and Sandra waited, the engine running.

On the way to Ravenna, Mama drove fast and talked nonstop, as if
to keep us kids from asking questions. We mustn't be shocked by the
sight of Daddy, she warned us, for he looked awful. There were tubes
and wires running out of him, and his skin was as pasty as bleached
flour. Still, it was important for us to see him, in case . . . But Mama
caught herself before saying in case what. Instead she told how Daddy
had stopped at Sly's store on his way home from work—don't ask her
why—and while he was there he suddenly collapsed, and Tommy
Thompson's brawny father, who also happened to be there wasting
money, carried Daddy to his truck and hauled him to the hospital,
where the doctors said it must have been a heart attack.

"But if he stopped at Sly's," I said, "it could have been—"

"It was a heart attack," Mama said firmly. She glared at me in the
rearview mirror.

Sandra was sobbing in the front seat. Glenn sat in back with me,
clinging to my hand. During one of Mama's lulls, he whispered, "Is
Daddy going to die?"

"He's too ornery to die," I whispered back.

"But if he does, will you be my daddy?" Glenn stared up at me
with his chocolate eyes. The older he got, the more he showed the
high cheekbones, coppery skin, and black hair passed down through
Grandpa Solomon from the ancient Assyrians. All I had inherited was
the Assyrian nose, humped as a hawk's beak.

I thought of a jokey answer for my scared little brother, but when I
tried to deliver it, my throat seized up. Likewise, I thought I had prepared myself to enter this hospital where I'd nearly bled to death at the
age of eight, only a couple of years older than Glenn was now, yet
when we actually reached the hospital and rushed into the tiled hall, I
caught a whiff of ether and my knees buckled.

"Hell's bells," Mama swore as she left me in the hands of a nurse and
went off with Sandra and Glenn to see Dad.

•   •   •

No one at school knew of Dad's troubles except Jeremiah, who asked me the next day how Mr. Sanders was doing. He never said "your daddy" or "your father," let alone "your old man," but always "Mr. Sanders." I supposed this politeness was a symptom of the color line that divided the world so much more clearly for Jeremiah than for me.

I had to admit we weren't sure if my father would live.

A couple of days later, between wind sprints at basketball practice, Jeremiah asked again, "Is Mr. Sanders doing better?"

Bent over, gasping for air, I answered, "They say he'll pull through."

"God's healing grace."

"More likely medicine."

Jeremiah turned his slick face toward me. "You pray to doctors, I'll pray to God."

The coach blew his whistle and bellowed, "Sanders and Pond, if you've got so much breath, why don't you run ten more sprints?"

As we ran, I thought about the truth in what Jeremiah had said. While I still prayed to God, the power I really counted on issued from the doctors, the scientists in labs, the periodic table of the elements taped to the wall beside my bed, the slide rule on my desk, the formulas in textbooks, the probes veering into space. My faith in science had crowded out my faith in religion. If Jeremiah could divine that shift in me, what other secrets might he detect?

I never did see my father during the ten days he spent in the hospital, although I tried several times. I never managed to get far beyond the reception desk without feeling woozy, for each time the syrupy smell flung me into my ether nightmare. So I retreated outside to wait in the fresh air until Mama, Sandra, and Glenn returned from visiting Dad. The first couple of days I was terrified he would die without my getting a chance to say all that remained unsaid between us, without my feeling ever again the warmth of his hand on my head.

When it was clear that Dad would live, I vowed to confront him the next time he came home drunk. I'd yell at him if I had to, heart attack or no heart attack. I'd seize hold of him if he tried to run away. Once I made him see how much pain he was inflicting on his family, he'd quit drinking. He'd have to, because he couldn't possibly love the taste of booze more than he loved us.

During that anxious week I hunted through Dad's car, the garage, the basement, the attic, and the barn, looking for bottles. I discovered an armful, tied them up in a gunnysack, and carried them clinking into the woods. There would always be more bottles in the store, yet I could bury at least this much of the poison. Although bare of snow, the ground was frozen, so the digging went slowly. When the hole was deep enough, I dropped in the gunnysack and pounded the lumpy cloth with my shovel, as if there were something inside I had to kill.

When Dad came home from the hospital, looking wrung out and unsure on his feet, I felt so relieved to see him alive that I wanted to throw my arms around him as I used to do when I was little. But at fifteen, I had come to feel awkward about hugging my father. Glenn came scampering in and did the hugging for me, nearly tipping Dad over with the force of his joy.

On doctor's orders, Dad stayed home from the office another week. He wasn't to drive the car, wasn't to do chores, wasn't so much as to step outside in the bitter cold. How cold? Morning and evening, before I could pour fresh water for the ponies, I first had to overturn their trough and dislodge a lump of ice as thick as a tire. On the West Branch of the Mahoning River, along where the raccoon used to wait high in her cage like a princess in her tower, even the riffles froze solid.

By then we were off school for the Christmas holiday, which left me cooped up at home along with Dad. The habit of watching him ran so deep in me, I found myself trailing after him from room to room as he gazed at the TV or read the paper or pored over his repair manuals or fiddled with designs for the shop he never had the money to build. Coon dogs didn't track their prey any more faithfully than I tracked my father. Sooner or later he would go looking for his stashed bottles, I felt certain, and I wanted to be there to say why they were missing. I rehearsed the speech I would make, a speech aimed at calling him back from sickness to his true self. At fifteen, I imagined I knew who my father truly was better than he knew himself.

If Dad ever looked for a hidden bottle, I never caught him. In the new year I started back to school and he started back to work in the Arsenal, where I could no longer follow him. When he came home in the evenings I studied his eyes, his walk, and the movements of his hands as he unbuttoned his coat, watching for telltale signs. And night after night he came home sober. When he passed by the dining room table, where I sat conjugating Latin verbs or working trigonometry, he paused to scrub my head with his callused palm, recounting some incident from the day, and his breath smelled neither of booze nor of mints.

Night after night he ate supper with us, and then he played his harmonica or watched the news or sat in his chair and regaled us with stories. Instead of tiptoeing around him as if he were a sleeping dragon, Glenn climbed into his lap, Sandra showed him her drawings, I asked him to check my math. We talked and teased with him as we had in the best of the old days, before he'd been seized by unclean spirits. Had Jesus healed him? Had the doctors? Sensing the change in him, Mama didn't complain about the broken washing machine, didn't bemoan the unpaid bills, didn't report on Sandra's spat with the art teacher or my dallying after basketball practice with a cheerleader. At bedtime, Dad retreated with Mama into their room without so much as a grumble.

At first I couldn't shake the habit of lying awake, listening for the clash of their voices. But as weeks passed without any shouts, I began to trust the darkness. Even the nightmare of oblivion, which had haunted me for seven years, gradually eased its grip, the way the ache of a broken bone slowly tapers away.

By summer, the flame had come back into Dad's face, the strut into his walk. And still he returned home sober every night. None of us breathed a word about the transformation, fearing to break the spell.

To judge from Dad's own silence, he'd never brushed against death and he'd never been drunk. One evening in that fall of 1961, I sat as usual at the dining room table doing homework. Dad spread newspaper on the table across from me and began cleaning his shotgun and oiling his leather boots. Mama came up behind him and announced in her old, peremptory way that a man who'd suffered a heart attack had no business going hunting.

Dad bristled. For the first time since he'd returned from hospital, I could see him slowly counting under his breath to keep from boiling over in rage. At length he said, with exaggerated restraint, "Don't you want a deer for the freezer?"

"I'd rather hang on to my husband," Mama said.

"I'm not planning to sit home for the rest of my days like a lame dog."

To my surprise and relief, Mama backed down. "Of course you want to get into the woods," she said soothingly. "I just hope you'll take it easy."

Maybe the alchemy that had turned Dad away from drink had begun to work a change in Mama as well, easing her compulsion to lay down the law for everyone within earshot. I was even willing to believe that the Holy Ghost, so often prayed for, had come to make peace between them. The upwelling of love didn't require the bending of nature's laws.

Whatever the cause, Mama stood behind Dad rubbing his shoulders while he rubbed the walnut stock of his gun, and they talked without anger, like old friends. He told her that some top brass from the Pentagon would be flying in for the annual deer hunt in the Arsenal the first weekend in December, and this year it was his turn to make sure the generals got some easy shots. This meant hiring local boys to beat the bushes and rustle up a herd and drive the deer past the blinds where the generals would be waiting. That didn't sound very sporting, Mama remarked. These were warriors, Dad said, not sportsmen. Just because generals wore medals on their chests didn't mean they could hit the broad side of a barn with a deer slug.

After Mama left Dad and me alone at the table, I asked him if I could go on the hunt. "Sorry, buddy," he answered. "It's only for VIPs."

"Then let me help scare up deer for the generals to shoot."

"I'd rather you wait a year or two."

"You said I could do it when I turned sixteen."

Dad pulled a cloth-tipped cleaning rod from the barrel, laid the gun down, and looked across the table at me. "Son, listen. It's not a picnic. When these guys get to drinking, they shoot every way but straight. Some of their kills aren't clean."

I'd never heard him criticize anybody for drinking, so I took a moment to absorb this remark. I knew the December hunt was a way of thinning the deer, which would otherwise starve to death in winter inside the Arsenal's high fences. So I said, "I'm not expecting a picnic. I know a lot of deer will die. I just want to go."

"All right, then." Dad clicked the shotgun closed at the breech. "You want to herd, you can herd."

"How about Jeremiah?"

"Jeremiah Pond?" Dad considered for a minute before saying, "Sure, why not? If he doesn't mind seeing deer guts and risking potshots from trigger-happy generals, he's hired. I can't pay you, but Jeremiah will get five dollars."

Five dollars proved not to be enough inducement to win over Jeremiah. On Monday of the week leading up to the Saturday hunt, I put the idea to him after basketball practice. Jeremiah responded cautiously, as he did whenever I invited him to my house. He wasn't sure, he thought maybe something was happening at church, he'd have to ask his father. The next day he thanked me for offering but said he couldn't go. If you change your mind let me know, I told him. Sure thing, he answered, avoiding my eyes.

Jeremiah never gave me a reason for saying no, and I never asked. But I sensed the reason on that Saturday morning as I rode along with some twenty other boys to a parking lot encircled by munitions bunkers in a far corner of the Arsenal. The army bus that carried us might have been the same khaki box I'd ridden back and forth to Charlestown Elementary, only now when I slouched in the seat my legs reached all the way to the floor. I had known some of the other boys since first grade. Their faces had filled out, and a few of them had begun to show a hint of beard. What hadn't changed was their complexion, which I had scarcely noticed in childhood. Now I could see that every single face on the bus was white. More than likely, all the hunters would be white as well. Jeremiah could have predicted as much. Why had I thought he might choose to spend his Saturday chasing deer through snow toward a nest of shotguns, the only black person in a mob of white?

We piled from the bus and stamped our boots while Dad, who had arrived here separately in an army jeep, instructed us in how to herd deer. He spoke well, as he always did, at ease yet forceful, with a sense of authority that came from knowing the crowd and knowing his stuff. I had listened to him speak many times over the years—at PTA meetings, Boy Scout roundups, sports banquets, school assemblies, family reunions—and I had watched every sort of audience get swept up in the smooth, witty, warm flow of his words. He was a charmer, as Mama often said. He could have coaxed a bear out of a den or a dollar bill out of a wallet with that voice of his, the way he had coaxed Mama into marrying him against her better judgment.

As Dad spoke on this cold morning, with just enough daylight to show the plume of his breath, I wondered how his Mississippi accent sounded in the ears of these Yankee boys. Would they lump him together with the southern sheriffs and governors and Klansmen who snarled on TV? Would they take him for a bigot, even if a charming one?

"So wear your hats," Dad concluded, holding up one of the bright orange stocking caps that a soldier was distributing to us, "and chase those whitetails until you get to Seven Lakes, where the bus will pick you up. Whatever you do, don't go anywhere near the shooting."

Without having paid any more attention to me than he would have to any other boy, Dad sped away in the jeep, off to join the generals in the blinds. Our orange-capped platoon fanned out with the wind at our backs and set off tramping past the munitions bunkers toward the meadow where Dad had told us deer would be munching hay. And sure enough, on reaching the meadow, we found maybe fifteen deer quietly feeding. A couple of bucks with antlers as wide as bicycle handlebars looked up at our advancing line, sniffed nervously, and stamped their front hooves. When we kept on coming, they whirled about and the whole bunch went bounding away. From the white flags of their tails, we could see they were heading downwind, toward Seven Lakes, as Dad had predicted they would.

"They'll want to keep your scary smell in their nostrils," Dad had said, "so they know where you are."

And so we pursued them for a mile or so, waving our arms, yelling, our boots crunching the brittle snow. The herd gradually increased as more and more deer were gathered up in the chase. By the time we came within sight of the first lake, perhaps as many as fifty deer wheeled and pranced before us, their eyes rolling, their breath coming in snorts. Following Dad's instructions, we formed a semicircle and funneled the herd onto a strip of land separating the last two lakes, and there we stopped while the deer poured on in the only direction available, straight past the blinds where the generals waited. Within seconds we heard the crackle of shots, like the rattle of hail on a tin roof, then a tapering off into silence, and then a chorus of celebratory shouts. The generals had made their kills.

But some of the generals, it turned out, had only wounded their deer, which ran away leaving trails of blood across the snow. Dad had taught me on our hunts for rabbits and squirrels that if you merely wound an animal, you must track it down if you can and put it out of its misery. To let it slowly bleed to death is lazy and cruel. But the generals argued over who had muffed their shots, and none of them would go in pursuit.

And so, before our ragtag platoon could board the bus, Dad fetched me and a few other boys to help him track down the stragglers. If the deer we found had already died, he told us, we were to drag the carcasses back here to the killing ground. If we found a deer fallen but alive, we were to cut its throat. Dad loaned his sheath knife to the one boy among us who hadn't carried a knife of his own. And we weren't to mess up the heads of any bucks, in case the generals wanted to mount the antlered trophies. Through all these instructions, Dad said nothing that might get him fired if it found its way back to the generals, but I could sense the fury in his face and voice.

Starting at the bloody, mired spot near the blind where men were gutting the downed deer, Dad set each of us boys to follow a separate crimson trail. My deer had left such a spoor of blood that I knew it couldn't have gone far. Entering a woods and weaving in and out among the trees, the hoofprints, at first punched cleanly into the snow and spread far apart in the panic of flight, soon became messy, wobbling side to side, as the deer had begun to stagger. I was so intent on studying the tracks that I came within a few yards of the deer before I saw it, and I saw it then only because I heard a low, keening sigh. It was a good-sized buck, with a rack of ten or twelve points, sprawled on its side in the snow. He'd been shot in the belly, and his entrails dangled out like grotesque pink and blue streamers. Red foam bubbled from his mouth.

As I approached, his legs were jerking in phantom flight, and his rib cage swelled and sank with each gasping breath. Fighting down nausea, I knelt at his shoulder, tugged off my gloves, pulled out my knife, and drew the blade across his throat. On the first pass I failed to cut through the dense pelt. The buck's head lifted, and his great glassy eye stared at me, unblinking. I asked his forgiveness. Pressing harder, I drew the blade again, and this time blood gushed over my fist. With a last sigh the head slumped. The black eye glazed over. I stood up and leaned against a tree and heaved until my stomach was empty. My only consolation was that Jeremiah hadn't come along to see this.

I couldn't stand the thought of the entrails snagging on brush as I dragged the carcass back, so I slit the belly and tugged out the steaming guts into a pile on the snow. Crows and vultures and smaller scavengers would feast on the offal. I scoured the blade with a handful of snow, wiped it dry on my jeans, then slid the knife into its sheath. Not knowing how else to honor the deer, I smeared a hand across my forehead so I could wear his blood. Even though I hadn't shot this buck, I had chased him into the line of fire, and I had finished the killing. It was my first deer, and it would be my last.

13

THE FOLLOWING DECEMBER, when my father asked me if I wanted to join the hunt again, I told him no. I understood the need for the annual deer harvest, as it was called. By wiping out big predators—wolves, mountain lions, coyotes, bears, lynx—both inside and outside the chain-link fence, and by creating millions of acres of prime habitat with our suburban sprawl, we had doomed the deer to multiply until they browsed every living shoot like locusts. And still they starved in winter. I had no quarrel with the hunt, so long as the hunters were skillful and the killing was quick. But the sleazy, shooting-gallery slaughter I had witnessed in the Arsenal cured me of ever wanting to see it again.

So I told my father no, I couldn't go. I had final exams coming up and papers to write. Dad never invited me again, and I never asked. He sensed my disgust, and I sensed his regret. Because he so rarely spoke of his feelings, I had to read them in his face and gestures. For instance, I knew more about his views on racial strife in the South from the way he glared at TV news broadcasts than from anything he said. And I learned about his regard for black people mainly from the way he treated them—the General and Aunt Minnie, prisoners in the cotton field, soldiers at the Arsenal, and Jeremiah Pond, among dozens of others. Years after I had lost track of Jeremiah, Dad was the one who telephoned a hunting buddy back in Ohio to find out that Jeremiah played basketball in college on scholarship, earned a degree in sociology, and went off to seminary in Atlanta. "Wherever he winds up," Dad told me, "I'd go hear him preach."

Dad himself never preached. Nor did he believe in rehashing the past. "Don't look back—something might be gaining on you," he liked to quote from Leroy "Satchel" Paige, the legendary pitcher from the Negro Baseball League. One of the few stories Dad recounted from his own past was about when he was a catcher in the bush leagues, and one night in an exhibition game he'd squatted behind the plate and caught nine innings of fastballs and fiendish curves from Satchel Paige. When I moped over losing a baseball game on my own wild pitch or a basketball game on a missed free throw, Dad would say, "Don't cry over spilt milk." When I mourned the end of a romance, he would quote Jesus: "Let the dead bury their dead." As a salve for any regret, he would recite his personal motto: "God invented mornings so we could start over."

Without ever mentioning his history of drink, Dad stayed on the wagon from that bitter cold December of 1960, when he landed in the hospital, right up through April of 1978, the month of his sixty-second birthday, when he retired. After his brush with death, he simply started over, turning a sober face toward the future. There was no need to make speeches about it.

By that April of 1978, my parents were living in Ontario, the fourth place the company had moved them since the Arsenal. Mama drove down from Canada with a carful of potted plants to our home in Indiana, while Dad stayed behind to help the movers. When the last of the furniture had been loaded in the van, the movers broke open a case of beer and invited Dad to join them in toasting his retirement. I learned this much from Mama later on, but I never learned if he'd planned all along to throw off his restraint, or if he merely succumbed to the euphoria of the moment. In any event, he celebrated his freedom by tipping a bottle back. The alcohol sank its hooks in him again, and for the remaining not quite three years of his life he drank every chance he got.

During those three years, while my parents clawed at one another like tigers in the house they'd built for their retirement in Mississippi, Dad wrecked the pickup truck he'd long dreamed of buying, he ran his car into ditches, slept on benches outside of taverns in nearby towns, got into fights, and more than once landed in the emergency room or jail. The company from which he had retired was still paying for his health care, and so, as the bills poured in, company officials persuaded him to enroll in a detox clinic. When the first cure didn't stick, they persuaded him to try a second time, and when that failed they gave up. Or maybe *he* gave up, because the drying out hurt too much.

Meanwhile, Dad did everything he could to stay out from under Mother's wrathful eye and sharp tongue. He drove away on trumped-up errands in his banged-up truck, with or without a valid license. He puttered on their three acres of scrubby land. He made sawdust in the workshop that he and Glenn and I had built for him, the one he'd never been able to afford when we all still lived under his roof. And when he could find no excuse to leave the house, he settled into his easy chair, cranked up the television to drown out Mother's harangues, and went to sleep.

Ruth and I witnessed these maneuvers on our twice-yearly visits to Mississippi with our two young children, at midsummer and Christmas. We might have visited more often, but Dad's bleary eyes, slurred speech, and palsied movements hurled me back into my own childhood, helpless before his addiction. The sight of him opened wounds I had thought were healed. When I tried talking with him about his drinking, about the misery he was bringing on himself and everyone who loved him, he clammed up. I usually cornered him in the shop, beyond reach of Mother's ears, the television babbling, the motor for his air compressor kicking in and out as the pressure in the tank fell and rose. Instead of answering me, Dad whistled or hummed, and turned back to his tools.

The day after Christmas in 1980, when I pleaded with Dad for what proved to be the last time, his hands were shaking too much to allow him the use of tools. On Christmas Day itself he had stayed sober, while my two children, three-year-old Jesse and seven-year-old Eva, opened their presents. Watching them with clear eyes, telling stories, laughing, Dad had seemed like his old self, redeemed from unclean spirits, the man I adored. It was as though he had vowed that morning to start over. And why not? He had stayed dry for eighteen years. All it required of him, I thought, was an act of will. All he had to do was to keep on choosing, day after day, the love of his family over a chemical fix.

And then on the morning after Christmas I went out early to the shop, eager to help Dad finish a jewelry chest he was making for Ruth. I envisioned a day like the best of our times together, joking, singing, swapping tall tales, doing skillful work. I found him seated on a stool at the workbench, his back to me. Before he said a word I could see in the way he sagged, head bowed, hands fumbling, that he had already made his choice.

Without looking around at me, he asked if I would glue together these blamed pieces of wood, the ones he'd been fumbling with. They were the parts of a drawer for the jewelry chest, cut from walnut, the wood he prized above all others. As I drew near to him, I could smell his sour breath. I picked up the pieces of the drawer, wanting to smash them. Instead I tried fitting them together, but I soon realized they wouldn't fit because they'd been measured wrong, and I told him so.

"These blasted eyes," Dad lamented—a plausible excuse, for his vision was clouding from cataracts.

I knew better. "You mean this damned alcohol."

"Don't give me that bull," he growled, but he couldn't get any menace into his voice.

My hope curdled into anger. Instead of trying to reason with him, as I had done for the past week, I denounced him as a weakling, a coward, a drunk. He cared only about wetting his throat. Guzzling that stinking booze. I shouted at him to look at me, tell me why he wouldn't quit, why he was torturing us, why he was killing himself. When he wouldn't face me, I grabbed his shoulder and he flinched away with a fearful gulp of air. My own father, the strong man, the boxer—afraid of me. I let go of his shoulder and stood back, ashamed.

Neither of us spoke for several moments. The television poured out drivel. The air compressor cycled on and off. Then Dad turned around and fixed me with his bloodshot eyes. "Your mother's the one who's killing me."

"Don't go blaming her."

"She's been trying to poison me for years."

"That's a load of crap."

"It's the gospel truth," he insisted.

He went on in a voice like the grinding of broken glass, asking if I remembered that heart attack, away long ago in Ohio. Of course I did. How could I forget? Well, he said, Mama had caused it by slipping some medicine in his food. Medicine prescribed by one of those quack doctors in the Arsenal, a kind of poison that tears your guts out and messes up your heart if you mix it with alcohol.

"Antabuse?" I guessed, because by then I had read about therapies for alcoholism.

"That's the stuff."

"She never told you?"

"Told me after I nearly died in Sly's store. Said she only wanted to scare me. Teach me a lesson."

I didn't believe him. I didn't believe any doctor would have prescribed Antabuse for an alcoholic without explaining the risks to the patient. At the very least, it would make a drinker violently nauseated; at worst, it could trigger a stroke. I didn't believe Mama would have laced Dad's food with such a dangerous drug, even if she had been able to secure a prescription. True, as a doctor's daughter, she thought there must be a medicine for every ailment, and for every character flaw, so visible to her eyes, there must be a cure. But she wouldn't gamble with Dad's life.

"You're only looking for an excuse," I said.

"She wants to lead me around by the collar. Wants to make a little puppy dog out of me. But I'm a man, you hear me?" He raked an arm across the workbench, spilling tools and wood onto the floor.

"Drinking yourself stupid before lunch makes you a man?"

"That's enough out of you, son."

"Look at you. Can't measure. Can't saw straight. Can't even stand up."

Dad tipped over the stool as he lurched to his feet. "There, I'm standing up. Keep talking back and see what happens."

I braced myself. "Are you going to shut me up?"

He swung toward me, and I lifted my fists as he'd taught me to do. I wanted an excuse to hit him, as if I could beat sense into him, as if I could snap the rope that was dragging him down. And if he pounded me, at least I'd have a reason for all this pain.

He lifted his own fists and circled clumsily, swaying to catch his balance, then dodged past me and staggered out the door. I let him go.

For a long while I stood there, my heart hammering.

The next morning, Ruth and I left for home with the children before Dad could begin his drinking for the day. So our parting was sober. He gave Jesse and Eva bear hugs that made them squinch up their faces in delight. After I hugged and kissed Mama, she said, What about your daddy? Doesn't he get a kiss? I bristled at her bossing, as Dad himself always did, but I obeyed, wrapping my arms around the stout barrel of his body and rubbing my lips against his whiskery cheek. That was the last time Dad and I ever touched.

What we had long feared came to pass six weeks later, when Dad slumped to the floor of Glenn's trailer in Oklahoma City, his heart finally giving up. Glenn was building solar homes in those days, and Dad had driven over from Mississippi to lend a hand. The hand would have been shaky, for Dad never quit drinking. Glenn couldn't be sure just when Dad had died, nor whether the end had been sudden or slow, for on that February morning when Glenn went to fix breakfast, he found the body already cold on the scuffed linoleum.

In the turbulence following his death, I couldn't bring myself to ask Mother if she really had slipped Antabuse into Dad's food. Months passed, then years, and I never put the question. I refused to believe she would have done such a foolhardy thing, but if the truth was otherwise, I didn't want to drag it out of her. Don't cry over spilt milk, I could hear Dad say. Let the dead bury their dead.

Now, of course, it's too late to get a straight answer from Mother about what she had for lunch today, let alone what she might have put in Dad's food all those years ago. Each morning and evening when the nurses bring her medicines, she eyes the little cupful of pills suspiciously. What is all this? she keeps asking Ruth and me. It's what the doctor prescribed, we keep assuring her. Are these people really nurses? Yes, we say. Even the men? The men are nurses, too, we say. What if they're trying to poison me? Nobody's trying to poison you, we tell her. We're all trying to help.

In the spring of 1962, my junior year in high school, when the miracle of Dad's sobriety was still fresh, I sent off applications to four or five science camps that were to be held that summer. A couple of them would be hosted at colleges in Ohio, one in Michigan, and one, the farthest afield, in southern Indiana. Such camps had proliferated in the aftermath of Sputnik, under the shadow of Soviet missiles. Our leaders believed we could defend ourselves against the Red menace only by training ever more physicists, chemists, mathematicians, and engineers to concoct ever more ominous weapons, and so they zealously funded efforts to draw young people into the study of science.

Every camp I applied to admitted me, and every one offered a scholarship. Which one should I choose? Mama wanted me to sign up for one in Ohio, close to home. Dad, who had itchy feet, urged me to go have a gander at a new stretch of the world. As a teenager, he had jumped on freight trains and traveled the country, like the bear going over the mountain to see what he could see. At twenty, after his only year of college, on a whim one Friday night he boarded a Greyhound bus in Memphis and rode to Chicago and got a job slicing cheese in a delicatessen, where, in his butter-melting southern drawl, he asked a pretty auburn-haired customer to write down her name and phone number on the wrapping paper, and she primly declined, but the following day she returned for more cheese and wrote beside the phone number all three parts of her name, Eva Mary Solomon, which became in the mouth of this Mississippi charmer the refrain of a song he often crooned to her when they danced—a song, for all I know, he sang to her when they made the love that blossomed into Sandra, Glenn, and me.

At sixteen I was more my father's than my mother's boy, so I chose the camp farthest away, at Indiana University. I could never have predicted, when Dad and I set out in our wheezing station wagon for the drive to Bloomington, that I would find in this place a girl to marry, that she and I would return here after graduate school and make our careers at the university, that our two children would be born and reared here, that our first grandchild would begin life here, that by living close to her parents this girl and I would witness the dwindling of her mother from Alzheimer's disease and of her father from congestive heart failure, that my own mother would spend over two decades after my father's death circling here in smaller and smaller orbits, that the two of us, this girl and I, would imagine spending the rest of our lives here, still in love.

What began that summer between Ruth Ann McClure and me did not yet deserve the name of love. It began as fascination. And Ruth was entirely worthy of notice, with a heart-shaped face surrounded by honey-colored curls, a rosy complexion, and a compact body that she carried with unself-conscious ease. The ease, I would learn, had been hard won.

If hormones made me gaze at her to begin with, some other impulse made me gaze a second time and a third. The girls I had known back home seemed to flaunt their looks, or apologize for them, or cover them up. Those familiar girls seemed to calculate their every move, as if they were auditioning for a part in a play. Ruth, by contrast, seemed to be fully and simply herself, gathered about her own center. When she moved or spoke, she expressed who she was rather than who she imagined others might want her to be. In the raucous throng of twenty or so campers—five girls and some fifteen boys—Ruth was quiet, composed, wearing a slight smile amidst the shenanigans, as if she were a grownup indulging the children. She was in fact the youngest camper, only fifteen, while the rest of us were sixteen or seventeen. She had started school a year behind me, but had skipped a grade, and still was at the head of her class.

These and sundry other facts about her emerged slowly over the course of the summer, and only in response to my questioning, for Ruth would be the last person in any crowd, then or now, to tell her life story without much prompting. So I discovered that she had been born in the town of Vincennes, along the Wabash River on the western edge of Indiana. One of her grandfathers had worked in the Vincennes post office, the other had farmed, and both grandmothers had kept house. Early on, Ruth had moved to Indianapolis, where she lived with a father who was an accountant for the Eli Lilly pharmaceutical company, a mother who was a mover and shaker in the Methodist church, and a brother who had been conceived just before her father shipped out to France during World War II. In France, her father had been entrusted with delivering liquor for the Allied officers' mess, because he was the only teetotaler in his unit.

When Ruth was four and her brother was five, they both came down with rheumatic fever. For the next two years she was confined to bed, where she learned to rely on her mind for entertainment, through books and games and make-believe. When at last she got out of bed, she had to learn all over again how to walk. She wasn't allowed to run. After missing kindergarten because of her illness, she completed first and second grades in a single year at a school for handicapped children, where she could take naps every afternoon. From then until she entered high school, the doctor forbade her to do any vigorous activity, because the rheumatic fever had left her with a heart murmur. She learned to play the piano, flute, and oboe. As she grew stronger she was allowed to join the marching band, but she never played sports or climbed trees or built snow forts, never learned to swim with abandon. She missed nearly all of childhood's wild romping. So the ease I sensed in her movements had been cautiously and painfully achieved.

All of this chronicle, as I say, emerged scrap by scrap over the course of that summer of 1962, in the sultry air of Bloomington, Indiana, under the sponsorship of the National Science Foundation. Ruth and I spent our days in laboratories, in my case purifying organic chemicals, and in her case dissecting the brains of rats. We spent our evenings in the dormitory lounge with other campers, lost in tease and talk, or strolling through the campus amidst the songs of crickets and cicadas, or simply reading in some quiet spot.

I realize how bizarre it must sound, in our electrified age, to say that reading could be romantic. But so it was for Ruth and me. Of course we went to movies, sipped milk shakes, held hands, and kissed, and on Sundays we walked downtown to the First Methodist Church, where we sat in a pew more aware of one another's closeness than of any words from the pulpit. And every bit of that was delicious. But nothing from the summer carries more lasting allure for me than the memory of sitting with Ruth on the bank of a stream on campus, taking turns reading aloud from the books we held in our laps, while the wind set leaves gossiping in the grand old trees above us and the creek rustled in its stony bed.

Ruth was the first girl I'd ever met who confessed to an unapologetic love of books. And the confession came in our first real conversation, which occurred on the opening field trip of science camp. One evening we all piled into a bus and rode into the hills north of Bloomington to the university's astronomical observatory. It was a clear night, the stars as distinct and fiery as they had appeared when I began wearing glasses.

Inside the observatory, each of us took a turn at the telescope. I managed to squeeze into line right behind Ruth, and so I was close enough to hear the catch in her breath as she gazed through the eyepiece. When my turn came, and my field of vision filled with light from galaxies billions of miles away, I felt dizzy, as if I might fall spinning into those unimaginable depths. I wondered how many of those remote suns had already burned out, how many life-forms had perished in the time it had taken this light to reach Earth.

I pulled away from the telescope to find Ruth studying me, bemused, a wisp of a smile on her face. Whatever she meant by that look, I felt challenged to say something adequate to the wonder she and I had just glimpsed. All I could think of were those proud yet fearful lines from the Psalms: "When I consider thy heavens, the work of thy fingers, the moon and the stars, which thou hast ordained; / What is man, that thou art mindful of him?" Quoting the Bible didn't seem the coolest way to approach a desirable girl, however, so I settled for saying, "Wow."

Ruth's smile changed from wispy crescent to full, which might have meant only that she found my utterance to be surpassingly dumb. Still, I chose to be encouraged. After a lecture on astronomy, to which I paid scant attention from a seat next to Ruth, we walked back to the bus together, and I found myself more intrigued by the glide of her white tennis shoes over the dew-damp grass than by the white sweep of the Milky Way overhead.

With a thumping heart, I sat next to her on the bus for the ride back to Bloomington. Perhaps sensing that she had an infatuated boy on her hands, Ruth drew from her purse a leaflet we'd been given with our other materials for camp, a listing of "114 Books for Pre-College Reading." I had already taped that leaflet above the desk in my dormitory room, vowing to work my way through from A to Z. Before the driver doused the overhead lights, Ruth and I studied the list, comparing notes on the books we'd read. Thinking to impress her, I told her how my rocketry had been inspired by Willy Ley's *The Conquest of Space*.

She laughed. "What a ridiculous title! It's like an ant sitting on its mound of dirt and writing a book called *The Conquest of Earth*."

Until that moment I hadn't realized how absurd it was for a two-legged mite on this dust mote of a planet to brag about conquering space. Our fastest rockets would take many human lifetimes to reach the nearest star in our own galaxy. Even traveling at the speed of light, the babble from our radios and televisions would take billions of years to reach the farthest of those galaxies we'd glimpsed through the telescope. And if, way out there, any listeners capable of understanding this babble happened to catch our broadcasts, what could they think of us, the supposed masters of the universe, except as a race inordinately fond of sitcoms, soap operas, pro sports, rock-and-roll, bloody news reports, and fatuous ads? If the Psalmist had known just how big and old the universe really is, could he have so easily believed that the Creator of all this splendor dotes on humankind?

Over the course of that summer and over the four decades since, Ruth would let the air out of countless gassy notions, quite a few of them mine. But this night on the bus, riding through the starlit Indiana countryside, was the first time I felt the force of her sane, serene, no-nonsense mind. After the lights were doused, we laced the fingers of our hands together, and kept on talking about books.

By summer's end, although I had fallen in love, I hadn't advanced the frontiers of science even a millimeter through my tinkering in the organic chemistry lab. Nor, as it turned out, had the American taxpayer secured in me another scientist to speed up the arms race against Communism. But Ruth did become a biochemist, and to this day she carries on medical research. Eva, our firstborn child, has become a biologist, specializing in the evolution of birds. Since Eva's husband, Matt, is a computer scientist, it seems likely that Elizabeth, the firstborn child of their love, will grow up puzzling over the ways of the universe. So I like to think there has been some return on the taxpayers' investment, if not in the field of weaponry.

As the camp drew to a close that August, I despaired of ever seeing Ruth again, let alone marrying her. The several hundred miles from her home in Indiana to mine in Ohio might as well have been the distance from Earth to Alpha Centauri, for all the likelihood that we could visit one another. Nor could we count on talking by phone, because we'd both been taught that long-distance calls were to be made only in cases of emergency—and our parents weren't likely to regard teenage romance as an emergency. So on our last evening together, which I imagined would be our last evening forever, I filled myself with the sound of her voice, the smell of her hair, the taste of her lips.

I was momentarily distracted from my heartbreak when Dad showed up to take me home in a 1959 Ford convertible, with a turquoise body and long white fins and a supercharged V-8 engine, a showboat of a car which he'd bought used when the crankshaft in the old station wagon cracked. Watching me give Ruth a despairing kiss goodbye, Dad drew his own conclusions, and made no comment when

I climbed into the car. As we cruised away from Bloomington, the weight of my grief increased mile by mile. We took turns driving. The feel of all that horsepower under my hands didn't console me. On our way home, we stopped over to camp and fish in an Ohio state park. Dad must have figured I'd be drawn out of my gloom by the water and woods. Or maybe he just wanted to get to know me again, now that he was sober and clear.

The nearest I came to speaking about Ruth was to ask if he had ever missed a girl so much it hurt. Sure, he told me, he had ached over plenty of girls until he met Mama, and then he made sure he'd never have to live apart from her again. I asked him how you know when you've found the girl you should never give up.

"With Mama," he replied, "it was like she lit up from inside. There was this crowd of other girls, and then there was Eva Mary."

The way he said it made me realize he still saw the love light shining in Mama, an unflagging radiance, as it shone for me in Ruth.

For the last leg of our trip, north from Columbus, Dad put down the convertible's top. While he drove, the rush of wind lulled me to sleep. By and by, a roaring and shimmying jerked me awake, and I looked over to see the dial on the speedometer topped out at 120 miles per hour. Dad grinned across at me, let up on the gas pedal, and shouted, "I just wanted to see what she could do!"

For the moment I was too happy to be scared, too glad of my father's company to be lonely.

WATER

14

WRAPPED UP IN Ruth during that Indiana summer, I had scarcely thought about the alarming changes under way back home in Ohio. Together with our neighbors on Esworthy Road, we had been forced to sell our house and land to the government, so the Army Corps of Engineers could build a dam on the West Branch of the Mahoning River and flood our valley with a reservoir. Eventually the house would be scraped away by bulldozers, along with the stable, pig-pen, orchard, fences, flower beds, and every other sign that we'd lived there. First to disappear under the flood would be the fat maples in the river bottom and the sugarhouse where sap boiled into sweetness. Then rising waters would erase the giant sycamore where the raccoon preened in her cage while dogs yapped below, the pastures where model rockets drifted down under their gaudy parachutes, the secret meadow where I used to lie in tall grass musing on clouds, and the woods and creeks where I learned to love the earth.

Displaced from our homes, my family and our neighbors got a mild taste of what the Indians must have felt when settlers armed with guns and Bibles drove them from this land that would become Ohio. Unlike the Shawnee, Wyandot, Miami, and other native peoples, we were paid for our land. We hadn't buried our ancestors here, hadn't woven the place into our rituals and lore. Still, the loss was wrenching.

There was no prospect of our moving to another farm nearby, be-cause Dad's company had decided to transfer him from the Arsenal to a factory in Lake Charles, Louisiana, where they wanted him to ease tensions between white and black workers. So Belle and her colts were sold to the milkman for his children to ride. Our farming gear was auctioned off. Dad went on ahead to Louisiana, living out of a suitcase, listening to death threats over the phone, shifting from one motel to another when a brick shattered the plate glass window of his room. In the fall, Sandra would resume her study of art at Kent State University, while Mama, Glenn, and I would spend the school year, my last before college, living once more inside the Arsenal.

On my return from science camp, I entered P Quarters, the same white clapboard house on the Circle where we had moved upon our arrival from Memphis eleven years earlier. I carried my bag upstairs to the bedroom where I had suffered ether nightmares. I looked out the window onto the familiar vista of lawn, spinning radar dish, and tangled woods where our collie had joined the pack of wild curs to hunt deer.

When I turned to put my things away, I noticed on the dresser a pastel blue envelope addressed to me in unmistakable handwriting. I opened it carefully with my pocketknife, to keep from tearing the paper in my excitement, and inside I found a letter from Ruth. I read it through in a kind of trance, hearing the feisty, funny, surprising turns of her voice. Then I read it through again and again. We had promised to write one another, but I had imagined letters would only deepen the ache of absence. Yet these pages conveyed a heady feeling of *presence*, as if Ruth were here in the room with me. How could I write to her anything equally vivid in response?

I mused on that question while I resumed work as a carpenter for the father of my old rocket buddy, Marty Sanford. Helping Mr. Sanford build houses, I had gradually advanced from lugging lumber and picking up scrap to framing walls, running wiring, hanging Sheetrock, installing cabinets, and finishing trim. When I returned to the jobsite that August, Mr. Sanford sent me up onto the roof to nail shingles. He believed in getting a day's work for half a day's pay, so whenever I paused in hammering longer than it took to open a new bundle of shingles, he called up to me, "You break an arm, Scott?"

I paused more often than usual, as I daydreamed on the roof while composing in my head what I hoped would be enchanting letters to Ruth. Yet the sentences I cobbled together seemed so gawky, so dull, I couldn't bring myself to write them down.

Then a second powder blue envelope arrived from Indianapolis, bearing a letter that began, "Darling Scott." I couldn't put off answering any longer, or Ruth might think I had forgotten her. And so, in clumsy script, in clumsy prose, I wrote my first reply.

Thus began an epistolary romance that continued for five years, at first a letter per week and soon a letter per day, through the end of high school and all of college, right up until our wedding in August of 1967. By the time Ruth and I exchanged our solemn vows, we had exchanged well over a thousand letters, all of which are stored in the attic above the room where I write these lines. That I am writing these lines at all owes as much to my apprenticeship in love letters as to any formal training.

The reams of paper I mailed to Ruth were filled with poems, stories, notions, news. They told about the books I read, plays I watched, music I heard, people I met. They traced the seasons by naming the flowers in bloom. They brooded on the civil rights movement, the nuclear arms race, the war in Vietnam, the mystery of God. They asked endless questions. They bared my soul. Striving to convey to this beloved audience of one what was going on around me and inside me during those five years, I learned the power of language to map a life, to overcome distance, to focus attention on what matters most.

"In the beginning was the Word," according to the Gospel of John, "and the Word was with God, and the Word was God." Theological friends, as well as footnotes in my dog-eared copy of *The Oxford Annotated Bible*, inform me that the Greek *Logos*, translated here as *Word*, means not simply language but the originating and organizing impulse of the whole cosmos. It signifies a shaping energy, intelligent and generous and inexhaustible. Like *Tao*, it is a finger pointing toward the Way of Things.

The Gospel of John goes on to say of Logos, "He was in the beginning with God; all things were made through him, and without him was not anything made that was made. In him was life, and the life was the light of men. The light shines in the darkness, and the darkness has not overcome it." I resist the Greek penchant for cleaving the world into contrary principles forever at war—light and dark, good and evil, soul and body, spirit and matter—yet I marvel, along with the author of these verses, over the miracle that *anything* shines forth in the void of space, let alone the intricate, exquisite life we behold all around us on this lowly planet.

Outside my window, the red oak we planted a year ago to celebrate Elizabeth's birth swells at every bud, thrusting out new leaves to lick the sun. It's April, and here in Indiana, Logos is putting on quite a show. Beyond the twiggy spire of the oak, a magnolia blazes with pink bloom. Our city lot glistens with spring beauties: trout lilies, cut-leaf toothworts, rhododendrons, woods poppies, rue anemones, Dutchman's-breeches, candytuft, tulips, trillium, phlox, daffodils, bloodroot, and spears of new grass. A fur of moss fills every damp spot. The nearby streets are aflame with redbuds, crab apples, cherries, pears. Birds break off their mating songs to build nests. Gauzy bugs, newly hatched, fill the air like constellations. Soon the seventeen-year cicadas will crawl up out of the soil in throngs, filling the night with their raucous cries. Out in the countryside, beyond houses and pavement, the creeks rush along, brimful of rainwater. Spring peepers croak from the rims of ponds. The woods glow with a fresh green light.

In the midst of all this ferment, in the middle of April, Elizabeth rounds out her first year of life. For the past month she has been taking the occasional shaky step or two on her own, without holding anyone's hand. Then suddenly last week she set off walking. Hearing of this breakthrough, Ruth and I hurried the few blocks over root-heaved sidewalks to Eva and Matt's house. The whole way I kept thinking what an achievement it is to walk on two legs. Lifting one foot, pivoting on the other, you tip off balance, and then swing a leg forward to catch yourself. Every step is a fall, interrupted in the nick of time by a well-planted foot. No wonder babies take many tumbles, practicing this risky venture, before they get the knack of it. No wonder old people shuffle cautiously, gripping a cane, a walker, a railing, or someone else's hand.

So long as Eva, Matt, Ruth, and I sat watching, Elizabeth wouldn't deign to walk. She had too much dignity to perform for us like a trained monkey. We coaxed and cooed, hands outstretched, but she ignored us. Only when the four doting grownups turned our attention away from her to talk about the latest bloody turn in America's latest war did Elizabeth take half a dozen staggering steps across the room. When she reached the couch, still upright, she flashed us a grin and loosed a triumphant shout.

A baby who falls will bounce back up with nothing worse than a bruise. An elder who falls may break a leg or the hinge of a hip and never walk again. Before her memory began to slip, Mother was squired around by a courtly retired journalist named Ed Moss. Because of a tricky hip he'd injured in World War II, during his last years Ed used a cane and took tiny steps. Mother often complained that his wary walk made him look like an old man. Why didn't he throw away that cane and stride along the way she did? Well, Ed replied with a patience I couldn't have mustered, he *was* an old man, and he didn't want to fall. Poppycock, said Mother. If you wish to stay young, you must act young. You'd never catch her shuffling around.

Then Mother's arthritic knees became so painful she had to have them replaced with artificial joints. After each surgery Ed helped nurse her through the convalescence. Year by year, Mother shortened her stride. She had to give up dancing and gardening. Reluctantly, she began to use a cane. She accepted help getting in and out of cars and climbing stairs. When Ed moved from his house into an assisted-living community, she moved there as well, lest some hussy steal away Ed's attentions. Then one night, after she and Ed had eaten supper together as usual, he fell asleep in his reading chair with a biography of Harry Truman open on his lap, and sometime before dawn his heart stopped. After Ed's death, more of the starch went out of Mother. With much grumbling, she agreed to use a walker. She began taking baby steps.

Mother's baby steps are a measure of her diminishment, while Elizabeth's are a measure of her growth. Still, Mother keeps moving. She relishes foods she can no longer name, hymns she can no longer sing. She notices the mint-colored haze of new leaves gathering in the woods outside her window. She praises the year's first flowers. What's remarkable about old age is not that we wear out but that we last so long in the grip of gravity.

What's remarkable about youth is that we rise up out of a smidgen of molecules into creatures capable of speaking, dancing, and singing. Who can look into the eyes of a newborn without a shiver of awe? Who can hear a baby's babble form into words without sensing Logos at work? Who can watch a toddler sally out on her first steps without rejoicing? Our April child, like every child, embodies the lavish energies of creation. Elizabeth's unfolding is every bit as marvelous to me as the stalks bursting into bloom and the twigs flickering into leaves.

"The light shines in the darkness, and the darkness has not overcome it," the Gospel of John assures us. If winter is darkness, a reminder of the void that precedes and surrounds all being, then spring proclaims the unquenchable light. It's the right season for Easter, at least in the Northern Hemisphere, as the early Christians knew. When better for a savior to rise from the dead than in the flush of spring?

Back in those days when Ruth and I began exchanging our fervent letters, I still felt that the resurrection of one man long ago in Jerusalem was more remarkable than the resurrection of the whole earth, year after year, as it awakens from winter's sleep. For this is the claim of orthodox Christianity—that the light shining in Jesus was a unique manifestation of the Source, the Logos, the Creator. As the Gospel of John puts it, "And the Word became flesh and dwelt among us, full of grace and truth; we have beheld his glory, glory as of the only Son from the Father." Two chapters later, we find the most famous promise of salvation in Christian literature:

For God so loved the world that he gave his only Son, that whoever
believes in him should not perish but have eternal life. For God sent
the Son into the world, not to condemn the world, but that the world
might be saved through him. He who believes in him is not condemned; he who does not believe is condemned already, because he
has not believed in the name of the only Son of God.

For those followers who, to this day, see Jesus as the sole vessel for God's
glory, it's as though they can perceive the miraculous nature of existence only by squeezing all sacredness into one person. It's as though
they can grasp the meaning of suffering only by regarding the death of
this hero on a cross as their ticket to paradise.

The Jesus who is quoted in the Scriptures never claimed to be the
only Son of God. His followers made the claim for him, and their version of the story was the one I absorbed from the pages of the New
Testament and the pews of country churches. In spite of the shimmer I
could see everywhere on this luxuriant planet, in spite of what I had
learned from science about the scale and splendor of the universe, when
I was seventeen I still believed that Jesus was the sole incarnation of
the Great Mystery at the heart of things, or at least the only one that
counted.

Now, believing otherwise, I can explain that stubborn clinging to
Jesus as a compensation for having lost my grip on God. By my last year
of high school, I had long since given up imagining God as a gigantic
and wizardly version of my father. I could no longer whisper into his
ear, crawl into his lap, shelter in his arms. Arms, lap, ear had all evapo-
rated, along with any tongue that might have dictated the Bible. In my
imagination, God shrugged off the flesh altogether, turned into vapor,
dispersed into gravity and light. The only role left for God in the universe described so convincingly by science was to spark the Big Bang
and frame the laws that govern how everything, from quarks to quasars,
would forever behave.

How could I worship a skein of rules or pray to a field of force?
How could I carry in my heart a God without substance or form? The

author of John understood our need for a tangible expression of the Creator: "No one has ever seen God; the only Son, who is in the bosom of the Father, he has made him known." In Jesus, that is to say, and only in Jesus, God took on a body we could touch. If we had followed Jesus around Palestine, we could have felt God's pulse, smelled God's sweat, heard God speak, gazed into God's eyes. The flowing of spirit into flesh is the mystery of incarnation, one of the twin pillars of Christian belief. The other pillar is the mystery of resurrection.

I have kept from my childhood Christianity a conviction that these are indeed the mysteries that frame our lives. Incarnation points to the astounding fact of Being itself, the sheer existence of the universe, which has given rise to life, which has given rise to consciousness, which gazes back in wonder at the whole show. Resurrection points to the power of renewal in things, the way the show keeps going on, even while countless actors shuffle on and off the stage, as Mother gives way to Elizabeth, as winter yields to spring.

Jesus, I now believe, was merely one of those actors. True, he made God known to us eloquently and memorably, but he was not himself God, nor the only son of God. Instead, he revealed a world saturated with divinity—the sea and its swimmers, the air and its fliers, the land with its rooters and runners, the sky with its host of stars. Jesus witnessed to the holy force incarnate in each of us, sinners as well as saints. He proclaimed the resurrection of life in every breath. Called *spirit* by Christians, *prana* by Hindus, and *ch'i* by Taoists, this animating energy flows through us constantly, renewing and sustaining us against the centrifugal tug of time.

When asked by skeptics when the kingdom of God was coming, Jesus replied, "Behold, the kingdom of God is in the midst of you." *Is*— right now—*in the midst of you*—right here. By living in communion with the Creator, he showed us what is true for every creature, in every moment. In fact, I sometimes wonder if all other animals, all plants, maybe even stars and rivers and rocks, dwell in steady awareness of God, while humans alone, afflicted with self-consciousness, imagine ourselves apart.

• • •

How else to account for the mayhem we wreak on one another and on the earth, if not as the result of some broken link between us and the source of life? During my last year in high school, the Army Corps of Engineers prepared a site for the dam just down the road from Wayland, where Reverend Knipe, rocking on the porch of the parsonage, had sought in vain to ease my fear of death. After the human residents were cleared from the valley, some of them escorted by sheriff's deputies, every other living thing was left to fend for itself. A few prime trees were felled and carted off before the reservoir began to fill, but most were left to go under the flood, like the fabled soldiers of Pharaoh who drowned when the Red Sea closed over their heads.

Once a week or so that fall, I drove by the dam site on my way home from school to watch the engineers at work. The ground quaked when dynamite loosened bedrock. Giant shovels roared in to scoop up the debris, and dump trucks hauled it away. I was excited by the harnessing of so much power, even while I was appalled by the devastation. The scourging of my home ground provoked in me the same mixture of astonishment and dread I'd felt at other pivotal moments in my life, ever since lightning shattered the front yard oak while I nestled in my father's arms. Only now *we* had become the wielders of lightning, shattering whatever stood in the way of our designs.

The energy that amazed and frightened me the most was bound up in the nucleus of atoms. Some of the best minds in America, working secretly during Hitler's war, had figured out how to set loose that cataclysmic fire. We demonstrated our might to the world in August of 1945 by reducing Hiroshima and Nagasaki to rubble, and tens of thousands of their citizens to charred corpses. Born two months after the blasts, I grew up under the sign of the mushroom cloud. Air-raid drills at school and persistent rumors about A-bombs stored at the Arsenal kept me from forgetting this new menace.

Then, in that fall of 1962, photographs taken by American spy planes revealed nuclear-tipped Soviet missiles being deployed in Cuba. President Kennedy announced the discovery on the twenty-second of October in a somber address, which I heard on a transistor radio during a break from dress rehearsals for a play at the high school. The United States would cut off Cuba by air and sea until the missiles were removed, the president said, and we would regard any attack on our forces as grounds for retaliating against the Soviet Union. With nightmare weapons in the skies, on land, and on all the seven seas, an outbreak of fighting between the two giants would almost certainly engulf the earth.

In our costumes and greasepaint, we hunched over the radio in the school cafeteria, our elbows braced on a table carved with profanities and vows of eternal love. When the president finished speaking, we all looked for guidance to the end of the table, at the sole grownup in the room, our dashing, witty, and irreverent English teacher, Eugene Fahnert. While directing the play, a snide comedy, he had kept up a joking banter to steady our nerves. If anyone could relieve our gloom, it was Mr. Fahnert. Now he returned our look without the hint of a smile, saying, "This could really be it."

A shudder of recognition went through me. I had been expecting this moment ever since I'd learned what happened in Hiroshima and Nagasaki, ever since I'd discovered that our government and the Soviets, instead of outlawing these awful weapons, were manufacturing them by the thousands and scattering them around the globe. It was as though the fences of the Arsenal had been stretched to encircle the earth, and every place had become treacherous.

"In the meantime," said Mr. Fahnert, standing up from the scarred table, "we might as well practice our silly play."

That was a Monday night. The real performance was scheduled for Tuesday. War seemed inevitable, if not tonight or tomorrow, then soon. But the play went on as scheduled, before an overflow crowd that guffawed at every turn of phrase or tilt of eyebrow. There was such hilarity in the air, we might have recited Latin poetry and still provoked laughter.

The rest of that week I skipped school. I couldn't bear to be cooped up indoors, discussing Camus and calculus, while the fate of the world hung by a thread. Each morning I left our house on the Circle at the usual time, but instead of catching the bus, I went hiking through the Arsenal. The guards had reported seeing on their patrols two albino deer, a doe and a buck, and I became obsessed with tracking down that ghostly pair. I longed to see them, as if the blaze of their white flanks against the russet of October leaves would be a talisman against war.

I suppose I was looking for evidence of sanity in a world gone mad. The Arsenal itself was a symptom of that madness—so much intelligence, labor, and wealth devoted to the machinery of death. In my wanderings I passed the humpbacked munitions bunkers, laid out along railroad tracks like rows of grass-covered graves, where sheep browsed on frostbitten grass. I passed lots full of rusting howitzers and tanks, their muzzles aimed at the horizon. I waded through an overgrown field where the fiery seed heads of sumac and the ruby leaves of blackberry glowed among the wrecks of vintage bombers. Just when I was beginning to hope that wildness might eventually reclaim the Arsenal, I discovered an oil-slicked pond where nothing stirred, and a fenced-off area posted with skulls and crossbones, a waste of raw dirt where nothing grew.

In my search I came upon hosts of deer, but never the albino pair. I began to suspect that the white doe and buck must have been dreamed up by the guards on their dull rounds of the Arsenal's perimeter. The ordinary, cinnamon-flanked deer should have been medicine enough to ease my anxiety, to reassure me about Earth's prodigal energies. Yet their very abundance reminded me of the vanished mountain lions and wolves, and the vanished hunters whose flint arrowheads glinted in the gravel of creeks. The Arsenal, which had seemed so vast and wild to me as a boy, such a sprawling paradise, now seemed a mere speck in the crosshairs of Soviet missiles.

On the Saturday following President Kennedy's somber threat of war and the performance of our silly play, a U.S. spy plane was shot down. Another U.S. spy plane wandered off course over Siberia and narrowly escaped the Soviet fighter jets that scrambled to intercept it. Soviet ships steamed toward the American blockade, with instructions from Premier

Khrushchev not to halt. Generals in Washington urged the president to bomb the Cuban missile sites, while Soviet commanders at those sites were under orders to hurl everything they had at the United States as soon as bombs started falling.

That night I wrote what I feared might be my last letter to Ruth. Who knew if it would ever reach her? Past midnight I went to drop the letter in a mailbox near the Arsenal's main gate. As I approached the guard shack, I startled the soldier on duty, who lifted his rifle and barked, "Who's there?"

I hoisted my arms, calling, "Hey. I live here. My dad's G. R. Sanders."

The soldier swore. "You're liable to get yourself killed, sneaking up like that."

"Sorry. I just wanted to mail a letter."

Lowering his gun, the soldier waved me on. I could see in the light from the guard shack that he wasn't much older than I was, and just as scared.

I took a roundabout way back to the house, across fields, trying to outwalk my panic. It was the dark of the new moon, and clouds shut out the stars, so the night beyond reach of the streetlamps was pitch-black. Though the ground was familiar to my feet, I stumbled often. No matter where I walked, I could find no refuge from the madness. So eventually I returned to the Circle, where the porch lights seemed laughably feeble in the face of so much darkness.

As I crept up the stairs of our rented house, Mama fussed at me from her bedroom. "Where have you been?"

"Out for a walk," I whispered at her door. "Any news about Cuba?"

"Don't talk to me about Cuba. You worried me half to death, wandering around out there in the night."

Before she could scold any more, I wished her sweet dreams and went to bed. If my walking had accomplished nothing else, it had made me tired enough to sleep.

The next day we learned that Khrushchev had backed down, ordering the Soviet ships to stop short of the U.S. blockade, promising to withdraw the missiles from Cuba. He and Kennedy exchanged conciliatory messages. In bunkers, cockpits, and control rooms, fingers moved away from the doomsday buttons. This time, the thread by which the fate of the world dangled did not snap.

Soon after deer season opened that December, an army doctor and his wife brought home the albino deer tied to the hood of their car. I was shoveling snow from the sidewalk out front of our house on the Circle when the hunters cruised up to show off their trophies. The doctor rolled down his window. "Aren't they beauties?"

"Yes, sir," I answered. "They sure are." I wanted to lay my hands on those white pelts, but I felt too heartsick to approach the car.

It would take me years to articulate the connections I sensed between the shooting of those snow-white deer, the building of that needless dam, the stockpiling of nuclear weapons, and the balancing of Earth's fate on the tightrope of fear.

15

THE SHOWDOWN OVER Cuba revealed, as in a lightning flash, our collective insanity. I've never forgotten what I glimpsed in those perilous days. While our leaders gathered in solemn assemblies, mouthing words of peace, our scientists and soldiers prepared for war. Maybe the motives for war hadn't changed much since our ancestors fought with stones, but our weapons had become ever more lethal. Proud of being rational creatures, we'd fashioned a civilization of laws and machines, stockyards and stock markets, all the while using the same cleverness to devise ways of destroying everything we'd built.

Even at seventeen, I began to see the deadly flaws in our intelligence. We would embrace a prophet—Jesus, say, or Muhammad or Marx—then declare all others to be frauds. We would embrace a creed—capitalism, say, or communism—then declare all others to be false. It was as though we could remain firm in our faith only by threatening to wipe out whoever believed otherwise. We invented spears or shotguns to kill game, and then started murdering our own kind. The same impulse that led us to shoot albino deer and make rugs from their pelts led us to shoot our human foes and hang their severed ears on our belts. Having learned to manipulate some portion of the world, we imagined the world exists purely for the sake of our manipulation. Having figured out how to dam rivers or split atoms, we barged ahead, heedless of consequences.

The prospect of my own death, which had driven me to the Bible

for consolation, seemed trifling compared to the prospect that everyone
and everything I loved might be annihilated. Ruth was reason enough
to cherish the earth. Yet every earthly creature was in jeopardy and
would remain in jeopardy so long as these terrible weapons existed. In
fact, even if the bombs and missiles were dismantled, they could be
made all over again. For they had come out of us, and so had the will-
ingness to use them. They had taken shape in our minds before they
filled our arsenals. The ingenuity that enabled us to invent language,
cure disease, launch satellites, and unriddle the plot of the universe had
pushed us to the brink of suicide. How had we gone so catastrophically
wrong?

Anxiety over the fate of the world drove me back to the Bible,
where I noticed how often the cry for God's mercy toward the faithful
is accompanied by the cry for vengeance toward enemies. In the
Psalms, for instance, the songs of love are shadowed by songs of hatred:

> Our God is a God of salvation; and to God, the Lord, belongs escape
> from death. / But God will shatter the heads of his enemies, the hairy
> crown of him who walks in his guilty ways. / The Lord said, ". . . I
> will bring them back from the depths of the sea, / that you may bathe
> your feet in blood, that the tongues of your dogs may have their por-
> tion from the foe."

Time and again the Psalmist pleads with God not merely to chastise but
to extinguish the foe:

> Pour out thy indignation upon them, and let thy burning anger over-
> take them. / May their camp be a desolation, let no one dwell in their
> tents. . . . / Add to them punishment upon punishment; may they have
> no acquittal from thee. / Let them be blotted out of the book of the
> living.

Although Jesus taught that we should love our enemies, in the letters of Paul his name became a sword for dividing the saved from the
damned. Paul described the work of Christ as a prolonged siege against

unbelievers, culminating in final victory for the only Son: "Then comes the end, when he delivers the kingdom to God the Father after destroying every rule and every authority and power. For he must reign until he has put all his enemies under his feet. The last enemy to be destroyed is death."

Death, that old bugaboo, crops up again and again throughout the Bible as the ultimate opponent. No sooner do we wake into this life than we realize that the universe will eventually grind each of us into a handful of dust. So we must work out our salvation in fear and trembling, as Paul remarked in another epistle. Could it be that we ward off fear of our own extinction by wishing death on our foes?

Certainly, the dread of God's exterminating power runs from the opening of the Hebrew Bible to the close of the New Testament, from the worldwide flood to the fiery last judgment. From beginning to end, while preaching forgiveness and love, the Bible envisions a God given to intolerance and spite. Although I kept reading this ancient book, seeking comfort and illumination, I was more and more troubled by the undercurrent of cruelty.

As American and Soviet forces armed themselves to blot out the opposing side from the book of the living, living itself seemed all the more precious to me. Against the backdrop of nuclear threats, the decisions I had to make—where to go to college, what to study when I got there, what work to follow after I graduated—seemed as trivial as those porch lights dotted like fireflies around the Circle in the dark of the moon. Still, through our last months in high school, Ruth and I wrote earnestly back and forth about such choices. We pretended the future was secure enough to plan for, and we began to dream of spending it together.

Ruth would go to Indiana University, study chemistry, and pursue a career in biomedical research, thereby fulfilling the fondest hopes of those who'd organized the science camp. My own plans seemed equally firm but proved to be largely pipe dreams. After reconnoitering nearby schools that were strong in physics and math, at the last minute I signed up to attend Brown University in faraway Rhode Island, because an alumnus of that place, having watched me play basketball in high school, thought I could play in the Ivy League. On the strength of my test scores, Brown offered me an academic scholarship that would pay my tuition and half my board and room. So I decided I would enroll there, play hoops, graduate with a degree in physics, and go on to design spacecraft.

Before I could begin at Brown, I had a summer's worth of midnight shifts to work in Lake Charles, Louisiana, where Dad had bought us a brick ranch house surrounded by gardenia bushes and banana trees. I was so eager to move there, one step closer to the great world, that I scarcely felt the pangs of loss when classmates I'd known since childhood said their goodbyes following high school graduation. We promised to keep in touch with one another from our new lives in the Army or Marines, in factories or shops, in hasty marriages or, some few of us, in college. Except for those joining the military, I was the only one headed far afield. I told my buddies I'd be sure to look them up whenever I passed through Ohio. None of us imagined that our friendships, woven through years of growing up together, could simply unravel. And so we blithely scattered.

Dad had lined up for me a vacation relief job driving a forklift at the factory where he was in charge of industrial relations. Over the past year, while he'd moved from motel to motel, dodging death threats and broken glass, his main task had been to persuade whites to accept the integration of blacks throughout the plant, from the lunchroom to the executive suite. His only tool was talk, delivered in a disarming Mississippi drawl, backed up with a threat of firing the worst bigots. By the time I clocked in for my first shift in June of 1963, he had achieved a tense truce. Whites worked alongside blacks in seeming peace, or at least in grudging tolerance.

The factory made synthetic rubber for use in tires. What began as raw chemicals at one end of a blistering hot shed emerged at the other end as fragrant bales of rubber about the size of a carry-on suitcase and weighing forty or fifty pounds. Loaders caught the bales as they rolled from the drying ovens and stacked them into cardboard boxes big enough to hold refrigerators. My job was to haul each carton to the warehouse, record its location, and then cruise back in my yellow fork-lift to wait for the next box. I spent much of the summer waiting, espe-cially on the midnight shift, the one most of the regular drivers chose to skip when they took vacation.

To while away the time between trips to the warehouse, I worked math problems on the backs of shipping forms, I drew designs for rockets, or I simply watched the big, sweating men who handled those heavy bales hour after hour. The biggest of these men, and the least boastful, was Hal Thibideaux, a black Cajun who'd grown up on one of the bayous. During his breaks he took a magazine from his lunch box and went outside to read, with his legs dangling over the edge of the loading dock. From week to week, the magazine changed, but the cover always showed professional wrestlers grappling or posing. Maybe that was the larger life Hal imagined for himself, his great body gleam-ing in the spotlight, as I imagined launching probes into space. It calmed me to see him sitting there, absorbed in his reading, while ma-chines back in the shed kept on clanking.

Most of the other men took no notice of me, nor could I blame them. For I was summer help, a kid passing through on his way to col-lege, while they were trapped here, or in some other plant just as noisy and hot, for the rest of their working lives. From my first day on the job, though, Big Hal looked out for me.

"You making it okay?" he asked me.

"So far so good," I answered.

"That's the ticket."

He told me if any of these jaybirds gave me a hard time, to let him know and he'd set them straight. He warned me to be sure and take my breaks, even when the work backed up, or else I'd wear myself out. "You work fast fast," he'd say, doubling or tripling his adjectives for em-phasis in the Cajun way, "and the machine she just go faster." As he mopped his face with a blue bandanna, he'd urge me to keep drinking water. "Mercy," he'd sigh, "but it's hot hot hot." I knew nothing about his life outside the factory, except that he was a deacon in a local church, he was married, and he had two young children.

One dawn near the end of my first week of midnight shifts, I paused in my forklift on the loading dock to watch the sun break the horizon. Fumes from an oil refinery across the road turned the sky blood red. Chimneys at a nearby explosives factory leaked violet smoke into the dawn sky. The witches' brew of vapors made the air smell like ripe bananas, reminding me of Ruth's hair after she'd worked in the lab at science camp.

As I idled there, another forklift drew up beside me and the driver leaned over to say, "Boy, you want to get along here, don't be talking with niggers." He was an older white man, his cheek swollen with chewing tobacco. He spoke matter-of-factly, as if, like Big Hal, he were advising me to keep up my strength by drinking lots of water. Message delivered, he drove away.

While my father had helped bring about an uneasy truce between whites and blacks inside the plant, tensions outside kept mounting all through that summer. George Wallace had just been elected governor of Alabama with the battle cry "Segregation now, segregation tomorrow, segregation forever!" Nine years after the Supreme Court had ordered integration of public schools, he vowed to stand in the schoolhouse door to prevent blacks from entering. The TV showed police in Birmingham turning dogs and fire hoses on peaceful marchers, including children. In Jackson, near my father's Mississippi birthplace, a field organizer for the NAACP named Medgar Evers was murdered with a bullet in the back. The Ku Klux Klan bombed black churches, meeting halls, businesses, and homes. In city after city there were demonstrations calling for the integration of restaurants, stores, buses, swimming pools, and schools, and everywhere they were met by violence. The South seemed poised for racial war.

When I heard at the plant one night in July that Hal Thibideaux was in the hospital with a bullet in his chest, I flushed with anger and shame, certain some white man had shot him. But I learned soon enough that the shooter was a black man, Hal's brother-in-law, who'd pulled a gun from a drawer when Hal showed up to stop the brother-in-law from beating his wife. At the hospital after work, I couldn't see Hal, who was in intensive care, so I approached every black person in the waiting room until I found his sister, the one Hal had been trying to protect. Several pink Band-Aids stood out against the caramel skin of her face.

"How's Hal doing?" I asked her.

She gave me a wary look. "Who're you?"

"A friend of his from the plant."

"He's dying," she said, turning away. "And he don't have no white friends."

I left the sister alone in her sorrow. She was right about me, at least, for my claim of friendship was wish rather than fact. She also proved to be right about Hal. Later that day, trying to stop the bleeding in his chest, the doctors wheeled him back into surgery, where he died on the table.

Even though he'd been killed by another black man, Hal's death seemed to me an emblem of the hatred seething in the South that summer. I could feel the rage gathering in me as well. Governor Wallace and his thin-lipped state troopers, the sheriffs and their club-wielding deputies, the police with their dogs and the firemen with their hoses, the vigilantes in KKK robes, all the white bigots inspired in me a contempt that wasn't far from hate.

A skinny white guy with tattooed forearms took Hal's place at the conveyor belt, straining to hoist the bales of rubber into shipping cartons. He was another Cajun, with a music to his voice that reminded me of Hal. When he had breath to spare, he talked about netting shrimp in Lake Charles and crayfish in the bayous. He wished aloud that God had made the Sabbath four days long, to leave a man plenty of time for fishing. He seemed harmless enough. Still, I resented him. It wasn't his fault he couldn't fill the space left vacant by Hal's death, yet I resented his scrawny red neck, sunburned from weekends on the water. My own neck was red from playing basketball on the blacktop court at a park near our new house. There was nothing outward to distinguish me from the white mobs I saw screaming at black marchers on the evening news.

The week before I set off to Brown, the news was filled with an ominous buildup for the March on Washington, which promised to be the largest civil rights demonstration in the nation's history. Fearing violence, President Kennedy urged the organizers to cancel the march, but they refused. The march went ahead as scheduled on August 28, attracting a quarter of a million people, a heartening number of whom were white. Gathered before the Lincoln Memorial, the crowd heard many rousing speeches, but none more inspiring than the one delivered by Martin Luther King, Jr.

I had followed the career of Dr. King since the Montgomery bus boycott, and gradually he'd become one of my heroes, as he had been for my high school friend Jeremiah Pond. I couldn't have imagined traveling to Washington for the march, but I made sure to watch the television broadcast of Dr. King's speech, and I could hear the biblical phrases and preacher's rhythms familiar to me from revival meetings. Echoing the prophet Amos, he proclaimed: "We will not be satisfied until justice rolls down like waters and righteousness like a mighty stream." And he echoed Isaiah when he said, "I have a dream that one day every valley shall be exalted, every hill and mountain shall be made low, the rough places shall be made plain, and the crooked places shall be made straight and the glory of the Lord will be revealed and all flesh shall see it together." I was primed to believe that all creatures could unite in harmony, praising the Creation, for it was the vision of God's peaceable kingdom, passed on from the Hebrew prophets through Jesus of Nazareth into this daring black minister.

When I read the text of Dr. King's speech in a newsmagazine, I copied into the journal I began keeping that summer the sentences that moved and puzzled me the most: "We must not allow our creative protest to degenerate into physical violence. Again and again we must rise to the majestic heights of meeting physical force with soul force." What kept him from calling for revenge, like the Psalmist or the lynch mobs? What was soul force, and how could it stand up against police dogs and bullets? The only hint of an answer I could find in the speech itself was another puzzling passage, also copied into my journal: "You have been the veterans of creative suffering. Continue to work with the faith that unearned suffering is redemptive." Here Dr. King must have been thinking not only of the nonviolent demonstrators but of Christ, the purest man or humblest god, nailed to a cross for our sins. Maybe soul force was another name for the Holy Ghost, a power of healing and renewal unaccounted for by science.

At seventeen, when I fancied I understood quite a few more things than I do now, I thought I grasped how suffering could be creative and redemptive. After all, I knew about Job, whose unearned troubles made him wise. His wife and children and livestock had been rubbed out, which was too bad for them, but at least Job got a chance to start over with a new family and a fresh appreciation of God's might.

Now that I've seen a lot of suffering up close, I no longer find much about it that's redemptive, especially when the sufferer is too young or old to comprehend the pain. When I visited Ruth in Indianapolis during my college summers, we often went to see one of her mother's best friends, whose daughter was dying of leukemia. The daughter, Laura, was three when I first met her and six when she died. Over that brief span she withered from a rambunctious child to a listless, hollow-eyed husk. I'm sure that her family, Ruth's family, and everyone else who knew Laura was moved by her vanishing. She may even have redeemed us, to some degree, from ignorance or callousness. But for Laura, too young to understand, her suffering was pure loss. So it is, I imagine, for the millions of children around the globe who are perishing right now, slowly or quickly, from disease, starvation, wounds, beatings, or neglect.

At the other extreme of age, the elderly who fade away from Alzheimer's, Parkinson's, emphysema, cancer, congestive heart failure, or the simple wearing out of organs and joints are frequently bewildered by their decline. Certainly this is true of my mother. For the past decade, the loss of mobility, memory, and language has vexed her.

When she could still summon up more than fleeting scraps of her past, she would recall how she used to dance, used to garden, used to tutor children in local schools, used to host international students from the university, used to gad about wherever she pleased. "Now I'm a stone," she'd say. "I'm a stick of wood."

She would insist on seeing a doctor, who surely could fix what was wrong. Yet after she'd been examined by one or another of a small army of doctors, she would dismiss the diagnosis with a scornful wave of her hand, saying they didn't know what they were talking about. She feared that her medicines were poison. She refused to do the prescribed exercises, or simply forgot them the moment the therapy stopped. "If it hurts, it's bad," she complained when I asked if she had done her leg lifts or stair climbing, "and this is torture." With every loss, she insisted she didn't need help, didn't need to move out of her house, didn't need to give up driving a car, didn't need to wear a hearing aid, didn't need to use a walker.

In the halls of the assisted-living complex, where the nurses could watch her, Mother dutifully braced herself on the walker, but in her apartment she pushed the despised contraption aside and teetered around without support. Then one night, getting up to use the bathroom, she fell, displacing her kneecap. The surgeon took a tuck in a stretched ligament of that knee and bound the leg in a foam cast. She was not to remove the cast for a month, not to walk on that leg, and above all not to get out of bed or the wheelchair on her own. As we repeated these instructions, Mother would nod her head, saying wryly, "I'll be a good little girl." Within minutes, however, she began loosening the Velcro straps of the cast and trying to stand up.

Night after night Ruth and I soothed her to sleep, urging her to call a nurse if she felt the need to get up. How do I call? Mother would ask. For the hundredth time we showed her the cord dangling beside her bed. She claimed never to have seen it before. Meanwhile, the nurses looked in on her once or twice every hour.

It's easy to see now that we should have taken more precautions. We should have insisted that her mattress be placed on the floor, with a railing installed to keep her from climbing out. But she found such restraints humiliating. "I'm not a baby," she said hotly. Wanting to preserve her last shreds of independence, we trusted in the nurses' vigilance and Mother's faulty memory.

And so one morning between three and four o'clock, Mother climbs out of bed, falls again, and this time snaps the ball joint of her hip. By the time she surfaces from the anesthesia following surgery, with an artificial hip to go along with her two artificial knees, she is lost in a fog of terror. "I'm dead, I'm dead," she mutters. "This isn't heaven. This is hell." She rocks from side to side, plucking at the sheet, moaning. Her white curls, one of her last sources of pride, tangle on the pillow. Her hands skitter over her throat and chest like frightened birds. She has no idea where she is, or why. She has fallen among strangers and cold machines.

Jesse, whom she doted on when he was growing up, drives from Maryland to see her, but she doesn't recognize this tall, broad-shouldered man her grandson has become. Nor does she recognize Eva, who made her a great-grandmother just over a year ago by giving birth to Elizabeth. Only Ruth and I can relieve Mother's panic by leaning close to her and speaking calmly, holding her skittish hands, stroking her forehead. We assure her over and over that she is not dead. She will not be abandoned. She is loved. We tell her about the fall, the broken hip, the surgery, the hospital. But each time it is news to her, and as soon as we cease talking we can see our words evaporating from her mind like water from a wiped table. Her agony soon wears me out, and I must walk in the hall to regain my composure, while Ruth, tougher and kinder than I am, stays by the bed.

One time when I return to the room, Mother surfaces from her trance long enough to sigh, "My son!" Another time she calls me by the name of her dead brother who once turned orange from eating carrots in an effort to pass the air force vision exam. Often she calls me Daddy. Whether by this she means her own father, my father, or me as father of Eva and Jesse, I can't tell. Whoever she has in mind—in what remains of her mind—she is comforted. So I stay with her as long as I can bear it, the way, on a dare, I once held my hand in a flame.

Jesse happens to be in the hospital room as Ruth and I hold Mother's arms while a nurse carefully inserts a needle for the intravenous tube, through which morphine will drip to ease the ache from surgery. Mother has pulled out four previous IVs, leaving purple blotches on her forearms. Now she cries out at the needle prick, as an infant does at a vaccination. We explain to her why she needs this tube in her arm, but she only quakes and whimpers until the morphine begins to ease her toward sleep. Ruth and I go home to rest, but not for long, because we know she will wake in terror. Although Jesse stays in town two more days, he doesn't visit Mother again. I don't ask him why. I sense he's less disturbed by death than by this pointless pain.

"I loathe my life," says Job of his torment; "I will give free utterance to my complaint; I will speak in the bitterness of my soul." Mother can no longer decry her losses, can only writhe and mutter, but I can say I loathe what her life has become. There is nothing creative or redemptive in such suffering, unless it speaks to those who keep watch. If there is to be any meaning in this pain, those of us who can still think and speak must find it.

16

"THIS SWELTERING SUMMER of the Negro's legitimate discontent will not pass," said Dr. King from the steps of the Lincoln Memorial, "until there is an invigorating autumn of freedom and equality." I pondered his speech as I rode Greyhound buses from Lake Charles to Providence late in that sweltering, turbulent summer of 1963. I didn't see how anyone who claimed to follow the example of Jesus could resist the call for human equality. Hadn't Jesus embraced tax collectors, prostitutes, lepers, and thieves? Hadn't he defied the biases of his time and place to honor women? Hadn't he insisted that we are all children of one Creator, all precious to God, all deserving of kindness and love, all worthy of life everlasting? The lessons seemed utterly clear to me. Yet across the South, white ministers and congregations either supported racial apartheid or held their tongues while thugs beat up peaceful demonstrators and governors barred the schoolhouse door.

I couldn't reconcile what I heard from the most vocal southern white Christians with what I understood from the teachings of Christ. And so began my estrangement from the church. Or perhaps it had begun earlier, during my years in the Arsenal, when I read about the destruction of Hiroshima and Nagasaki, and I realized how few followers of the Prince of Peace ever spoke out against the insanity of the nuclear arms race. How could you love your enemies while preparing to exterminate them? How could you spend your nation's wealth and talent on ever more weapons while children went to bed hungry and the poor slept in the streets?

That fall, my first semester in college, was not to be the "autumn of freedom and equality" that Dr. King had envisioned. Classes had barely begun in September when yet another black church was bombed in the South. This time it was Birmingham's Sixteenth Street Baptist Church, where dozens of worshipers were injured and four young girls—preparing for Sunday school in the basement near the hidden dynamite—were killed. Surely now, I thought, every white minister in the country, every white Christian, would denounce this madness.

To be fair, some did speak out, including the chaplain at Brown University, Charles Baldwin, whose witness and counsel would be profoundly important to me over the next four years. But most religious leaders, and most of their followers, kept silent. At first I took that silence to be proof of hypocrisy—the gap between what Christians professed to believe and how they actually lived. But what did Christians believe? What did *I* believe? Distant from the country churches in which I had been reared, distant from home, increasingly troubled by the vengeful and xenophobic strain in the Bible, I thought harder about those questions than about any of my college assignments.

At freshman orientation I learned that Brown had been founded in 1764 by Congregationalists and Baptists as a seminary for training ministers. They had chosen Rhode Island because the colony welcomed all religious faiths, unlike neighboring Massachusetts, where the Puritans ruled. I didn't learn until years later that the wealthy, philanthropic Brown family for whom the university was named had made much of their fortune by trading in slaves and by employing slaves in their factories. The university's motto was the same pious one that Americans would later read on their coins, *In Deo speramus*—In God we trust. In keeping with those religious origins, weekly attendance at the chapel had been required of all Brown students until a few years before I enrolled. Like every requirement, this one had been resented, and the alumni who remembered those days spoke of chapel as tedious and barren.

So on Sundays that fall, instead of worshiping on campus, I tried out one after another of the big, stone, half-empty churches in downtown Providence. The city was then in the doldrums, much of the downtown dingy, boarded up, many of the surviving businesses run—so rumor went—by the Mafia. On Sunday mornings it looked like a city abandoned after a plague. The few other worshipers making their way to the old churches might have been survivors slinking through the ruins.

Although I sat through many sermons, I heard no references to the latest bombing in Alabama, no references to the Cuban missile showdown or nuclear weapons, no references to poverty. What I did hear, in service after service, was the Apostles' Creed:

I believe in God the Father Almighty, Maker of heaven and earth. And in Jesus Christ his only Son our Lord; who was conceived by the Holy Ghost, born of the Virgin Mary, suffered under Pontius Pilate, was crucified, dead, and buried; he descended into hell; the third day he rose again from the dead; he ascended into heaven, and sitteth on the right hand of God the Father Almighty; from thence he shall come to judge the quick and the dead. I believe in the Holy Ghost; the holy catholic Church; the communion of saints; the forgiveness of sins; the resurrection of the body; and the life everlasting. Amen.

I had long since memorized the creed, had recited it on countless Sundays, but that fall, as I sat in those echoing churches, I examined it closely for the first time. How much of it did I actually believe? I believed the heavens and earth weren't accidental but were the handiwork of an unimaginably vast and subtle power, which I still felt comfortable calling God. I also believed that a Jewish prophet named Jesus had lived and taught two thousand years before and had died on a cross. But as I probed my childhood faith, I discovered I no longer believed that Jesus was the one and only son of the Creator, nor that he had been born of a virgin, nor that he had risen, bodily, from the dead.

If I doubted the resurrection, how could I believe in the prospect of everlasting life? If I doubted the central promise of Christianity, how could I call myself a Christian? Everything in the Apostles' Creed pointed toward the denial of death and the longing for immortality. Left out entirely was any mention of how we should *live*, how we should treat one another, how we should deal with the poor, the sick, the weak, the mad, the old, or with the millions of other species on our planet. And those were the questions that concerned me. The creed said nothing about justice, healing, peacemaking, or compassion. And those were the impulses that moved me, as I encountered them in Jesus and Isaiah and Amos, in the writings of Mohandas Gandhi and the speeches of Dr. King. Nor did the creed convey anything of the awe I felt in the woods, along the stony beds of creeks, or in the company of storms and stars.

I would have been happy to save my soul—assuming I had one, and assuming it was salvageable—but I couldn't accept that we were born into this world merely to angle for a favorable deal in the next one. Surely there was work we should be doing right here, right now, in this amazing flesh and brimming instant. Surely there must be some purpose in life larger than one's own private salvation. Surely the fate of one's soul is bound up with the fate of one's neighbors and neighborhood.

All of this came to me slowly, fitfully, during that fall of my freshman year, as I sampled one church after another in the desolate downtown of Providence, a city named for the benevolent guidance of God.

On the eve of my eighteenth birthday in late October, I went to the selective service office in Providence to sign up for the draft. Standing in line with other boys my age—and I thought of myself as a boy, not yet as a man—I wondered whether I could fight in a war. The question seemed idle. I realized we had troops stationed around the globe, including some military advisers in a country called Vietnam, but so far as I knew America was at peace. The soldiers I remembered from the Arsenal had seemed less like warriors than like indentured servants, putting in their time until their real lives resumed. From reading comic books and watching war movies, I had once dreamed of wearing a uniform and fighting enemies; but that dream faded in the Arsenal, and it melted away entirely when I tracked down the generals' gut-shot deer in the bloody snow.

I felt no swell of patriotism as I filled out the government forms. The law required me to register for the draft, so here I was. Instead of listing my college address in Rhode Island, I wrote down my parents' address in Louisiana. That casual decision would complicate my life five years later, when having thought harder about my country's penchant for war, I would declare myself a conscientious objector, and my Louisiana draft board, doubting that conscience could prohibit any red-blooded man from killing for his country, would reject my appeal. During those five years, the handful of U.S. military advisers in Vietnam would be replaced by hundreds of thousands of troops. And my disillusionment with our government, like my disillusionment with the organized church, would grow in proportion to the mounting violence.

In October of 1963, however, it was still possible to believe that the grownups who ran our nation, if not those running other nations, earnestly desired peace. Many politicians in the South were clearly racists, but maybe those in the North really did wish to serve the needs of all people. John Kennedy, in particular, struck many young people as sincere. We took him at his word when he declared, in his inaugural speech, that we should ask not what our country could do for us but what we could do for our country. We trusted him when he promised to lift up the downtrodden and make the United States a beacon of justice and freedom.

If I could no longer convince myself that the universe was ruled by a benevolent God, concerned for the welfare of every last soul, I still persuaded myself that our country was ruled by a benevolent president. I could do so only because, at eighteen, I knew little about American politics or history aside from the sugarcoated accounts in textbooks. Trusting in grownups to run things, therefore, I could remain a boy awhile longer, absorbed in my studies, my plans, my romance.

The bitter news from Dallas, which convulsed the nation on November 22, broke through my complacency. That Friday afternoon I was crossing the green at the heart of the Brown campus on my way to physics class when I noticed clusters of students huddled here and there along the sidewalks, their heads bent together, unnaturally still. They seemed to be listening, not to one another but to some distant voice. Pausing near one of these groups, I saw a transistor radio in their midst and I heard an announcer repeating in a strained tone, as if to convince himself, that President Kennedy had been shot. The huddle opened to admit me, and I stood there shivering, the physics class forgotten. Minutes passed; the radio voice kept rephrasing its dire news. Then a reporter at a hospital in Dallas came on the air to say the president was dead.

Moans went up from our group and from others nearby, the first sounds any of us had made. Instinctively, we looped arms across one another's shoulders and drew into a tight knot encircling the radio. Through tears, I looked at the other students, all of them strangers to me, trying to figure out what to make of this terrible fact. Their faces revealed only shock and grief.

On Sunday morning I couldn't bear to walk downtown to one of those cold stone churches, yet I craved company, so I went to worship for the first time in the Brown chapel. Entering between tall fluted columns, passing a memorial to students and alumni who'd died in the Civil War, I climbed to the sanctuary on the second floor. Everything was white—the walls, the altar cloth, the barrel-vaulted ceiling, the painted pews. The pews that morning were crowded, one of the few times I would ever see them so. Large mullioned windows admitted the clear light of day. Without stained glass, statues, banners, or any sign of a cross, the chapel was even plainer than the Methodist churches where I had begun my hunt for God.

I can't remember what the chaplain said that morning, but I can remember how he sounded, this man who insisted on being called not Reverend Baldwin, not mister or sir, but simply Charlie. He sounded like a person in pain. He sounded like the Psalmist trapped down in a well of sorrow. But unlike the Psalmist, he didn't couple his anguish with anger, didn't cry for vengeance against whoever had caused this woe. I sensed in him, as I sensed in Dr. King, a tough-minded compassion, as if he knew the worst about our kind and still would not give up on the healing power of love. With a mild voice, a ruddy face, and thinning corn-silk hair, Charlie Baldwin didn't radiate the charisma of Dr. King, but he seemed to speak from the same deep springs. I longed to drink from that source, and my thirst drew me back to the bright upper room Sunday after Sunday for the rest of my time at Brown.

Classes were canceled that Monday, November 25, in observance of a National Day of Mourning. Sick of the grievous images, I watched only enough of the funeral coverage on television to see the late president's son, John Jr., who turned three that day, standing in a blue coat out front of the cathedral and saluting the coffin as it rolled by.

The world seemed, suddenly, a much more precarious place. Without mushroom clouds, with merely a couple of bullets, the stability I had taken for granted had been shattered. Of course I had been naïve to take it for granted. My confidence in the grownups running our nation was only an extension of my faith in the honesty and decency and competence of my own parents. It was a vestige of childhood. Once broken, it could never be restored.

The last article of childhood faith I would surrender was my belief in the certainty of science. After I had come to question the benevolence of God, the integrity of the church, and the reliability of government, I still believed that science could provide unerring, exhaustive knowledge of the universe. I still imagined that I could extract a guide for living from the clear, clean, dependable rules obeyed by energy and matter.

The physics classes I missed on the day of John Kennedy's assassination and on the day of his funeral were the only ones I missed all that year. The more precarious the human world appeared to be, the more obsessed I became with learning the laws of nature. I threw myself into the study of gravity, electricity, magnetism, optics, atomic structure, all so precise and sure. I wielded my slide rule like a wand that could open every locked door. I no longer needed to keep the periodic table of the elements taped to the wall beside my bed, for I had memorized the orderly scheme. So many protons, neutrons, electrons, so much mass, gave rise to knowable properties for each element, which gave rise to everything in heaven and earth. No one could undo these certainties with a bullet or a bomb. Bullets and bombs, in fact, slavishly obeyed nature's laws.

One consequence of my enthusiasm for science was a decision not to play basketball at Brown. In those days before college sports became semiprofessional, freshmen weren't allowed to play with the varsity, and so they formed a team of their own. When I discovered that practices for the freshman team were scheduled at the same time as the first-year honors physics lab, I had to choose between devoting myself to basketball or devoting myself to the universe, and the universe won. Basketball can hardly be said to have lost, since even in the humble arena of Ivy League sports, I would have been no better than a journeyman point guard.

Meanwhile, the literature I was reading in freshman English class, from the *Iliad* to *The Waste Land*, seemed chaotic, fractured, riddled with mysteries, seething with the very passions that roiled our days. I could see nothing noble about the Trojan War, for all the beauty in the telling. Fair Helen was only an excuse for the Greeks to hack away at their foes, and for a blind bard to commemorate the butchery in song. Achilles was merely a long-winded precursor of G.I. Joe. Except in scale and sophistication, the *Iliad* was no different, I decided, from the war comics I'd read on the porch of our farmhouse in Memphis. As for *The Waste Land*, despite its canny artifice and four hundred footnotes, what was it but a cry of despair, a heap of fragments that wouldn't cohere?

By contrast, the universe revealed by science cohered magnificently. From the tiniest wisp of matter to the largest array of galaxies, everything in the cosmos was bound by rules to everything else in an ancient, elegant dance. Here was a vision far grander than anything imagined by the authors of the Bible. The six days of creation outlined in Genesis seemed paltry beside the twelve or fifteen billion years of cosmic evolution outlined by physics. The shaping of Adam out of clay, as if he were a vessel on a potter's wheel, seemed far less wonderful than the shaping of *Homo sapiens* by three billion years of earthly evolution.

The parting of the Red Sea or the turning of Moses' staff into a snake seemed like conjurers' tricks beside the fusing of heavy elements in a supernova or the fashioning of proteins by the millions in a single living cell.

Over the course of my first year in college, I came to feel that the religion I had taken in through my pores in childhood was simply too small and tame. As a response to awe, science outdid everything I had read in the Bible or heard from the pulpit. The more I learned from astronomy, chemistry, physics, and biology, the more preposterous I found the claim that the whole sweeping cosmos was designed expressly for *us*. I refused to believe that the far-flung stars, more numerous than the sands of the sea, and the prodigious burning of our own sun and the untold millions of species that flourished and died on this planet before the rise of our two-legged ancestors were all mere backdrop for the drama of our salvation. Clearly, we humans were latecomers to the cosmos, and minor characters at that. If we had a meaningful role to play, it was to decipher the history and lawfulness of the cosmic show, and to praise our glorious home. Doing some small portion of that praising and deciphering seemed like a worthy ambition for a life's work.

17

A s I L I N K the beginning of college with the assassination of President Kennedy, so I will always link the final phase in Mother's decline with the onslaught of cicadas. Just as astronomers can predict eclipses to the very minute, so biologists predicted the outbreak of the largest known brood of periodical cicadas, if not to the minute then to the exact week of their emergence in May of 2004.

After seventeen years as flightless nymphs underground, where they sucked sap from the roots of trees, the cicadas known as Brood X crawled up through the soil on schedule, boring holes the diameter of a pencil. How many holes? An average of 100,000 or so per acre, according to estimates, spread over portions of fifteen states, from New Jersey to Missouri and Georgia to Michigan, totaling perhaps ten trillion insects. One biologist, heralding "this tsunami of life" in *The New York Times*, calculated that all these cicadas taken together would weigh about twice as much as the population of the United States; each day they would produce enough excrement to fill three hundred Olympic-sized swimming pools; and in one square mile of forest near the center of the outbreak, they would lay as many eggs as there are stars in the Milky Way.

Maps reveal that here in the hardwood hill country of southern Indiana we're near the center of the outbreak. Ruth and I first noticed the cicadas in our yard the week before Mother broke her hip. By the hundreds and thousands, they swarmed onto our purple coneflowers and oxeye daisies, shed their old husks, spread their translucent new wings, and took flight. The males soon began rasping out courtship songs. Up close, the sound was like pebbles clattering in the surf or coins jingling in a pocket. From farther away it sounded like the rushing of wind through pines. As the number of singers increased, the chorus grew louder and louder, until now, in the heat of midday, it's like the pulsing of thunder or the revving of an engine as large as the sky. At the height of their frenzy, in fact, the cicadas hereabouts have been measured at 100 to 120 decibels, roughly the same level as thunder, an ambulance siren, a chain saw, or a crying baby.

After mating with the loudest singers, the females scrape through the bark of twigs on trees, lay their eggs in the slits, then die. The youngest of the trees chosen for their egg laying may also die. Oaks, it turns out, are among their favorite hosts. By the first of June, the red oak we'd planted to celebrate Elizabeth's birth began to wilt. First a quarter, then half, and now in June three-quarters of the leaves have turned brown. I'm not superstitious enough to connect the health of the oak with the health of the baby, but I do fear we will lose this tree, twig by twig, cell by cell, as we are losing Mother.

Mother knows nothing of this living storm. When I describe the cicadas for her, she gazes into space, eyes unfocused, mouth slack. That is her usual pose these days. Although disturbing, her vacant look is an improvement over the terror she displayed in the hospital. When she sees Ruth or me approach her in the nursing home, her face lights up just long enough to reveal that she still knows us, if not as her son or daughter-in-law, then as loved ones. When I hold her hand, she draws me down for a kiss. But soon she lets go and resumes plucking at her blouse or pants. Her legs twitch, beating a tattoo on the footpads of her wheelchair. Her gaze drifts away, and her face relaxes into the mildly amiable expression she wore before spying us. It's a look not unlike the one often carved into statues of the Buddha.

What does she feel? A drowsy twilight broken only by meals and occasional visitors? A stoic sense of loss? An agony kept hidden, except for those jittery fingers and quivering legs, so as not to inflict it on others? How much does she remember of her nearly eighty-eight years? I ask her how she's feeling, what she's thinking, but she cannot say. I try prompting her by recalling people and events from her past, but she returns only that blank agreeable look. The few words she manages to utter are garbled and hoarse.

Occasionally she will surprise me with a complete sentence, as when she asks, during my latest visit, "How did you know I was here?" Twice in a week, out of her dazed silence, she exclaims, "This is my birthday!" The first time I gently remind her that her birthday is in August, two months away; the second time, I congratulate her on looking so pretty, and I feed her some ice cream to mark the occasion. She falls asleep with the spoon in her mouth. I watch the pulse in her throat, wondering at its stubborn persistence, as I wonder at the storm of cicadas.

Toughened by decades of dancing and aerobics, Mother just may have enough resilience in her heart and limbs to get back on her feet once more, yet even if she does manage to walk again, she'll be in constant danger of falling. Whether or not she ever walks, it's certain she'll never speak again in a way that tells us much about her interior life. She has lost touch with the part of her brain where words dwell. Piece by piece her mind is being whittled away, as twigs fall from the oak.

The eggs laid in Elizabeth's red oak and in trees across fifteen states will soon hatch into nymphs, which will tumble to the soil, burrow down among roots, suck sap, and begin the seventeen-year wait for their reemergence. The bodies of their parents, the chorusing males and egg-laying females, now litter the ground and gather in windrows along the curbs of streets. One can't walk outside without crunching them underfoot. The brown-leaved broken tips of branches also litter the yards in town, as if a fastidious wind had swept through, neatly pruning every tree.

If cicadas were as edible as salmon, we might have braided their astounding life cycle into our ceremonies. If they were as dramatic as eagles, we might have carved their likeness into totem poles. If they were as beautiful as monarch butterflies, we might have formed clubs to monitor their stupendous eruption. But cicadas haven't captured our imagination, perhaps because they are falsely identified with locusts, that biblical plague; perhaps because their prolonged underground sojourn strikes us as grim; perhaps because, unlike monarchs and eagles and salmon, they are thriving without our help.

I suspect there is not nearly as much mind present in the emergence of ten trillion cicadas as in the emergence of a single human child, but there is the same insistent energy, the same scrambling to *be*, as I see in Elizabeth. She turns thirteen months old near the beginning of the outbreak and fourteen months old near the end. Her walk, once cautious, now accelerates to a gallop when she's in a hurry. She easily follows directions or, when feeling contrary, shakes her head vigorously no. She investigates every new item that falls within her reach, whether a bug on the carpet or a shard of brick at a building site. Whatever is beyond her reach—a chalky moon on the horizon, a clock in a tower—she stares at intently. And about everything within her ken she freely comments, sometimes in the hand signs Eva has taught her, sometimes in words, more often in a language known only to babies. Listening in, we can translate many of her utterances, but others are as mystifying as the broken sounds made by Mother.

Like Mother, Elizabeth can't grasp the epic history of cicadas; unlike Mother, however, one day she will. For now, she notices their red-eyed, iridescent bodies expiring on sidewalks as we stroll through the neighborhood. She squats down to look at them, collecting husks in her hand, and I squat down beside her. Aren't they beautiful? I say. Elizabeth strokes the translucent wings. By the time Brood X returns, this toddler will have grown into a young woman of eighteen, ready to begin college, fully capable of understanding anything, I predict, that science has figured out.

When I was eighteen, I still counted on science to reveal in precise equations everything God—if there was a God—had in mind in making the world. This article of my childhood faith was the one I clung to most doggedly, and nothing I had learned in high school or in the first year of college challenged my belief. Of course I had read popular accounts of relativity and quantum theory, but only during my sophomore year at Brown, after another summer of driving a forklift in Louisiana and another romantic visit to Ruth in Indiana, did I begin to study those subjects in depth. What I found unsettled me. For the more I studied, the more I realized that uncertainty is woven into the very fabric of the universe.

I knew that Einstein had dissolved the distinction between energy and matter, showing them to be transmutations of the same fundamental reality, like steam and ice. But now I learned from quantum mechanics that we can never know what the ultimate reality *is*, because in the act of observing it we change it. Down at the smallest scale that science can reach, there is no essential "stuff," no underlying substance, only waves of probability shimmering in a field of potentiality. Beneath the last veil, it turns out, there are no solid particles, nothing like the billiard balls of classical physics, but only events, flashing in and out of existence like evanescent thoughts.

Newtonian physics presented the universe as a grand machine, made up of durable cogs and wheels interacting by measurable forces, as predictable in its movements as a well-made clock. A scientist could stand apart from this machine and know it objectively. But now I learned such objectivity was an illusion, or at best an approximation that held up reasonably well in the everyday world. Classical physics was adequate for calculating the shape of an airplane wing or the orbit of a satellite, but it couldn't explain the curving of light from distant stars or the gambols of subatomic particles. At very large and very small scales, modern physics offered more accurate descriptions, yet only by admitting that what we're describing isn't nature in itself but the response of nature to our way of questioning. Our consciousness is entangled with the phenomena we study.

Einstein himself taught us there is no privileged spot from which reality can be observed. Space has no center, time has no regular beat. According to relativity theory, nothing is fixed and firm except the speed of light, and some physicists, my teachers announced, were proposing that even light speed might be fickle. In rejecting quantum mechanics, Einstein famously said he didn't believe God played dice with the universe. But all the evidence suggests that, at the finest grain of things—a grain unimaginably finer than the biblical mustard seed—dice are indeed being rolled, if not by God then by the impersonal, implacable scheme we call nature. Down at the quantum level, the behavior of reality is random, and therefore unpredictable, not just in practice but in principle. We can describe those events mathematically, yet between our symbols and the events themselves there is an unbridgeable gap. Some of Einstein's own equations in support of the theory of relativity led to singularities, points where the laws of physics break down. He spent the latter decades of his career trying to erase those singularities and refute the implications of quantum mechanics, and he failed.

Over the course of my second year in college, I was forced to accept that the language of science, no matter how precise and confident it seems, is no more capable of capturing reality than is the wayward language of poems and stories. No matter how many formulas we devise, no matter how many words we add to the dictionary, nature slips through our finest nets. As far as they go, our various languages are useful; they simply cannot go all the way to the source. They can only point to an unfathomable potency, a torrent of forms arising and perishing and ever newly arising.

With the reluctance of one stepping away from shore into a flood, I let go of my faith in the clockwork universe. Modern physics convinced me to see the universe as an ebullient flow of energy, radiating outward from the Big Bang, casting into existence myriad forms—protons and galaxies, cicadas and persons—then dissolving them back into the flow.

Physics can explain why the universe might gradually run down as entropy increases, but it cannot explain why, since the Big Bang, the universe has run *up*, proliferating more and more complex structures. Whatever its ultimate fate—contracting to an explosive kernel or expanding forever—the universe has shown itself to be persistently creative for twelve or fifteen billion years. Why? This question is distinct from the even more fundamental puzzle of why there should be a universe at all. Why *this* kind of universe, so vigorous in casting up new forms, so dynamic, so beautiful?

Only after finishing college and graduate school, and after becoming the father of two children who changed at dazzling speed before my very eyes, would I discover in the world's mystical traditions a way of ascribing meaning to this cosmic flow. For science, the flow, however fascinating, does not bear any meaning; it can be analyzed but not evaluated; it can be monitored but not revered. In the same way, for science, life itself can be no more than a curious, transient pattern in matter, like an eddy in the energy stream, and consciousness can be no more than a by-product of biochemistry.

The tide of cicadas surging out of the ground, briefly filling the air with their calls, then subsiding to litter the ground with their myriad husks, seems to proclaim that life is abundant and cheap. It may be, at least here on our planet, and at the wholesale level of the species. But so far as we can tell, life in the cosmos is rare, perhaps unique. And at the level of individuals—a slain president, an ailing mother, a blooming granddaughter—life is precious. And not just human life. The half-ounce chickadees nesting in the hemlock tree outside my window defend their young from hawks and owls as fiercely as any human parents protecting a baby.

Some biologists claim that the intense affection we feel toward our offspring is merely a stratagem for passing on our genes, no more significant than the gravitational tug of Earth under our feet. I can't disprove that claim, but I don't believe it. The claim, in fact, suggests why science will never provide us with a guide for living. Of course scientists love their children, but they can't account for their love through science, except as a survival instinct masquerading as a genuine emotion. Nor can they account for their burning curiosity about the workings of nature, except as an exaggeration of some adaptive trait, analogous to the fiddler crab's grotesquely swollen claw. Nor can they say, through science, why they should or should not be loyal to a spouse, compassionate toward the weak, loving toward people of another race, or for-giving toward enemies. No amount of knowledge about how nature behaves will tell us how *we* should behave.

In the spring of my sophomore year, I had a conversation with a physics professor whom I admired. I was trying to imagine myself following in his footsteps, conducting experiments, collaborating with other scien-tists, publishing what I'd found. Like anyone contemplating a life in sci-ence, I wondered how I would fare in the scramble for research dollars. As he told me about his own study of lasers, I asked who was funding his work.

"The Department of Defense," he answered.

"Why are they interested?"

"The military likes to deliver lots of energy in small packages."

"Lasers might be used as weapons?"

"That's what I keep telling them." He laughed. "Thank God for the Cold War."

Wasn't he worried that his discoveries might be used in a hot war? How his discoveries might be used, he said, was for politicians and gen-erals to decide. His job was finding new knowledge, and to do that he drew money from the largest available pot.

He gave me an amused look. "You have a problem with that?"

"I guess I do."

"Then maybe you'd better think of another career."

By then I'd begun to learn how our latest weapons were ravaging Vietnam. I hated the prospect of spending my life begging for handouts from the Pentagon and seeking knowledge that could make the war machine even more deadly. But how could I justify my dismay? There are ethics implicit in the *practice* of science that tell you how to conduct research once you've chosen a problem—to demand evidence for any claim, to report findings honestly, to be exact in procedures, to ac-knowledge the contributions of others—but there is nothing in science to tell you how to choose between one research agenda and another.

Should we experiment on prisoners in a concentration camp? Should we experiment on rats in a lab? Should we invent new life-forms by manipulating genes? Should we patent organisms and turn them into property? Should we brew toxic chemicals that will be released into water and air? Science cannot say. Our answers to such questions have to come from elsewhere. But where?

What I realized, midway through college, was that science could not ask the questions that kept me awake at night. For me, even more urgent than the metaphysical puzzles were the ethical ones. How should we treat other people? How should we treat other species? How should we treat the earth, our one and only home? And what, oh what, should I do with my life? In April of 1965, near the end of my second year at Brown, I copied into my journal a line from the American poet Theodore Roethke: "Whoever you are, be sure it's you." But how could one be sure? How could one discern a true identity out of all the bewildering possibilities?

Aside from my devotion to Ruth, no theme figures more prominently in my journal from college than my search for an authentic self. Who was I? What was I called to do? Although I had discarded the supernatural trappings of my childhood religion, I still understood a "calling" in religious terms. Having a vocation implies there is a Caller summoning you to a particular task, which means you aren't free to choose whatever path seems most lucrative, prestigious, or easy. You must find the correct path, like the one and only trail through a labyrinth. What might mine be?

I considered theology, but from a sampling of books I'd read over the summer, theologians seemed either abstract or presumptuous, concocting airy empires out of words or making confident assertions about God on the basis of dubious Scriptures. I considered philosophy, but the reigning school of thought in the academy at that time was logical positivism, which imposed the same limitation as physics: whatever can't be measured can't be profitably thought about. I considered history, but it ignored everything in the universe beyond the bounds of Earth, and practically everything on Earth aside from our own upstart species.

Then, in the fall of 1965, I took a class called "Literature of the American Renaissance." The works we read by Emerson, Thoreau, Hawthorne, Melville, and Whitman were a revelation to me. Of course I'd read plenty of stories and poems, including dozens of classics from the list of great books Ruth and I had picked up at the science camp. But I'd considered all that reading to be a source of pleasure or polish rather than knowledge. I'd thought of literature not as a way of discovering truth, like science, but as a way of expressing emotion, like painting or music. Now for the first time I began to see—in *Nature* and *Walden*, in *Mosses from an Old Manse*, *Moby-Dick*, and *Leaves of Grass*—how literature might not merely entertain but illuminate. Ambitious for their art and for their young country, these five writers had set out to probe the depths of existence. They asked the questions that kept me awake at night—about nature and God, about good and evil, about democracy and vocation and the elusive self. Unlike the authors of the Bible, they claimed no divine sanction for their insights, only the authority of experience, imagination, and reflection.

Scattered throughout their pages were passages that reminded me of my own experience of awe, moments brimming with the power and glory of things, when the small self disappeared. There was Hawthorne's Young Goodman Brown, cowering before the tangled and seemingly endless New England woods. There was Melville, through his narrator Ishmael, contemplating the blank forehead of the whale. There was Whitman, singing the body electric, at one with the teeming American people. And behind them all, their intellectual grandfather, was Emerson: "Standing on the bare ground,—my head bathed by the blithe air, and uplifted into infinite space,—all mean egotism vanishes. I become a transparent eye-ball; I am nothing; I see all; the currents of the Universal Being circulate through me; I am part or particle of God." I couldn't, or wouldn't, have said it so grandiloquently, but I knew in my bones what Emerson was talking about.

Above all, I thrilled to *Walden*. I read that brash, cranky, extravagant book as I had read the Bible, with a mixture of perplexity and clairvoyance. Much I did not understand. But I shivered in sympathy when Thoreau chased loons across the pond or traced the shapes of thawing mud or tracked the moon. When he proclaimed, "Shams and delusions are esteemed for soundest truths, while reality is fabulous," I murmured yes, yes. Many passages lifted me out of my chair and set me pacing, as when he confided, "Nearest to all things is that power which fashions their being. *Next* to us the grandest laws are continually being executed. *Next* to us is not the workman, whom we have hired, with whom we love so well to talk, but the workman whose work we are." Other passages sent me outdoors to walk the streets of Providence, as when he exulted, "This is a delicious evening, when the whole body is one sense, and imbibes delight through every pore. I go and come with a strange liberty in Nature, a part of herself."

In the chapter where Thoreau celebrated the gift of reading, I found a description of the impact *Walden* had on me: "There are probably words addressed to our condition exactly, which, if we could really hear and understand, would be more salutary than the morning or the spring to our lives, and possibly put a new aspect on the face of things for us. How many a man has dated a new era in his life from the reading of a book." I dated a new era in my life from the reading of *Walden*. For here was the testament of a man who sought to live a purposeful life, who sensed the fashioning power at work in all that he saw and in his own depths, who never ceased to be astonished by reality, and who strove to record those moments, in the midst of ordinary nature, when he shook with a sense of awe.

It wasn't that scientists lacked a sense of awe; they simply couldn't *talk* about such feelings, or any feelings, within the confines of science. In poems and novels, essays and plays, by contrast, writers could talk about anything humans were capable of experiencing. For literature, nothing under the sun, or beyond the sun, was taboo. I had sensed this all along, of course. But the Bible was my primal book, and once I'd begun questioning the veracity of Scripture, I came to doubt the truthfulness of any book not grounded in science. Now that science, too, had revealed its limitations, I finally allowed myself to see, in the works of these five great writers, how fully literature could address my deepest questions and most powerful yearnings. If the answers I found in poems and stories could not be tested in laboratories, they could be tested in life.

So I was pulled as well as pushed away from the study of physics. When I announced the decision to my parents, in a rare long-distance phone call, Dad came on the line first. "English?" he said. "You already know English."

"I mean studying poems and novels and talking about them."

"And somebody's going to pay you to do that?"

"I don't know."

"Then you don't know how you'll keep a roof over your head."

"I could build houses. I could put up my own roof and sleep under it."

"Go to college and become a carpenter?"

"Maybe I could write for a newspaper," I added quickly. "Or I could go to law school." I didn't mention the idea of becoming a teacher. Dad's opinion of that profession was summed up in a saying he liked to quote: "Those who can, do. Those who can't, teach."

There was a long pause. I eyed the stack of quarters on top of the pay phone in the stairwell of my dorm, wondering if I'd have enough change to make my case.

Finally Dad broke the silence. "You've been saying you wanted to be a scientist practically since you learned to talk. You're giving all that up?"

"Dad, believe me, I've thought hard about this."

"Well," he said, "it's your life. All my folks ever heard me talk about was boxing and farming. Now look at me, wearing a white shirt and riding a desk. You do what you want to do, and we'll stand behind you."

At this point, Mama came on the line. "Daddy's right. Study whatever your heart desires, so long as it makes you happy."

By the summer solstice in this year of Brood X, the din of cicadas has dwindled to a whisper. About two-thirds of the branches on Elizabeth's oak have died. As I prune them, I notice green shoots flickering from every live twig, like tiny green flames. The new leaves are flawless.

The sky is also flawless on this first day of summer, the air surprisingly mild. When I visit Mother at the nursing home, I wheel her outside to show her the dark-eyed pansies, the grackles and cardinals squabbling at the feeder, the sunlight snared in the needles of a pine, the horsetail clouds. Look, I say, look! She wears her usual vague smile but doesn't respond to my enthusiastic pointing.

I've come to accept this vagueness, this blurring of her feisty self, as a blessing. Over the past decade or so, her most intense pain has sprung from her clinging to the person she once was. Why can't she pack up a suitcase and travel? Why can't she teach aerobics at the senior center? Why can't she dance, drive, shop, or cook? Why can't she read? There must be something wrong with her eyes. Why can't she tell time? The clocks must be broken. Why can't she hear? People must be keeping secrets from her. Why can't she bathe or dress herself? Why can't she find words to say what she's thinking? Why can't she think straight? She has agonized over every loss, and we've agonized with her.

Now Mother seems to have forgotten who she used to be, and this forgetting has eased her pain. Her *self* is breaking up, just as Elizabeth's is forming. The zeal Elizabeth shows in shaking her head no betrays her delight in choosing to go against some grownup's wishes. This power to choose is the essence of selfhood—a power that Mother has all but lost. She is dissolving into the flow of things, even as Elizabeth is gathering into a focus of curiosity, preference, humor, and desire.

On this afternoon of the summer solstice, Mother and I pause for a while in the sunshine. When she begins to fidget in her wheelchair, I take one of her dappled hands in mine and rub it. After a spell I turn to the other hand, which she has knotted into the front of her blouse. As I gently pry open the fist to massage it between my palms, it's as though I have uncurled Mother from her daze. Suddenly she grins up at me and says, "You're a little monkey!"

It's what she used to say when I teased her as a child. It's what I said to my own children and what I say now to Elizabeth when she's being mischievous.

"You think I'm a monkey?" I ask with mock indignation.

"I do," Mother snaps.

"Well, who taught me to be a monkey?"

"*I* did!" Her grin widens.

Is she happy? I believe she is, for the moment. And for the moment so am I. These are the first coherent sentences I've heard from her in a week. To hear them come out of her is as startling as to see those bright green shoots flicker from the wounded oak.

18

IF GIVING UP the study of science meant I'd starve, as my friends assured me, I figured I might as well go all the way to ruin and become a poet. This ambition was abetted by visits to the Brown campus during my senior year of four quite different poets: Richard Wilbur, a buttoned-down formalist still willing to rhyme; Stephen Spender, an old English lefty still battling fascism and the bourgeoisie; Andrei Voznesensky, a Russian accustomed to roaring his verses in stadiums before tens of thousands of spellbound fans; and James Dickey, a onetime advertising copywriter transformed into a guitar-strumming bard. "The poet lays down words in the right order, and they stay there," Dickey said, "the way God planted trees just so in the Garden of Eden." About each of these visitors I wrote long passages in my journal, trying on their poses and voices to see if they fit. I tried rhyming like Wilbur, decrying injustice like Spender, roaring like Voznesensky, chanting the vernacular like Dickey.

During my last year of college I was also imitating a handful of poets whom I'd met only in books, from word-drunk Dylan Thomas to occult William Butler Yeats, from crabbed Robert Frost to ecstatic D. H. Lawrence. I read most of them in a course taught by a professor who'd published several collections of his own poetry, a world-weary man in his fifties who was still jittery from his time battling General Franco and the fascists in the Spanish Civil War. He wouldn't sit with his back to a window or door, for fear someone might sneak up behind him and pitch a Molotov cocktail into the room. His languid speech, his woebegone look, his threadbare corduroy jackets, everything about him suggested that the feast of history was over, and those of us who came along after would have to make do with the crumbs. This Professor Morse, as I'll call him, spent the semester trying to persuade me I had no future as a poet.

More than vanity kept me from immediately accepting his verdict. To begin with, I hadn't absorbed enough good poetry to recognize the flaws in my own. I was also reluctant to give up on poetry because I thought of it as the most exact, difficult, and potent mode of writing, just as physics was the most exact, difficult, and potent mode of science. By comparison with poetry, fiction seemed lazy and sprawling, just as biology seemed messy and easy by comparison with physics. Anybody could watch birds or read a novel, but only the initiated could decode quantum equations or modernist verse.

To be difficult in writing, it turned out, was simple. All you had to do was leave out links between one image and the next, or drag in private memories the reader knew nothing about, or bury literary allusions here and there the way a squirrel buries acorns, or use words purely for the sake of their sounds while ignoring their sense. I tried every trick. When I saw how thoroughly my offerings baffled my classmates, however, I soon outgrew this craze for the obscure. What was the point of writing if you couldn't even speak to other aspiring poets, let alone ordinary mortals? The ordinary mortals I had in mind were people like my rocket-launching partner Marty Sanford, my basketball teammate Jeremiah Pond, the coon hunters and farmers on Esworthy Road, the factory workers in Lake Charles, my father and mother, my first heartthrob Vicki May Langston, and the Indiana girl I hoped to marry. To be lucid, I decided, was more generous to readers, as well as more demanding of the writer, than to be obscure.

I also stuck with poetry because it seemed better than prose at evoking the experience of awe. What novelist or essayist had ever come as close as Wordsworth, for example?

> . . . And I have felt
> A presence that disturbs me with the joy
> Of elevated thoughts; a sense sublime
> Of something far more deeply interfused,
> Whose dwelling is the light of setting suns,
> And the round ocean and the living air,
> And the blue sky, and in the mind of man:
> A motion and a spirit, that impels
> All thinking things, all objects of all thought,
> And rolls through all things.

Except for leaving out the dread, which showed up elsewhere in his poetry, Wordsworth had captured the intuition I'd felt since earliest childhood, of a power that surges through bone and rain and everything.

When I asked Professor Morse what he thought of this passage from "Lines Composed a Few Miles Above Tintern Abbey," he said he didn't much like it, and for the same reasons he didn't much like my verse—too fancy, preachy, and abstract. If Wordsworth had left out the woolly metaphysics and stuck to describing nature in short lyrics, he might have amounted to something.

"Poetry isn't for telling stories or delivering messages or maundering on about the mysteries of life," Professor Morse advised me. "A poem should be an object of contemplation, as sharply cut, as hard, as free of emotion as a diamond." To illustrate these virtues, he quoted a two-line poem by Ezra Pound, which compared the faces in a crowd at a Paris Metro station to petals on a rain-darkened branch. "Don't think saga, Mr. Sanders. Think haiku. And whatever you do, forget philosophy." Here he quoted William Carlos Williams: "No ideas but in things."

In the portfolio of poems I turned in at the end of his course, I broke every one of his rules. More than half the portfolio was taken up with an epic history of the cosmos, from the Big Bang to yesterday, told in slant rhyme over some two hundred lines. Here's the opening quatrain:

> In the beginning was the egg,
> Ylem, proton welter,
> Primordial mother dug,
> Womb of all matter.

It got worse. In the remaining 196 or so lines, I settled the dispute between the scientific and biblical worldviews by declaring physics the winner, dragging in a troop of natural philosophers, from Ptolemy and Galileo to Newton and Einstein, to support my case. As if to balance the account, I also included in the portfolio a series of poems about figures from the Hebrew Bible, such as tongue-tied Moses and defiant Job. The only good lines were the ones I stole from Scripture, as when the prophet Amos described God as "he who forms the mountains, and creates the wind, and declares to man what is his thought; who makes the morning darkness, and treads on the heights of the earth."

The rest of the portfolio consisted of love poems addressed to an unnamed *You*, who was receiving copies of them folded up in the letters I kept mailing to Indiana. Ruth had the tact, or the kindness, to accept these fervent gifts without commenting on their quality as literature. Feeling no such restraint, Professor Morse crossed through one love poem after another with strokes of a red pen. His summary advice: "Spare poetry. Tell her in person."

I did tell Ruth of my love in person every chance I got. I just didn't get nearly enough chances to suit me. In the four years since the end of science camp, we'd seen one another perhaps a dozen times, never for more than a few days. Each reunion was more joyful than the one before and each parting more painful. The exhilaration we felt in one another's company seemed like a taste of the life we were meant to lead, and we wanted to taste it always. Ruth would turn twenty that October of 1966, and I would turn twenty-one—quite old enough, we both imagined, to plan a marriage.

During the previous two summers, I had stopped through Indianapolis on my way to and from Lake Charles, courting Ruth under the watchful eyes of her parents. When I arrived for a visit on the eve of my senior year at Brown with an engagement ring in my pocket, I asked Mr. and Mrs. McClure for their blessing before I offered the ring to Ruth. They gave their blessing, but they made clear without ever saying so that they expected us to remain chaste until the ceremony took place. Necking on the couch was permissible, so long as we retired to our separate beds at a respectable hour. That hour was announced by the sound of slippers shuffling down the hall, the clearing of a throat, and either Mr. or Mrs. McClure turning up in the archway of the living room to declare surprise at how late it had gotten to be.

Ruth's parents left many things unsaid. As devout Methodists, they didn't gossip, gamble, smoke, drink, dance, or quarrel. Ruth had never heard them raise their voices in anger, or even mildly disagree at the dinner table. They would have been scandalized by much in the behavior of my parents, about whom I was careful to reveal only innocent details. Nothing about hidden bottles, poker parties, coon hunts, jitterbugging contests, or muffled shouts from behind the bedroom door. Nothing about Dad stomping off to sleep in the Bachelor Officers' Quarters, or about Mama left behind sobbing in the dark.

Unlike my father, who told stories with relish and struck up conversations with strangers, Mr. McClure was reticent. At meals, rather than ask for more pork chops or pie, he would stare at what he wanted until someone noticed where he was looking and passed the dish to him. The rare stories he did tell always had a point, as when he relayed how his father, a postal clerk in the Indiana river town of Vincennes, had sorted thousands of postcards but had never read a one of them, out of respect for the privacy of his neighbors. Mr. McClure himself would never pry. Although he must have been shocked by some of my outspoken views on civil rights, women's rights, the Vietnam War, the hypocrisy of churches, and the wickedness of corporations, he would merely say, "Well, people have all sorts of opinions."

Mrs. McClure made up for his quietness with her own readiness to talk, yet she never spoke about her innermost thoughts or inquired into anyone else's. She kept up a cheerful commentary on people and events, without sorting the significant from the trivial. A squabble on the church finance committee might weigh as much in her narrative as the Cold War. The fact that her father had abandoned the family when she was a girl, leaving her mother to rear four kids and run a dairy farm alone, aroused no ire in the telling. Nothing upset her, and nothing much excited her, aside from faith healing and Indiana basketball. Even following a close game on television, she didn't yell but only turned red and trembled. And the healing she practiced involved no shouting preachers but rather a laying on of hands and silent prayer. Among the many biblical instructions she took seriously was the one that warned "Judge not, lest ye be judged." I never heard her say a harsh word about anybody.

Mrs. McClure's live-and-let-live manner took some getting used to, because my own mother passed judgment on everyone and everything that came within her view. A girl sashaying down the street in hot pink shorts, a man swaying out of a bar with his gut sagging over his belt, a house painted a hideous green, a yard grown up in weeds—any and all violations of Mama's standards would come in for her scorn. She wouldn't let you cross the room without telling you to stand up straight, put on a sweater, fetch yourself a glass of milk, or do something else she had decided you needed to do.

Mrs. McClure let you do whatever you pleased, so long as you did it politely. Her own politeness, and that of Mr. McClure, kept them from asking what had possessed me to abandon hardheaded science for frivolous literature, or how I proposed to support their daughter, or why I considered going to jail rather than fighting in Vietnam. They could see how bedazzled I was by Ruth, and evidently that was assurance enough.

I took what I was feeling for Ruth to be love rather than infatuation because I never felt so intensely alive, so alert, so open to every sensation, as when I was with her. She affected me the way my friends at school spoke of being affected by psychedelic drugs. My doors of perception were cleansed, as when I'd first put on a pair of glasses, only with Ruth the effect didn't wear off.

While I never felt so alive as when I was in Ruth's company, I never felt so alone as when I was apart from her. By my last year at Brown, the ache of separation had become almost unbearable. At night, when the pain was acute, I took long, melancholy walks, often stopping on a terrace overlooking downtown Providence, where the swarm of lights spread out like a cheap imitation of the stars, which were hidden by the city's pall of smoke. Just so, I imagined, any companionship I felt among friends at college, however bright and warm, was a pale substitute for the joy I felt with Ruth. Many of the poems I sent her week after week were composed on those midnight rambles. Yet even as I folded my earnest verses into letters, before Professor Morse crossed through them with his scornful pen, I knew they failed to convey more than an inkling of what I felt. Writing letters to her didn't ease my loneliness but only made me long to share my days with her instead of describing them in words. And Ruth's own frisky letters only made me yearn to reach through the pages and hold the woman herself.

The winter of our senior year, I got another chance to hold her. After the end of classes that December, I met her in Indianapolis and we drove to Lake Charles for Christmas with my family. Our staying in a motel along the way was out of the question, so we stopped overnight with one of my aunts in Mississippi. My parents assured Mr. and Mrs. McClure that we couldn't have been in safer hands, morally speaking, if we'd stayed with the founder of Methodism, John Wesley himself. True to her reputation, Aunt Ludi made up a bed for Ruth at one end of the house and a couch for me at the other. She kept watch in between by staying up for the late-night movie on TV.

In the morning, she greeted us with enough eggs, sausage, biscuits, honey, grits, buttermilk, and German chocolate cake to fuel a crew of lumberjacks. Aunt Ludi herself had already eaten, and her husband, one of my father's older brothers, was away driving a freight train, so all of this food was intended for Ruth and me. Ruth ate what she could, then looked to me for help, and I dutifully cleaned her plate after cleaning my own. All through the meal, Aunt Ludi kept switching her gaze from Ruth's face to mine and back again, grinning broadly, as if, though a straitlaced Baptist, she were sipping sweet wine.

At the doorway as we left, she hugged us both and said, "Don't ever forget what you're feeling right now. Love is the Lord's gift. Cherish it always."

Beginning in childhood, I heard and read that God is love. At first I understood this to mean God was like my own parents, kind and caring, only much bigger and older. Then Sunday school taught me that God's love meant the gift of Jesus, his only son, for the redemption of our sins. For a while I thought Jesus and God were different names for the same person—the way my father could be called G.R., Sandy, Greeley, or Dad—and this greatest of all persons had made the whole world for our sake. Since the Creation was filled with everything we needed—food, houses, creeks, ponies, trees, books, friends—it was proof of God's love for us. Eventually the study of science persuaded me that the world wasn't made for any purpose whatsoever, least of all for the benefit of *Homo sapiens*; that no kind parent or savior watches over us from heaven; that whatever we might call the impulse animating the universe, it has nothing to do with love.

Then Ruth and I fell in love, letter by letter, year by year, until Aunt Ludi could see the radiance in our faces over breakfast, older couples passing us on the sidewalk could break into smiles and reach for one another's hands, our parents could trust us to marry. This kindling of fire between a man and a woman—or between a man and a man, a woman and a woman—is as old as our species, yet to Ruth and me it was brand new.

"The love of the body of a man or woman balks account, the body itself balks account," Whitman conceded in *Leaves of Grass*. "That of the male is perfect, and that of the female is perfect." But if Whitman felt humbled before the mystery of the body and its yearnings, scientists boldly explained this incandescence between lovers as another side effect of neurochemistry, like ether nightmares or seesaw moods. "Hormones induce mating, breeding, and the self-sacrifice needed for parenting," as one of my teachers put it in a psychology class. "The emotions associated with such behavior are the genes' ploy for replicating themselves." I duly recorded his words, but I didn't believe them. If that was all science could say about my feelings for Ruth, then I would have to look elsewhere for insight, because I trusted the authority of my experience, which told me love was real.

Next to the psychology professor's remarks, I copied into my journal a line from an eighteenth-century American Quaker, John Woolman: "Love was the first motion." Woolman was speaking here of his desire to travel among the Indians, "that I might feel and understand their life and the spirit they live in, if haply I might receive some instruction from them." From the rest of his journal, however, it was clear he believed that all genuine feeling, every calling, every spiritual opening, indeed every living creature and the world itself, arose from love, which he took to be the defining trait of God.

In light of Woolman, whom I read in one of those subversive literature classes at Brown, I decided my psychology teacher had things backward. I thought of what my father would say when contradicting what he took to be a harebrained notion: "If you turn that kitty around, you'll be rubbing it the right way." Instead of seeing chemistry as primary and emotion as derivative, I began to see love as the primary impulse, which gave rise to hormones, genes, and other ingenious devices for the unfolding of life. Nothing seemed more certain to me than this upsurge of life, whether in Ohio woods or Louisiana bayous or Rhode Island tidal pools or in the beating of Ruth's heart against my chest. And why shouldn't this urge be the same one that set the universe in motion? Why shouldn't it be the same tumultuous energy that bubbles at the quantum level and whirls galaxies in their billion-year dance?

At first I don't recognize Mother across the dining room, where an aide patiently holds a spoon before her closed mouth. Mother's face has shrunken toward the contours of her skull, and her white hair, backlit by sunlight from a window, appears as finespun and frail as milkweed down. She brightens when she recognizes Ruth and me, but whatever she tries to say comes out as a hoarse croak. We clean her face and remove the bib, as we do with baby Elizabeth after meals; then we ask if she'd like to go for a spin in her wheelchair. Mother nods, yet even as she does so her eyelids droop.

She is sliding fast down a steep slope. Only a week ago, on one of my solo visits, I found her in the physical therapy room, leaning forward in the wheelchair, mouth puckered in concentration, batting a pink balloon back and forth with a chipper young woman. "Good!" the therapist cried. "Very good!"

As the fat balloon floated lazily toward her, Mother waved at it with her palsied left hand, sometimes connecting, often not. I was afraid she'd be embarrassed to have me see her struggling at such a childish game, but she beamed as usual on spying me, and loosed a scratchy laugh when I bragged on how well she was doing. To be embarrassed, I realized, you must have a strong enough sense of self to imagine, and care, how others perceive you. That's why adults who return Elizabeth's frank gaze as we ride between floors in an elevator look away before the baby does. Elizabeth hasn't yet fully arrived at self-consciousness, while Mother has drifted beyond it.

The therapist encouraged Mother to use her right hand for a change, and Mother dutifully lifted the other arm, but then merely held it upright, stiff as a dead branch, while her left arm chased the pink balloon.

"Look at you!" I said. "Pretty soon you'll be playing volleyball."

Again Mother gave her wheezy laugh, much like the sound Elizabeth makes when we play hide-and-seek.

Today, however, as Ruth and I wheel Mother about, nothing we say or do sparks any light in her. Nothing outdoors can rouse her—not a kingfisher giving its rattly cry from the nursing home's antenna, not a tiger swallowtail nectaring on the butterfly bush, not a brisk wind hustling the clouds. So we roll her back indoors to the lounge, where half a dozen piebald fish, orange and white, glide back and forth in a tank. Mother ignores the fish but gazes up at a flounce of burgundy cloth draped across the top of a nearby window, just the sort of Victorian froufrou she has always liked. She surprises us by suddenly rasping, "Whose house is this?"

Ruth and I exchange a look, worried Mother will ask to be taken home, as she has after every previous move.

"This is *your* house," Ruth assures her. "You live here."

Mother says firmly, "I like this house."

Even as she speaks these reassuring words, Mother writhes in her chair, clearly in pain—whether from the two recent operations on her knee and hip, from the bedsores she picked up during her latest hospital stay, or from the constraints of her diminished life, it's impossible to know. I rub her shoulders, hold her hand, lean down to ask where she hurts. She only shakes her head and turns on me a crimped smile.

In that spring of 1967, Ruth and I were both offered graduate fellowships at Harvard, she in biochemistry, I in literature. We made plans to study there together for a year before getting married, to reassure ourselves—by living in the same place if not in the same apartment—that our commitment might be deep enough to last a lifetime.

Our plans were thrown into confusion when I learned I'd won a Marshall Scholarship to study at the University of Cambridge in England. What to do? Should I decline the scholarship, turn my back on the land of Shakespeare and Wordsworth, and go to Harvard anyway, so as to be near Ruth? Or should we study apart the first year, with Ruth taking a leave the second year and joining me in Cambridge while I finished a master's degree, both of us then returning to Harvard for our Ph.D.'s? We spent her spring vacation together in Providence, and spent mine the next week in Bloomington, trying to make up our minds. The bliss of being together for those two weeks made the prospect of dwelling apart for another year all the more agonizing, yet that is what we decided to do.

Meanwhile, I was meeting with Charlie Baldwin, the chaplain at Brown, to decide whether I should declare myself a conscientious objector if I was drafted to fight in Vietnam. For me the question was not a practical one—there were easier ways to avoid the draft—but a moral one: Could I take part in a war I saw as flagrantly immoral, simply because I was ordered to do so by my government? Charlie's own views were no secret, for he openly denounced the war, but he made sure I examined my own convictions. And what if my convictions landed me in exile or prison? What if they kept me from ever teaching at a university? What if they put my name on a publishers' blacklist? How much grief would that cause for my parents, how much alarm for Ruth's, how much distress for Ruth herself?

My feelings about the war were also complicated by the discovery that one of my favorite uncles—the one who'd eaten too many carrots in an effort to pass the air force eye exam—had helped develop Agent Orange. This virulent herbicide was being sprayed from U.S. planes on the jungles and farm fields of Vietnam, killing crops and forests, poisoning streams, exposing the soil to erosion, and leaving who knew what legacy of damage in every living thing in that battered country. Here was chemistry in service to killing, the very perversion of science that had prompted me to abandon physics. I had already lost several high school classmates in Vietnam, but this news about my uncle made me feel an even more personal stake in working to end that ghastly war.

Then one Sunday in April, at the invitation of Charlie Baldwin, Martin Luther King, Jr., came to speak at Brown. I arrived at the hall an hour early to make sure of getting a seat, and I was still sitting there an hour after Dr. King had finished, turning over in my mind all that he had said. He said that as a man of conscience and a Christian, he must speak out against the mayhem in Vietnam, against our government's policy of stifling liberation movements all over the world, against the sending of our poor abroad to fight and die in defense of America's economic interests. He felt bound to say these were the interests mainly of the rich, the very people who, as owners of the media and giant corporations, held us in thrall to a mindless materialism that was corrupting our souls. He was proud to report that dozens of young men from his own alma mater, Morehouse College, had chosen conscientious objection rather than join the killing. If he was called unpatriotic for opposing his government's policies, well then, he would have to suffer the name, because his religion required him to love all people, not merely those of his own country. His religion called on him to be a peacemaker, to denounce injustice, to uphold the cause of the poor. And if, in obedience to that call, he offended those in power, if he upset those believers who refused to carry their religion beyond the church doors, if he angered those self-proclaimed patriots who believed America could do no wrong, that was a risk he had to run.

Dr. King said a great deal more, some of which I scrawled in my journal, all of which I drank in like much-needed medicine. For he made my dithering over the price of conscientious objection, over where to study and when to marry and how to earn a living, seem petty. Here was a man who took his convictions so seriously he was willing to die for them. I knew from accounts in the press that bullets had been fired through the window of his house, just as bricks had been hurled through the window of my father's motel room. I knew that Dr. King's phone—like Dad's, during his tense early days in Louisiana— often rang with threats, and his mail brought messages of hate. Yet he wouldn't keep silent. He wouldn't back down. No one I'd ever seen in person helped me to imagine so vividly what it might have been like to meet one of those Hebrew prophets, who delivered unwelcome news to the privileged, or to meet Jesus, who kept defying the authorities even in the shadow of the cross.

On the way back to my room, I saw clearly that I could not serve the American war machine, and I could not bear to live apart from Ruth another year, whatever the consequences. Long after we both should have been asleep, I called her to ask if she'd be willing for us to postpone our studies at Harvard, get married that summer, and go to England together.

"Yes," she answered before I'd quite finished the question, "yes, let's do. I was just lying here dreaming the same thing."

In the valedictory address I wrote for delivery at the Brown commencement in June, I quoted Dr. King, whose words helped me say what I felt too young to say in words of my own. Much of what I wrote was commonplace among my classmates, who were less intent on making a good living than on making a good life. We believed that making a good life for oneself alone, or for one's family, was impossible without creating a decent society for all. And we believed that creating such a society meant shifting our nation from the relentless pursuit of war to the pursuit of peace, meant fighting for civil rights and women's rights rather than the almighty dollar, meant curbing the abuses of business, meant lifting up the poor, meant caring for the earth. And if our elders dismissed us as too naïve to voice opinions on such weighty matters, we answered that no one has a greater stake in shaping a country fit to live in than we who will inherit it.

Like my poems, the speech was heartfelt, clumsy, and brash. The best lines were those I borrowed from Dr. King, calling on us to live in fellowship with all people, regardless of race, class, or nation, in unconditional love. "When I speak of love," said Dr. King, "I am not speaking of some sentimental and weak response. I am speaking of that force which all of the great religions have seen as the supreme unifying principle of life. Love is somehow the key that unlocks the door which leads to ultimate reality."

The dean insisted on reading my remarks before I delivered them, to make sure I wouldn't say anything inflammatory to the parents and alumni. He politely suggested that I tone down passages here and there, and I politely refused. "Oh, well," he sighed, "nobody listens to graduation speeches anyway."

I couldn't have said whether many in the audience listened as I spoke, there in the sunlit sanctuary of the First Baptist Meeting House just down the hill from Brown, for when I looked out over the audience my gaze slid across the tops of the mortarboard caps emblazoned with antiwar slogans, and the only faces I saw were those of my close friends scattered among the graduates, a few of my teachers in their garish doctoral robes, and in a side pew near the front, my family and the woman I would marry.

19

AFTER THE ORGAN MUSIC, the flowers, the exchange of vows and rings, the drinking of punch in the parlor of the church, the rain of rice on our heads as we descended the steps to the idling car, the parting hugs for our friends and the kisses for our families, Ruth and I drove away into our mysteriously conjoined life. I kept both hands on the wheel to make sure my joy didn't send us careening off the street. In the rearview mirror I could barely make out the well-wishers crowding the sidewalk behind us, for the back window was nearly obscured by white letters proclaiming JUST MARRIED. From the artistry of the lettering, I figured this was Sandra's work. The string of cans tied to the tailpipe and the clatter of stones in the hubcaps were most likely the work of my college buddies who had made the trip to the heartland to see me get hitched.

We swung by Ruth's house to change into our traveling clothes. It was odd and thrilling to be in this home where I had courted her, to hear the clock in the living room chime the quarter hour, and to realize that no one ever again would shuffle down the hall at midnight to make sure we retired to our separate beds. Thoughts of sharing one bed tonight, in a motel on our way to a honeymoon in New Orleans, made my hands shake as I untied the string of cans, pried off the hubcaps to remove the stones, and scrubbed the news of our marriage from the rear window.

On our drive south from Indianapolis, I could barely quit looking at

Ruth to look at the highway. We talked of our trip to England, which would begin in a month, skipping over the sweet, nervous time between now and then. At the motel near Louisville I almost wrote our separate names on the registration slip, before I remembered to use *Mr. and Mrs.* I took the first shower. The pajamas I put on were still creased from the package. I couldn't quite believe that Ruth had actually married the man who peered so awkwardly from the steamed-up mirror. As presentable as I was going to be, I tiptoed out of the bathroom as she tiptoed in. "Don't go away," she said. The sheets felt cool against my skin. While I listened to the water pouring on Ruth, my heart thudded as though I had been running sprints. In a few minutes she emerged wearing a lacy white gown and drying her hair with a towel. Then she slid into bed beside me, I drew her into my arms, and our long waiting came to a fearful, delicious end.

We live in a universe in which every mass, from electron to galaxy, is drawn to every other mass—by gravity, in Newton's formulation; by the curvature of space, in Einstein's; or by love, in Woolman's, Wordsworth's, and Whitman's. And just as surely we live in a universe in which things eventually fall apart. Stars burn up or explode, mountains erode, species vanish, parents and partners age and die. The gathering impulse then makes new things from scraps of the old, like our earth from the debris of supernovas, like an infant from atoms that have passed through many previous lives. Looking upstream into this perennial flow, you see fresh forms arising; looking downstream, you see them dissolving. Well past midlife, as I am now, watching my mother die by inches, watching my granddaughter grow, remembering my own younger selves, I look both upstream and down.

On the Fourth of July in the summer of cicadas, Ruth, Eva, and I take Elizabeth, nearly fifteen months old, to visit Mother in the nursing home, to see if the baby can stir her dwindling spirits. The bedsores have festered into open wounds. One hole is large enough, a nurse tells us, to hold a fist. Inside, you can see the tip of her tailbone. Even doped up with painkillers, Mother can no longer bear to sit up in a wheelchair or lie on her back. So we find her curled on her side, eyes half open, staring at the wall.

Holding the baby in my arms, I lean down to catch Mother's gaze. She brightens momentarily, acknowledges Elizabeth with a raspy chortle, and then lapses into staring at the wall. I hand the baby to Eva and kneel beside the bed to rub Mother's shoulders. Through her skin the bones feel like stones in a thin cloth sack. It's difficult to imagine she will ever walk again, or even sit up to bat a pink balloon. Into her ear I speak news of her family, friends, casual acquaintances, anybody whose name might coax a response from her. But she says nothing. Two or three times her mouth opens, her tongue moves, but no sound emerges. The Buddha smile is gone, replaced by a grimace.

Meanwhile, Ruth places a bouquet of flowers, freshly cut from our yard, in the vase beside Mother's bed. A dog on a leash passes down the hall, its claws ticking on the linoleum. Elizabeth lets out an excited "Woof!" and then toddles off to give the dog a pat, with Eva in pursuit. Mother's eyes register none of this—the dog, the baby, the flowers, my hands on her shoulders, my voice in her ear. Every now and again the lids drift closed, and then drift halfway open. Every now and again her body jerks with pain.

Ruth senses my own pain and says it's time for us to go. I'm relieved—and abashed for feeling so. Kissing Mother on the cheek, I tell her I love her, and she rewards me with the flicker of a smile. Ruth combs Mother's hair as best she can against the pillow, also gives her a kiss, and says goodbye. Eva returns with Elizabeth in her arms, and the two lean down to Mother. When they straighten again, Mother's gaze follows them, twisting her face away from the wall. Sunlight angling through the window strikes a green spark in her eyes.

Ruth talks with the head nurse while Eva, Elizabeth, and I mosey out to the car. I carry the baby, and Eva walks beside me with her arm around my waist.

"It's hard, seeing her like that," Eva says.

"It sure is," I confess.

"I want to remember her alert and full of zest, the way she used to be."

"In her prime, she was about the most alive person I've ever known."

Eva tightens her arm at my waist. "You're doing all you can, Daddy."

Elizabeth suddenly grabs my chin and points the other arm skyward. "Burr!" she cries, her whole body wriggling with excitement.

"Bird!" I agree, as a kingfisher goes rattling by overhead. Looking from the baby's wide-open eyes to Eva's, I see they both have the same crazy mix of green and gray and brown as Mother's.

"You know," I say to Eva, "Wonder Girl here might turn out to have her great-grandmother's eyes."

"And mine, too," says Eva, this fruit of my love for Ruth, "and yours."

In August of 1967, in sexually liberated America, few grooms could have been as ignorant of the intimacies of marriage as I was. Like my knowledge of quantum mechanics, what little I knew about sexual mechanics had come almost entirely from books. Almost—but not quite.

I must have been ten years old or so when a rawboned boy named Solitude Jenkins, who lived in a shack near us on Esworthy Road, asked if I knew how babies were made. Sol and I were in the same grade at school, but he was a couple of years older, because he'd been held back. Dim, everybody agreed, and we blamed his fits. Now and again in the lunchroom or on the playground, his eyes would roll back and he'd keel over and jerk like a frog on the tile or dirt. One of us would fetch a teacher, who'd come running and pry open Sol's mouth to make sure he didn't gag on his tongue.

The day Sol asked me if I knew how babies were made, he and I were collecting hickory nuts in the woods behind our place, and each of us had pretty well filled a pail.

"Sure," I fibbed. "Everybody knows that."

"How, then?" he demanded.

"You tell first."

Sol eagerly told, but his description sounded so much like what I'd seen of the stallion mounting our mare that I refused to believe him. Surely people couldn't make babies the same way horses did.

"You're telling me a whopper," I said.

"Cross my heart and hope to die. Sis told me, and she's got a baby to prove it."

"Liar!" I cried, and flung a handful of hickory nuts at him.

Sol ducked, reached into his own pail, and hurled a fistful at me. "You're the liar! Don't know a thing about making babies."

We took cover behind trees and kept flinging nuts until both of our buckets were empty. Then it occurred to me that with all the excitement Sol might have a fit right there in the woods, and I'd have to reach in his mouth and uncurl his tongue, and what if he was only pretending and he decided to bite down hard on my fingers.

"Okay," I shouted, "I believe you!"

"Say I'm not a liar!"

"You're not a liar!"

We stepped out from behind our trees, shuffled toward one another with our empty pails, and resumed gathering nuts.

I knew better than to check Sol's account with Mama, who didn't approve of him, or his teenage sister with her fatherless baby, or his whole derelict clan. In those days, Mama herself had just recently brought a baby home from the hospital, little Glenn with his rosy chin and squinched-up eyes. The only clue she'd revealed about where Glenn came from, aside from the hospital, was to say that no matter how much she and Daddy fought, they loved one another very, very much.

So I never meant to breathe a word to her about Sol's unsettling news. But that night as Mama sat beside my bed in the darkened room while I fought off sleep, exhaustion overrode caution and I blurted out the whole scene, from Sol's opening question to the hurling of hickory nuts.

"Is it true?" I asked Mama in the darkness.

She kept silent for a moment. "It's part of the truth," she said at last, "but it leaves out a lot."

"Like what?"

"Like kindness and joy."

Mama never elaborated on her nighttime confession, and Dad seemed to count on my drawing the needed lessons from watching horses, cows, chickens, and dogs go about their business. Dad may also have counted on my learning what I needed to know about female anatomy from the girlie calendars displayed in the feed store and lumberyard.

Until I entered high school, therefore, the breathless account of Solitude Jenkins was the fullest introduction to sex I'd ever received. What I learned in high school came not from teachers or textbooks but from boys bragging in the locker room or in the back of the bus. For the boys who bragged the loudest, sex was another sport, with girls as the opposing team, and with every conquest, real or imagined, counting in the score. At least some of the conquests were real, since a handful of girls from our class became pregnant and had to drop out before graduation. The boys who kept quiet about sex either knew too little to say much, as in my case, or knew a particular girl too tenderly to boast of conquering her.

I had known a few girls tenderly before meeting Ruth, and I knew a couple of others in the years between our meeting and our deciding to marry. But what I learned of their bodies, and of Ruth's, was circumscribed by clothes, parents, chaperones, the girls' sense of decorum, and my own restraint. It wasn't lack of desire that held me back. Since Vicki May Langston had awakened me to girls, I had taken a passionate interest in their every contour and move. But the nearest I had come to seeing what lay beneath all those clothes was on the beaches of Lake Erie and the Gulf Coast of Louisiana, where a few daring beauties paraded up and down the sand in two-piece suits.

On entering my freshman dorm at Brown for the first time, I found that my roommate had already plastered the ceiling over his bed with *Playboy* centerfolds. I flushed when I saw them and looked away; then I studied them carefully as soon as my roommate left to buy some beer. He flunked out by midsemester, and took his photos with him. Long after he'd moved out, I could still imagine the expanse of bare skin overhead, the gravity-defying breasts and buttocks floating there like so many balloons in the Macy's Thanksgiving Day parade.

For all my burning desire, I still didn't press Ruth or my earlier girlfriends to open their zippers or thighs. Caution held me back, and so did simple respect for the girls' own wishes—not to mention the wishes of their parents. But I was restrained as well by a sense that the naked meeting between lovers is so powerful, so holy, it needs to be surrounded by ceremony and obligation. I believed that a wedding, with its cloud of witnesses, would provide the ceremony, and the vows of lifelong fidelity would provide the obligation.

These prim notions largely derived, I suppose, from the Bible, Methodist preachers, and my puritanical mother. Still, despite its occasional diatribes against the flesh, especially in the killjoy letters of Paul, the Bible as a whole was if anything an incitement to be fruitful and multiply. King David's dalliance with Bathsheba loomed larger in my imagination than the asceticism of Paul. As for preachers, more than one of those I'd come across had been forced out of the pulpit by amorous mischief. And my mother's warnings about the wickedness of the body were belied by her own clear delight in the senses, by her affection for my alcoholic father, and by her devotion to the fruits of their union, including this nightmare-ridden son.

Whatever the reasons, my knowledge of sex on our wedding night was largely anecdotal, or in the case of the airbrushed pinups, mythological. Ruth seemed willing to forgive my ignorance, then and forever after.

Having made love now for almost forty years with one and only one woman, and having joined with Ruth to rear two children, I've also known many happy couples who've chosen quite different sexual paths. I don't hold up my own history as any sort of standard. It is simply my history. What I do still believe, however, is that the union of lovers is holy and risky, a tapping into the power at the heart of things. Any lesser use of this power—for recreation, say, or merchandising—is toy-ing with fire. Nothing we do will put out the fire, which was burning long before we came along and will keep on burning long after our kind is gone. But if we treat this holy flame without reverence, we may lose the warmth and light of it.

Making love carried me as close to the center of awe as anything I'd ever experienced. It gathered into one fearsome rapture all my earlier transports of terrified wonder—from thunderstorms to starry nights, from the chill brink of death to the dawn chorus of waking birds. Although "making love" may serve as a polite name for an act that has many rude ones, it's misleading. For lovers do not so much *make* love as they are remade *by* love—dipped into the fire, melted down, reshaped. If they're devoted to one another, love will transform them, dissolving the shells of their old separate selves and making them anew.

Needless to say, I didn't have the presence of mind to realize any of this on my wedding night, or for a long while thereafter. In those early weeks of marriage I was so overjoyed to be with Ruth that I could scarcely think of anything else. The discovery that I wished to spend my life with her had been one of three great openings during my college years. The other two had been my turn from science to literature as a way of understanding and my awakening to the anguish caused by racism, poverty, and war.

For a spell after the wedding, the bliss of marriage shut out these other concerns. Then, on the eve of our departure for England, Ruth and I attended a weeklong retreat for recipients of the Danforth Fellowship, which I had won along with the Marshall. One of the presenters was a Jesuit priest named Daniel Berrigan, who had the sharp-featured, ferocious quality of a hawk. Then in his mid-forties, Father Berrigan had not yet run afoul of the law by destroying draft records, as he would do the following year, or by pouring pig's blood on nuclear-tipped missiles, as he would do a few years later. But he emanated a zeal for peace and justice like an electrical charge. I saw in him, as I saw in Dr. King, as I sensed in Gandhi and Jesus, an unwavering compassion. It was a quality I admired but also feared, because of the way it both clarified and consumed these lives.

At the close of our final session, Father Berrigan told us about having met recently with Vietnamese Buddhist monks who had been expelled from their country for trying to rescue and comfort the wounded in the midst of the war. Because they ministered to everyone, refusing to distinguish between friends and enemies, many of their fellow monks back in Vietnam had been thrown into jail and some had been killed. To protest the suffering, a few monks had set themselves on fire, as had a few Americans, although you'd never know it from the newspapers. In his own religion, Father Berrigan acknowledged, suicide was a sin. But how did the sacrifice of these awakened souls differ from that of Jesus? And who were we to tell others how much pain they should take upon themselves?

After letting the image of human torches burn in our minds for a few seconds, Father Berrigan went on to say, "Buddhists take a vow to relieve the suffering of all sentient beings. All—without exception. Nonhuman as well as human, stranger as well as neighbor. That is the essence of morality. That is the essence of good work."

Then he asked us to stand in a circle holding hands, keeping silent, and to consider how we might use our own lives to carry on that work. Since I happened to be standing next to Father Berrigan, I held his hand on one side, Ruth's on the other. As I pondered his words, suddenly all the world's grief came rushing back into my consciousness, and the force of it made me stagger, sway, and faint dead away.

I opened my eyes to find Ruth bending over me, looking distressed, and beside her Father Berrigan, looking nonchalant, as if he were accustomed to having people faint in his presence.

"What happened?" Ruth asked.

"Those monks," I murmured.

It was more than the monks, of course. It was the pain and courage and sacrifice they stood for. Spinning in the grass as a boy had made me dizzy, and smelling ether in the hospital had made me woozy, but nothing before had ever knocked me out. What laid me low was no mystical vision, no message from God, but a blow of compassion. In a wakeful mind, no force is more terrible, or precious.

•   •   •

Like her father, who waited in silence for someone to pass him the dish he wanted at supper, Ruth waited for me to explain, in my own good time, whatever was baffling in my behavior. It was just as well she never asked further about my fainting spell, because the answer, insofar as I understood it, might have upset her. Except for her rheumatic fever, nothing in her tranquil growing up had prepared her for the moodiness, crankiness, world-saving ambition, or conscience-stricken turmoil of her new husband. Whenever I lifted the lid on that inner turmoil, it scared her, so I tried keeping it covered, even though I knew that water comes to a boil faster in a lidded pot.

I counted on our sojourn in staid old England to calm me down. The several books of history I'd read in preparation told of a long, bloody struggle for power in the British Isles, stretching from the Druids who'd built Stonehenge, through the Romans, the Normans, medieval warlords, marauding clansmen, rebellious Celts, conniving archbishops, vengeful kings, merchant princes, Cromwell and his Puritan hooligans, and a string of imperial prime ministers, right up to Winston Churchill steadying the nation through World War II. Since then, as I read the history, England had surrendered its empire and its claims to worldly dominion, and had settled into genial, fusty retirement. The royalty had become actors in a costume drama. The soldiers had put on furry hats to stand guard before shuttered castles. The pirates had become corporate executives. The dreaded Tower of London had become a tourist trap. In such a quiet place, I imagined, safely distant from race riots and antiwar protests and all the miseries of America's nightly news, maybe I could see my own vexed country in a clear light, and maybe I could imagine a way to help in the healing once I returned.

Along with the twenty-three other new Marshall Scholars—only one of them married—Ruth and I sailed late in September from Montreal to Southampton on the British ship *Carmania*. As cruise ships went, it was dowdy and old, within a year or two of being taken out of service. But to Ruth and me it seemed like a floating palace, with nightly dances under chandeliers, white-jacketed waiters delivering snacks between meals and five-course feasts at the meals themselves, a swimming pool, game room, and bar. And for landscape, horizon to horizon, we had the swaying ocean and the ever-changing canopy of sky.

We avoided the bar, since Ruth didn't care for alcohol and I positively feared it, due to my father's addiction. I shunned not only drink but people under the stupefying influence of drink. That aversion, plus my empty wallet, had kept me away from parties at Brown. In fact, it had kept me from even so much as tasting beer or wine, not to mention any stronger liquor. I knew that as the son of an alcoholic I had a good chance of inheriting the disease—if it was a disease and not a moral failing, as Mama believed, and not evidence of buried sadness, as I sometimes thought. The only way to find out whether I risked my father's affliction was to take a few swigs and then see if I could stop.

Each evening at supper aboard the *Carmania* our waiter offered us wine with our meal, and each evening Ruth and I—alone among the boisterous young scholars at our table—refused. Then, on the last evening before landfall, our companions urged us to try the Chardonnay, so they could toast our marriage and the adventure we were all about to undertake in England. Ruth accepted half a glass of wine, and so did I, thinking now was as good a time as any to make the test. We clinked glasses around the table, gave a toast, and sipped. My mouth filled with a burning sweetness. I sipped again. No craving seized me, so far as I could tell, but I drank the rest. When the waiter returned with his bottle, however, I shook my head no, just to be safe.

To everyone else at table it must have seemed a trivial, even a silly rite of passage. But this tasting of alcohol was nearly as momentous for me, as fraught with dread and excitement, as that first lovemaking on our wedding night. In a way I couldn't have explained to the others, not even to Ruth, I sensed I was gambling with my father's fate as well as my own.

Next day, crammed into the bow of the ship with Ruth and dozens of other passengers, peering ahead through fog to glimpse Land's End, I thought of my father, whose ancestors had emigrated from the British Isles, and I thought of my mother, whose ancestors had come from elsewhere in Europe and, in the case of Grandpa Solomon, from the

Middle East. Neither of my parents had ever been able to visit the Old World, as they called it. And Grandpa Solomon, after fleeing his Assyrian village to escape massacre by the Turks, had never seen his homeland or family again.

Gulls appeared out of the steel-gray fog, a sure sign of land. Suddenly the passengers at the rail began to stir, and someone cried out, "There it is! Look!"

Cheers went up. And sure enough, there in the mist ahead of us, a long, low shadow broke the horizon—the cliffs of Cornwall, westernmost flank of England. Ruth and I exchanged glances, to be sure the other had seen. What we found in one another's eyes made us laugh aloud amidst the cheers. In that shared seeing, the Old World, like the New, seemed more luminous and fine.

EARTH

20

H OW MAMA WOULD HAVE LOVED the flowers, I thought as Ruth and I made our way by train from the port in Southampton to London, and how Dad would have itched to repair nearly every building in sight. Though the air of early October was alarmingly cool, flowers glowed in market stalls, in window boxes, in backyard gardens and sidewalk planters, in the arms of people waiting at stations, in the lapels of gentlemen striding along with rolled umbrellas, all as fresh and bright as a full moon on a clear night. Between towns, the countryside might have been one continuous park, a brilliant green, the trees carefully planted to call attention to streams, the grazing cows and sheep mere ornamental pets rather than livestock destined to be milked or sheared, let alone butchered, and the hills neatly placed so as to improve the view.

By contrast, everything humans had made, as opposed to what they had gardened, looked timeworn and shabby, like the battered antiques Mama brought home from auctions for Dad to fix. The row houses, warehouses, shipping yards, and shops were all covered in grime, which I imagined to be the residue from centuries of coal smoke. The churches hunkered down like toads under the weight of moss-covered roofs. The stone steps leading up to buildings had been cracked by weather and gouged by generations of feet, the railings had rusted, and many of the buildings themselves were leaning out of plumb, with ill-fitting windows and chimneys askew. Even the billboards, which I would learn the English call hoardings, advertised products that appeared to date from before the last war. The clothing people wore in the streets and aboard the train was a drab mélange of grays and browns—with the exception of miniskirts, which were as common and often as colorful as the flowers, and which, I couldn't help noticing, bared more of the female leg than was ever exposed in America this far from a beach.

Noplace were bright miniskirts and dingy buildings more in evidence than in London, where we spent a few days of orientation with the other Marshall Scholars. We were given a crash course in British etiquette. We shook hands with dignitaries over glasses of sherry, which I warily drank. In the House of Lords we met bewigged elders who seemed puzzled as to who these young Americans might be. We sat on back benches in the House of Commons—a room so small we could hardly believe a quarter of the earth had once been ruled from this place. We met Members of Parliament who had voted the funds for our scholarships, and in the streets and shops and pubs of London we moved among ordinary citizens whose taxes actually paid our bills. I felt an immense gratitude to these strangers for bringing me and my new wife to this storied land.

Our last outing before we all scattered to our various colleges was a visit to the British Museum. Since we had only enough time to sample a few of the hundred or so galleries, Ruth and I dipped into a room filled with literary manuscripts, where we read the opening page of *Mrs. Dalloway* in Virginia Woolf's own handwriting; we looked at the Rosetta stone, which had unlocked the code of Egyptian hieroglyphics; and then, on my urging, we toured the Assyrian collection. I wanted to glimpse something of the ancient people from whom Grandpa Solomon had descended.

Maps showed us how the Assyrian Empire, beginning from its heartland along the Upper Tigris River in what is now Iraq, spread out to encompass nearly the whole of the Middle East. At the height of their power, between about 800 and 600 B.C.E., the Assyrians controlled all the lands from Turkey in the north to Egypt in the south, from the Mediterranean Sea to the Persian Gulf. Ruth and I entered the gallery by passing between a pair of enormous stone bulls, each one sporting wings and a human head. According to the label, these monstrous figures would have flanked the entrance to a throne room, the better to intimidate anyone who approached the king. Along the gallery walls, bas-reliefs carved with exquisite detail into limestone slabs showed a parade of ambassadors groveling at the king's feet, suppliants bringing tributes of silver and gold from the far reaches of the empire, emissaries presenting booty from conquered towns, and strings of slaves captured in battle.

One roomful of panels showed a king slaying lions with arrows and sword, his wavy hair flowing over his shoulders and his beard curling halfway down his chest. The king's legions of warriors also wore beards, although never as long or robust as his, for the king stood alone at the summit of virility. While their names changed over the centuries, these rulers always appeared as gods, and like gods they held absolute sway. In one sculpture after another, they were attended by servants, priests, and guardian spirits, cooled by fans made of palm fronds, sheltered by awnings, plied with food and drink. It was all quite grand—and ghastly.

In the sculpted images of those warriors, I fancied I saw the profile of my grandfather, the curly mane of an uncle, even my own humped nose. Grandpa Solomon was full-blooded Assyrian, Mama and her brothers were half, while I was only a quarter; but that was a higher percentage of my ancestry than I could trace to any other source. So I had long been curious about the Assyrians. On the one hand, they were pioneers in astronomy and mathematics, which appealed to the scientist in me. They held trees to be sacred, along with sun and moon and stars, which appealed to the nature lover in me. They were among the earliest people to use written language, spiky letters pressed into clay tablets like bird tracks in mud; they recorded proverbs and tales; they amassed great libraries; and they included in their pantheon a god of writing—all of which appealed to me as an aspiring writer. On the other hand, I knew from reading that in their heyday the Assyrians, or at least their leaders, had been a bloodthirsty lot. I didn't realize just how bloodthirsty until I toured these galleries.

Before we finished viewing the collection, I had seen all I could bear to see of my ancestors. I didn't believe that genes could transmit guilt, the way they could transmit the shape of a nose or the color of an eye. Still, I felt entangled in that murderous history, as I felt implicated in slavery by virtue of my southern birth and pale skin. While I admired Assyrian art, I was appalled by most of what it depicted. There were peaceful interludes—a man grooming a horse, a woman nursing a child, a genie cradling a deer—but the sculptures as a whole glorified war and exalted the king, celebrating his power over animals, armies, enemies, slaves, and geography. It reminded me too much of Hitler, with his death camps and his Thousand-Year Reich. The pageant of booty and slaves reminded me of the poor, mainly dark-skinned people laboring to fill America's coffers and coddle the rich. The lion hunt reminded me of the generals from the Pentagon boasting as they slaughtered deer in the Arsenal. The celebrations of war reminded me of B-52s raining bombs on Vietnam.

So we cut short our tour of the Assyrian galleries and went outside to sit on the museum steps. Ruth sensed my agitation, although she couldn't have known, and didn't ask, the cause of it. Instead, she ran her palm along my cheek and mused, "Would your beard be that curly?"

"Like one of those bloody kings?" I asked sullenly.

"I was just wondering," she said, lifting her hand from my cheek.

"Well, there's one way to find out."

By the time we reached our flat in Cambridge a few days later, a rusty shadow had begun to show on my unshaved face. Within weeks it had come in curly and dark, like steel wool left in the rain.

During the time I've been tracing these encounters with awe, my nation has been at war in the Assyrian homeland, now known as Iraq. The official reasons given for launching this war have all turned out to be false. People are dying just the same. As the body count rises, the true reasons for the war come clear, and they are the ones recorded on those bas-reliefs in the British Museum: the lust for power, the craving for treasure, and the cosseting of rulers far removed from the bloodshed.

American troops are only the latest wave of conquerors to sweep over that region since the Assyrian Empire collapsed of its own brutal weight 2,600 years ago. When they captured Baghdad in the spring of 2003, our soldiers stood by while looters ransacked museums and other public buildings. Within days, cultural treasures that had accumulated over thousands of years, including the world's premier collection of Assyrian artifacts, had been stolen, smashed, or burned. While I've been piecing together one person's spiritual history, the history of a whole people has been torn apart. And every day's news brings word of more destruction—arson, bombings, mortar attacks, assassinations, roadside ambushes, kidnapping, torture, rape—as various ethnic and religious factions battle for supremacy. Among those factions are the Assyrians, descendants of the onetime conquerors, although now reduced to such small numbers that they're battling not for supremacy but for survival.

I suspect Mother would grieve if she knew anything of the war in her father's ancestral land. But she knows nothing of Iraq, or of any other place beyond the walls and grounds of the nursing home. In fact, it appears that she is no longer able to register much of anything beyond the confines of her own skin. Today when I visit she is asleep, as usual, propped on her side with pillows and facing the wall. The fist-sized wound has begun to heal, the nurse assures me, but complete healing will take months, and in the meantime it must feel like a flame scorching her back.

"Hey, there," I murmur, brushing the hair from Mother's forehead. One eye cracks open, revealing a hazel glint. "Look what I've brought you," I say, offering a bouquet of gaudy flowers from our yard, a riot of yellows, purples, pinks.

Her face, with its sunken cheeks, turns a few inches, and her eyes swim into focus. "Oh, how gorgeous," she whispers, and gives a wan smile.

Encouraged by this rare response, I point to a cluster of lavender, crown-shaped blossoms. "Look at this bee balm. I had to chase away a hummingbird to cut a few stalks of it for you this morning. Isn't it pretty?"

But the smile has already blown out like a candle in a gust of wind. The eyes have lost focus. She coughs.

"Are you thirsty?" I ask.

Her chin dips to signal yes, a gesture that came to baby Elizabeth months later than the wag of head to say no. I pour ice water from a pitcher into a cup. Unwrapping a straw, I bend the tip and place it between Mother's lips. Her teeth clamp shut as though guarding her throat. I remind her to close her lips and suck, but instead she chews on the straw. I remind her again, and she keeps chewing. She can't drink straight from the cup without sitting up, and I'm reluctant to move her, for fear of rousing her aches—for fear of snapping her like a brittle twig.

"Well," I say, giving up, "they'll take you to lunch pretty soon and give you lots to drink."

Her mottled hands fumble with the edge of the sheet, pulling it to her throat, pushing it away, pulling it back. The bewildered look comes over her face.

"Are you okay?" I ask.

Her chin jerks sideways, and she mutters "No" with an almost humorous intonation, as if to say, *Look at me, for God's sake, and tell me what you think.*

I realize I'm the one hoping to feel okay, to be relieved of her pain. "What's the matter?" I say. "Do you hurt somewhere?"

"I feel so—" she begins, then falters.

I wait, hoping she'll finish her sentence. What do you feel, Mother? Pain, anger, resignation, despair? What is life like for you, moment by moment, day by twilit day? If I were to stay here beside you, holding your hand, pouring a familiar voice into your ear, instead of slipping away to my separate life, would that relieve your agony, or mine?

When she says nothing more, I repeat back to her, "You feel so . . . ," followed by a pause. Two times I say it, three times, four. Her jaw trembles but will not open.

In our dank little flat near the train station in Cambridge, Ruth's jaw trembled whenever I began to rant or brood. She took my usual high spirits in stride, but if I railed too long against injustice or sank too deep into melancholy, she wept. Her weeping in turn deepened my dejection, because I wanted nothing more than to make her happy.

Although she had witnessed my moody extremes in letters, until we began living together she had rarely seen them up close. Perhaps she had imagined, as I had, that marriage would damp down these wild emotional swings. My raving was usually about some public outrage, from the napalming of Vietnamese peasants to the burning of America's ghettos. My brooding was usually about some fresh evidence that I would never amount to much as a scholar, never amount to anything as a writer, never accomplish a lick of good work in this needy world.

I assured Ruth that she wasn't the cause of my volatile moods; on the contrary, she was the steadying force that kept me from swinging even further toward the extremes. Her calm temper balanced my mercurial one. Her focus on the present moment, dealing with whatever came along, balanced my obsession with past and future. Her contentment with who she was helped to restrain my own constant grasping after a new and vastly improved self. Without her, I might have shaken to pieces, like an out-of-kilter machine.

It took Ruth most of our first year of marriage to accept credit for my joy without also blaming herself for my gloom. It took me much longer to recognize my darkest gloom as depression, and longer still to identify its buried sources.

A few reasons for gloom were obvious, and temporary. I missed my family and would likely not see them, or any of our stateside friends, for two years. We didn't know a soul in England, except the Marshall Scholars whom we'd briefly met and most of whom were studying elsewhere. Our flat in the downstairs of a row house was lit only by a bay window in front, a single window in back, and a handful of dim bulbs. The sun itself, rarely seen through breaks in clouds, seemed like a dim bulb. A space heater near the bay window and another in the kitchen, set on timers to run at night, when electric rates were cheaper, barely kept the apartment warmer than the outside air. The sole other source of heat was a gas fire in the living room, which burned only when we fed it shilling coins. Since we had no coins to spare, the place was dark and damp. On moving in, we scrubbed mold from the walls, but it soon grew back. Sheets fresh from the laundry turned clammy within hours. From out there beyond the railroad tracks, to do anything in town we had to bicycle a couple of miles along busy streets, dodging among buses and lorries, as often as not through rain.

Since my father had carried me out to watch thunderstorms from the porch of our farmhouse in Memphis, my favorite weather had always been rain, the harder and louder the better. In Ohio I had savored the daylong buildup of surly clouds that suddenly cracked open and loosed a downpour. In Louisiana I had thrilled to the storms that flashed up from the Gulf and burst overhead with a roar. Drizzle would do, but the rain that sent chills up my spine was the ripsnorting kind that flooded creeks and washed the world clean. English rain, by contrast, never raised its voice, never got excited, never fell hard enough to loosen the grime. Rarely amounting even to a drizzle, it was more like heavy fog, not sure whether to fall or simply mill about in the air, an all-pervading mist that worked its way into every crevice.

Undeterred by damp, Ruth and I explored Cambridge on bicycle or on foot, and occasionally we rode the bus to nearby villages in East Anglia. When we'd saved enough coins in the dish we kept on the kitchen table, we splurged and rode the train to Oxford or London. We often had to choose between feeding those coins into the gas fire, to take the edge off the perennial chill, or saving them for train fare, tickets to plays, or books.

The books we bought used from shops in the warren of alleyways at the center of town. Many of these volumes bore the bookplates and marginal notes of previous owners, sometimes in three or five different hands, with dates stretching back a hundred years or more, and in one case all the way back to 1650. Reading these pages, I felt as though I were delving down through layers of mind. Most of the plays we watched in one or another of the Cambridge or London theaters. But we saw a stirring production of Shakespeare's *Richard III* in a college courtyard that was older than the play itself. And we saw medieval mystery plays acted out on the cobbled market square, where goods had traded hands for more than a thousand years.

Everywhere we turned, we encountered a depth of human habitation, layer upon layer, like the strata of rock exposed in a road cut. As a boy growing up in Ohio, I'd been fascinated by every trace of the Indians who'd lived there for thousands of years, the arrowheads turning up in plowed fields, the burial mounds, the names on the map. But I felt no living connection to those ancient people. So far as I knew, they had vanished entirely, leaving behind only their stories in books and their artifacts in museums.

But in England the reminders of earlier human presence weren't merely objects in museums, like Indian tomahawks or Assyrian sculptures. They were living presences. Centuries-old books circulated hand to hand. Some of the churches, built more than a thousand years earlier on ground where aboriginal Britons had worshiped fire, still rang with song on Sunday mornings. Some of their bells had been marking the holy hours since before any European set foot in the New World. In those churches were tombs of knights who'd fought in the Crusades, their stone effigies complete with chain mail and swords, their surnames still prominent in the local phone book. Classes had been taught at the university since the thirteenth century, and some of the authors studied by those early scholars were still in the Cambridge curriculum. The black gowns we students wore to class, with long sleeves trailing like bat wings, derived from those worn by clerics in the Middle Ages.

In a corner of the courtyard where Ruth and I went to see *Richard III* stood an ivy-covered turret, which one of our companions identified as Erasmus's Tower. I knew that Erasmus was a humanist and theologian who'd helped ignite the Reformation by publishing a Latin edition of the New Testament early in the 1500s. But I also knew he was from Holland, so I asked why this tower in Cambridge bore the name of a Dutchman.

"Because that's where Erasmus lived while finishing his New Testament," our companion answered.

I looked back at the tower with new respect, trying to imagine the search for knowledge going on there continuously for half a millennium. Students lived there still, laboring away at their own discoveries. Elsewhere in Cambridge, students conned their science and math in rooms once occupied by Isaac Newton, Charles Darwin, and Bertrand Russell. Those who aspired to make literature, as I did, carried on in the wake of literary legends, ranging from Shakespeare's archrival, Christopher Marlowe, through John Milton, Samuel Pepys, John Dryden, William Wordsworth, Samuel Taylor Coleridge, Lords Byron and Tennyson, on up to C. S. Lewis and Vladimir Nabokov.

E. M. Forster, celebrated for his writing since the 1920s, still occupied rooms in his Cambridge college, decades after publishing his last and greatest novel, *A Passage to India*, which I had studied at Brown as if it were holy writ. Then close to ninety, Forster was reputed to be senile—or dotty, as the English would more politely say. But when I was invited along with a handful of other students to have lunch with him, I found him witty and captivating. He was a contemporary, and in many cases a friend, of the great modernists, such as T. S. Eliot, Ezra Pound, D. H. Lawrence, and Virginia Woolf. When Forster was twenty-two—my own age when I met him in the winter of 1968—Henry James and Joseph Conrad and William Butler Yeats were in their prime. He spoke familiarly of them all. He told anecdotes about Virginia Woolf, for example, as if he'd seen her only the other day, even though she had been dead since wading into a river with her pockets full of stones early in World War II.

The teacher who guided me through my initial studies at Cambridge was a veteran of both world wars, a portly, kindly, gimpy, red-faced Anglo-Irishman, well advanced in years, named T. R. Henn. Mr. Henn, as everyone called him—for he'd never completed a doctorate or been elevated to a professorship—invited his students to a literary soiree in his rooms once a fortnight. I attended every session, along with ten or fifteen other apprentice writers. Usually we took turns reading aloud our latest attempts at poetry or fiction, upon which Mr. Henn would comment by quoting from Virgil or Donne or Austen or others of his favorites.

When quoting prose, he would rise from his chair, limp heavily on war-battered legs to a bookshelf, draw out the relevant volume, open to the exact page, and declaim the passage in a sonorous voice. Poetry he would recite without budging from the chair, for he carried a good portion of English literature in his head. While a prisoner of war in Asia, he had passed the time by memorizing reams of poetry, including much of Chaucer, most of Shakespeare, and all of Yeats. Mr. Henn felt especially close to Yeats, for as a young man he'd known the great Irish poet well.

At one of these literary evenings, in the book-lined study lit only by candles flickering on the windowsills, Mr. Henn announced that he would try to summon up the shade of Yeats. Those of us in attendance exchanged skeptical looks. Mr. Henn began by reciting a few of Yeats's poems; then he closed his eyes and began muttering in a language that might have been Gaelic. Suddenly the candle flames wavered, as if a draft had blown through the room, and out of our teacher's mouth poured a voice higher-pitched and fussier than his own rumbling brogue.

The sort of chill usually aroused in me by thunderstorms spread up my spine and lifted the hairs on the back of my neck. The voice spoke in English, yet I could scarcely make out the words. There was something about ectoplasm, something about karma and reincarnation, and then one clear sentence: "The river of words flows on."

After a few minutes the voice abruptly ceased, Mr. Henn shook himself slightly and opened his eyes, and the candle flames steadied.

By and by, we resumed the reading of our own compositions, which seemed no better than before the séance, and yet seemed also more dignified, as if they were tributaries, no matter how small, to the one great river of words.

That night, as I bicycled home to Ruth, I remembered a line I'd copied into my journal from William Faulkner's *Requiem for a Nun*: "The past is never dead. It's not even past." I had understood this as a truth peculiar to the South, with its grievous legacy of slavery. But now, pedaling through rain-slick streets, I realized it was true everywhere and always.

Not only in Germany, say, with its malign inheritance from the Holo-
caust, but also in my own country, haunted by the ghosts of slaughtered
Indians and buffaloes. And true not only of human atrocities casting
their curse forward through time but equally of human achievements,
all those layers of discovery, artifice, and reflection that we the living
had inherited. We made nothing from scratch, but drew on ideas and
inventions and materials bequeathed to us. The words in my head and
clothes on my back, just as surely as the genes in my cells, were a gift
from generations past.

Atop the bridge that crossed the railroad tracks near our flat, I pulled
over to lean my bike against the railing and watch a lit-up train chug
south toward London. I could hear from the clatter of wheels that the
joints in the rails needed mending. Since arriving in England, I'd been
able to perceive only that nearly everything needed mending. Now it
struck me that my perceptions were peculiarly American, ignorant of
history, tuned to the shiny present. I'd been deluded into believing that
each of us is born as a blank slate into a world forever new. Yet here in
England, in the streets and rooms of Cambridge, the past kept insisting
on its presence. On hearing the voice of Yeats, or perhaps the jesting
voice of Mr. Henn, I realized that what I'd seen as decay—the buildings
in ill repair, the layers of grime—was also the compost of deep human
time. Whatever I did with my life would be planted in that soil, and
would either deplete or enrich it for those who came after.

I could never be sure whether what happened at Mr. Henn's séance
was a parlor trick or a genuine communing with the dead. Even as a
trick, it revealed how the past, literary and otherwise, saturated the air
of Cambridge. The literary heritage, in particular, humbled and inspired me. Humbled me, because I was so unlikely ever to achieve anything worthy of comparison with the work of Yeats or any of the
luminaries who'd studied at the university. Inspired me, because I realized that each of them had once been young, uncertain, just setting out
in life. This didn't mean I had any prospect of reaching their level of
achievement, but it did mean I should aim high.

21

IN MARCH OF 1968, a series of warm, dry days lured the daffodils into blooming and the birds into nesting, and fooled Ruth and me into spending our weeklong holiday bicycling through the fen country of East Anglia. By eating bread and cheese and staying overnight at youth hostels, we could just afford the trip. Soon after we set out from Cambridge on our laden bikes, however, the balmy breezes gave way to bitter ones; the sunshine gave way to sleet. No matter which direction we turned, we always seemed to be riding into the wind. And we turned often, because the roads in that low-lying country twisted hither and yon to avoid hummocks and bogs, the way animal trails do. The only straight roads were those built on top of Roman highways, for Caesar's engineers had laid out their turnpikes with rulers. In the face of persistent wind, our yellow slickers acted like sails to hold us back. On we pedaled, through village after village, taking refuge in any building that charged no admission, our teeth chattering and legs aching.

We arrived at our first overnight destination a couple of hours before the hostel was scheduled to open. Too weary to wander about in the cold wind, we hunkered down to wait under a thatch-roofed pavilion on the village green. I put my arms around Ruth to still her shivering. From a boyhood of sports and outdoor work, I was used to driving my body hard. Meanwhile, rheumatic fever had kept Ruth in bed for two years of childhood, and the resulting heart murmur had kept her from strenuous exercise for years afterward. I worried that I had dragged her on a foolhardy trip. When I suggested we could get a good night's sleep and then head back to Cambridge the next day, she said, "Don't be silly."

Presently a woman about the age of my mother approached us carrying a basket of groceries, and from her look of concern I fancied she was going to invite us home to supper. I gave her a smile and prepared a little speech of thanks. But this wasn't Ohio or Tennessee, where such a thing might have happened. This was England, where the woman strode on by, remarking amiably, "What a pathetic little sight."

Rising to her feet, Ruth declared, "I'm not going to sit here looking pitiable." So we hunted up a tea shop, where we treated ourselves to hot chocolate and scones. The price of this luxury consumed our budget for the whole day's food.

At the hostel we met young people from Scotland, Australia, Canada, France, Germany, and Spain, all eager to talk about their travels. A few sleek men had bicycled up from London, fifty or sixty miles, while Ruth and I had labored to cover twenty miles through the beastly weather. Even the fittest travelers huddled near the coal fire in the common room, rubbing their hands. I made sure Ruth found a seat on the hearth. As everyone traded stories, the color gradually came back into her cheeks. By bedtime, however, she hadn't stopped trembling. We set off toward our separate floors, in keeping with youth hostel rules, which required men and women to sleep apart. But as soon as Ruth had found a bunk in an unoccupied room, I stole down to join her, shut the door behind me, and propped a chair under the knob. Then I crawled beneath the covers with my beloved and held her all night long.

By morning she had recovered some of her strength; then by the next evening she was exhausted and shivering again. Yet she wouldn't hear of turning back. And so it went for the whole of our weeklong trip. Whenever we could evade the wardens at the hostels, Ruth and I slept together. Sometimes her trembling woke me, and I lay there fretting. What if she caught pneumonia? What if her damaged heart acted up? I felt as never before the full weight of our vow to care for one another, through sickness and health, until death parted us. And death *would* eventually part us, a fact that tormented me whenever I allowed myself to think of it.

During the day, when sleet chilled us or the wind wore us down, we took shelter in churches. In one place we listened to an organist practice; in another we listened to bell ringers sound hundreds of changes on their bells; and everywhere we hunted for curious inscriptions. My favorite epitaph appeared on a tomb in Tetbury: "In a vault underneath lie several of the Saunderses; particulars, the last day will disclose. Amen." Admirably terse, these folks were either reluctant to pay the cost of inscribing a longer memorial or confident their laundry would prove spotless on Judgment Day. Since the English could not pronounce my surname without making it sound like "Saunders," I took this clan as my own.

One noontime we stopped to eat our lunch in the lee of a house where two men were tiling a roof. In answer to my questions, the older of the men, who wore a threadbare suit coat and flat brown cap, told me he'd salvaged the tiles from a collapsed barn. "The ones as they make nowadays don't have the character of these old ones," he said, holding up a tile for me to admire. When I asked how long this job would last, he answered, "Two hundred years." The pride in his work and the battered look of his hands reminded me of my father, and of the farmers and carpenters on Esworthy Road.

Another noontime we ate lunch in the ruins of a priory where it had once been the custom to give a flitch of bacon to any couple who had "not repented them, sleeping or waking, of their marriage in a year and a day." Reading that provision, Ruth and I laughed. So far we'd been married seven months, without a moment's regret, and we felt sure, had the custom survived, that we could have claimed the bacon.

The priory had been sacked by Oliver Cromwell's troops during the Civil War between Parliamentarians and Royalists in the seventeenth century. Born in this part of England, Cromwell returned here with his Puritan zealots intent on destroying everything that smacked of idolatry or aristocracy. They burned mansions belonging to nobles. They set fire to whatever would burn in stone churches—roof beams, tapestries, altars. They smashed icons, hacked heads from statues, shattered stained-glass windows. For lack of money or will, some of the wrecked buildings had been left to molder, like the rubble from Nazi bombing in parts of London or the ruins of medieval castles and Roman forts throughout the country, all scars from a violent history.

In one of the sacked churches, now restored, we found a rose window, as round and mesmerizing as a mandala, which had been pieced together from shards of stained glass left by those who'd waged war in the name of God. Staring at this window, with its crazy-quilt pattern of purples and reds, I felt an overwhelming sense that everything now in existence had been cobbled together from scraps of things demolished—tiles from a fallen barn covering a house, stones from a Roman temple used to make a church, the stones themselves made from the ground-up bits of mountains or the shells of sea animals, our bodies fashioned from remnants of other lives, the earth and sun compounded from the dust of earlier generations of stars. Did this mean that our own acts of demolition—mining, logging, bulldozing, butchering, bombing—were the norm, the way of the universe, while acts of loving care were the aberration? If so, then Jesus had sent his followers on a fool's errand, for the dream of peace was a vain delusion.

Every now and again during our trip, U.S. Air Force jets from one of the East Anglia bases roared overhead, practicing for war. No matter how many times their thunder broke over us, Ruth and I always flinched. As we pedaled into the village of Saffron Walden, our last stop on the way home to Cambridge, a fighter squadron was piercing the air in a V formation like a skein of geese. The part of me still infatuated with big, bold, ingenious machines jerked my head up to gape at them. I had to shield my eyes against the sun, for the foul weather had finally broken. The jets hurtled on by.

Feeling proud for having covered some two hundred miles on our own power, and feeling grateful for the early April sunlight, Ruth and I decided to indulge ourselves with a pub lunch. As we rolled down the main street of Saffron Walden, we debated whether to choose shepherd's pie, Welsh rarebit, or some other hearty dish. Before we reached the pub, however, we saw out front of a news agent's shop a signboard bearing the headline MARTIN LUTHER KING ASSASSINATED. The shock of it brought immediate sobs, as if Ruth and I had been saving our sorrow for just this moment. We stopped, straddled our bikes, and leaned against one another, while the life of the village streamed on by. The tears were still running down my face when I went in the shop to buy a newspaper. The clerk gave me the paper but wouldn't accept my coin, saying, "It's a great pity, sir." Before I could read any details of the killing, my eye snagged on the dateline—Memphis. This peacemaker, this follower of Jesus, had been slain in my birthplace. Riots had broken out there, and in dozens of other American cities. I felt the sting of shame, as if I were complicit in the murder.

We forgot about the pub lunch and bicycled on toward Cambridge. I longed to keep going all the way to America. A scrim of grief cut me off from the sunlit countryside. This loss felt more personal than the assassination of John Kennedy. Dr. King had stood up against the white bigots who postured on television during my boyhood. On my bus trip to college, his words had echoed in my head, giving me hope that the dream of a just and loving world might come to pass. Only a year ago I had sat in a crowded lecture hall at Brown, watching and listening to him, spellbound.

Had Dr. King been shot because he was a black man who spoke up for equality? Because he defended the poor against the rich? Because he advocated nonviolence in a society enraptured by violence? Because he denounced the war in Vietnam? Everyone whose heart was lifted up by knowing he was in the world must have feared this murder would happen, just as the disciples must have feared that the ruling elites whom Jesus challenged would not let the savior live.

Two months later Robert Kennedy was shot while campaigning for the Democratic presidential nomination. He had just won the California primary and was leaving a hotel ballroom in Los Angeles following his victory speech when a gunman opened fire at point-blank range. Because he didn't die right away, the British newspapers carried headlines saying KENNEDY FIGHTS FOR LIFE or KENNEDY DEATH DRAMA. Several papers ran the same grisly photo, of the once vibrant Bobby Kennedy lying on the floor of that hotel, his chest bared, face contorted in pain, hand gripping a rosary, as he waited for an ambulance.

The day after the shooting, Ruth and I traveled to Stratford-upon-Avon for a performance of *King Lear*. As we rode the bus I tried keeping my eyes on the green countryside to avoid thinking about the misery back home, but every time one of the passengers rattled a newspaper I was reminded of the shooting, and every time I glanced across the aisle I saw the ghastly photo. By the time we reached Stratford, the headline on news kiosks had changed to KENNEDY DIES.

The rest of the afternoon, Ruth and I paid homage at the literary shrines. In a pasture beside the footpath leading to Anne Hathaway's cottage, sheep that had been newly sheared leapt about in tall grass, looking as carefree as toddlers romping naked on a lawn. The sheep might be headed for slaughter, but they didn't know it. All they knew was the lightness of their bodies prancing in the sunlight. I wished I could share their oblivion for a few hours, long enough to enjoy visiting Shakespeare's town. But everywhere we turned we kept meeting that stark announcement—KENNEDY DIES—and every time it brought us to a standstill. Later, watching the play, I couldn't tell how much of the twisting in my gut was caused by the sad story of King Lear and how much by the death of another one of my heroes.

As in the murders of John Kennedy and Dr. King, one could only guess the reasons for Bobby Kennedy's assassination. Because he promised to negotiate an end to the Vietnam War if he was elected? Because he vowed to fight poverty and racism? Because he sympathized with one side or the other in the strife between Israelis and Palestinians? Because he had white skin or a Boston accent or a famous name?

Less and less of what happened in America, at least what we could learn of it from across the ocean, made any sense. Ruth and I and our American friends in Cambridge talked endlessly of the turmoil in our homeland—assassinations, race riots, burning cities, body bags arriving from Vietnam, antiwar marches met with tear gas and truncheons, sit-ins on campuses, marauding gangs, drug busts, wiretaps, overflowing prisons. Home was such a mess, a few of our friends decided they would never go back. But Ruth and I and most of the American students we knew felt it was *our* mess. Now in our twenties, we were the adults we had long aspired to become, which meant it was time for us to share in the responsibility for our nation's future.

During that chaotic summer of 1968, Ruth and I made some decisions that would shape our own future. I kept asking myself how I could remain in England, cultivating my mind, sipping tea, while America fell apart. Yet what could I do if I went back home now, with a bachelor's degree in English and a pile of unpublished manuscripts? With a doctorate I might become a teacher, and with practice I might become a writer. Maybe that way, in classrooms and books, I could lend my hand to the healing of my country. After a year of working in a biochemistry lab at the university, Ruth decided she didn't want to pursue a Ph.D. in this field, or any field, which meant she had no intention of returning to Harvard for graduate school. This freed me to forgo Harvard as well, and to stay on in Cambridge for my own Ph.D., as Mr. Henn—conveying, as he said, the wishes of Yeats—had urged me to do.

Our other big decision was more fraught with risk. From the moment I'd begun hearing of America's role in Vietnam, it had roused in me a deep revulsion. I soon learned to give reasons for my feelings, but the feelings came first. I grew nauseated, thinking of napalm scorching children, Agent Orange poisoning jungles and rice paddies, tanks firing into grass huts. I explained to Ruth why I could no longer hide behind my student deferment, why I had to declare myself a conscientious objector. She and I decided that if the draft board accepted my application, I would do alternative service; if they refused, I would appeal; and if the appeal failed, either I would go to trial, and most likely to jail, or we'd both go into exile. Under no circumstances would I fight in Vietnam. I owed that much to the memory of the Kennedys and Dr. King.

The working out of that decision would send convulsions through our second year in England. We began the year by moving into a new flat, this one bright and airy, with high ceilings, tall windows, and French doors opening onto a garden. It had been fashioned from the parlor and butler's pantry of a grand house known as St. Chad's, once belonging to Geoffrey Keynes, brother of the Cambridge economist John Maynard Keynes. In the garden, amidst leggy bushes and perennial flowers, was a bomb shelter dating from World War II. The grass-covered, hump-backed shape of it reminded me of the munitions bunkers in the Arsenal. All one could see through the rusted grate covering the entrance was a cricket bat resting in the shadows down below. I wondered if a child had left it there after a game, or if a mother, with her husband away at war, had thought to use the bat as a last weapon against Nazi invaders. From the table where I sat writing early in the morning while Ruth slept, I looked out on that hunched shape and thought how my whole life had been haunted by bombs.

Ruth found a job she liked much better, working as an aide in a school for handicapped children. Because of her rheumatic fever, she had spent her own first five grades in such a school, so she felt drawn to children who needed extra care. I persuaded the graduate faculty at Cambridge to allow me to pursue a Ph.D., focusing on the novels of D. H. Lawrence—another scholarship boy who'd grown up on the back roads in a countryside blighted by machines, with an alcoholic father, a strong-willed mother, and a passion for nature and words.

During the day, when I wasn't attending lectures or scouring the library, I often stayed in our bright flat, straddling a boxy space heater to capture its waning warmth while I hammered away on a portable typewriter Ruth had used in college. Strapped into its case, this machine had been one of two pieces of luggage I'd carried with me in our stateroom as we sailed from America. I hammered away rather than pecked on the keys because the letters were badly worn. But they held up well enough for me to type several thousand pages of notes, thesis drafts, correspondence, book reviews, and stories.

On that battered machine, I also drafted memos and manifestos for a network of American students whom Ruth and I helped to organize in support of U.S. soldiers, stationed in England, who opposed the Vietnam War. We formed the group after meeting GIs at antiwar marches in Cambridge, Oxford, and London. Mainly from the Air Force, these men and women didn't wear their uniforms, yet they still risked their military careers by showing up at demonstrations, where British and American agents photographed the crowds. If an officer recognized their faces in the photos, they could be busted to lower ranks or shipped off to some dead-end post. In spite of the risks, they wanted to rally their fellow GIs against the war, and they asked if we could help by doing things the military rules forbade them to do—printing and circulating newsletters, renting halls, arranging speakers and films, handing out leaflets, picketing.

A number of American students, many of us Rhodes and Marshall Scholars, decided to help. We began meeting at a pub near one of the air bases, until the military police started hassling us, and then we gathered in our flat at St. Chad's. By the fall of 1968, neighbors reported seeing trench-coated men eavesdropping outside our windows during meetings. We began locking our doors while away from the flat, but this didn't prevent agents from coming in and pawing through our papers. Since we had no phone, there was nothing to tap; but others in the group heard telltale clicks on their lines. Those with cars were often tailed by black sedans when leaving our place. Several times I was followed on my bicycle, until I veered from the street into paths too narrow for a car.

None of the spying was disguised; it was done blatantly, to make sure we knew we were being watched. Since our meetings were open to anyone who wished to attend, we had no way of protecting ourselves from informers. No sooner would a GI emerge as a leader in the antiwar effort than he would disappear—transferred overnight, we later learned, to Alaska or Korea or Guam, his identity betrayed by a snitch who had infiltrated our group.

So there we were, a few students handpicked from America's universities to represent our country in Great Britain. Why did we provoke such scrutiny? We caused some minor embarrassment to the U.S. government—then headed by Lyndon Johnson, soon to be headed by Richard Nixon—by helping to publicize how many of our soldiers opposed the war in Vietnam. But we practiced nonviolence. We betrayed no military secrets. We acted openly, exercising the principles of free speech, democratic deliberation, and dissent, for which the war was supposedly being fought. We broke no laws, except the unwritten one that says opposition to a war declared by one's own government will not be tolerated.

Duly warned, a few students withdrew from our group. Most of us stayed, however. Still, I thought it prudent to find out what might happen if the British or American authorities decided I was too much of a nuisance. A lawyer in London who counseled dissidents told me that my draft board could revoke my student deferment and call me up for duty. Prospective employers, such as universities, could blacklist me. The State Department might cancel my passport, to keep me from going into exile. The Marshall Aid Commemoration Commission might withdraw my scholarship, whereupon I would lose my right to remain in England. Goons hired by military intelligence might snatch me from my bicycle some night and crack my skull. Or I might be charged with spreading disaffection among the troops, and be imprisoned for up to ten years.

"You're exaggerating," I said.

"I am citing case histories," said the lawyer.

"Ten years in prison for handing out a newsletter?"

"May I remind you, Britain guarantees neither freedom of speech nor freedom of the press."

On a long walk that evening, I explained the risks to Ruth and asked if she was willing to share them. She kept silent awhile, pondering, before saying yes.

The next morning I sent my letter to the draft board in Louisiana, telling them I would perform any public service they chose, would clean toilets in a hospital or sweep floors in a school, but on the grounds of conscience I would not serve in the armed forces so long as our nation was at war in Vietnam. The draft board responded by ordering me to report for a physical exam at a nearby air base, where our peace group often picketed.

There were dozens of ways to fail a physical—fasting, gorging, tanking up on caffeine, going without sleep, drinking various concoctions, sniffing glue, scarring one's wrists, feigning schizophrenia—but the same conscience that kept me from joining the war kept me from try-

ing any of those dodges. So I rode a bus to the air base on the ap-
pointed day and presented my unadulterated body to the doctor, who
noted only one defect—a joint in my left big toe shattered in a basketball injury, betrayed by a three-inch scar where a surgeon had sliced in
to clear the bony debris.

"Does that cause you much pain?" the doctor asked, bending the
toe.

"When it rains," I said, although in truth the foot ached much of
the time.

"Then why are you in this soggy country?" He gave a rowdy American laugh, which made me homesick.

When I showed my papers at the gate on the way out, the guard on
duty recognized me from the picket lines. "Do the ladies like those
whiskers?" he asked.

"My wife does," I answered, brushing knuckles along my jaw.

"I wish they'd let us grow beards."

"You'd look good in one."

As he handed back my papers, he jerked his chin at the spot across
the road where we usually stood with our placards. "Hey, listen. Don't
you guys give up."

Again I thought of the Arsenal, remembering the guard who'd challenged me at gunpoint while the Russians were deciding whether to
launch missiles at us from Cuba. "We won't quit," I promised.

22

THE AIR FORCE DOCTOR must have pronounced me fit, because within a week the draft board reclassified me 1-A, meaning they could put me in uniform any day. What about my conscientious objector application? I asked them. Denied, they said. So I appealed, and a date was set for a hearing in the summer of 1969, around the time America's astronauts were scheduled to land on the moon.

We sent the news to our parents, who wrote back demanding that we call home collect. I stood in a phone booth near our flat, watching boys in little cutaway tuxedos and top hats stream out of the King's College choir school while I tried to reassure my parents that I wasn't ruining my life by risking prison. My father, who'd built bombs during World War II, urged me to sign up for the Navy and apply for a job in electronics or computers. He said I'd score so well on the tests, the Navy wouldn't put me anywhere near a battlefield. I told him I wasn't going to serve the war machine.

Then Mama broke in. "War machine? Where did you get these radical ideas? From socialists in England? From books?"

"I got them from growing up in your house," I said. "I got them from reading the Bible and going to church."

"Don't just think about your principles. Think about your sweet wife."

"I think about her night and day," I said evenly, then rang off before I lost my temper.

Ruth took her turn in the phone booth, leaving the door ajar so I could hear her side of the conversation with her parents. Mainly she said, "No, he's not. That's not true. That's not fair." Within a minute, she was crying, and I looked away. Here was more trouble I had dragged her into, only this was a lot worse than bicycling through wind and sleet. I watched the choirboys come trooping back from wherever they'd gone in their tuxedos. Except for the top hats and tails, they were like little boys anywhere, horsing around, yelling. When I turned back, Ruth was saying goodbye with dry eyes.

In bed that night I asked Ruth, "What did your parents say? That you'd made a big mistake in marrying me?"

"They said they just want us to be happy."

"And are you happy?"

She snuggled against me. "I am when you are. When you're miserable, I'm miserable. Where you go, I will go. It's in the Bible. Book of Ruth."

"And where you go, I'll go. Book of Scott."

Just then, caressing her breast, I felt a hard knot under the skin. Ruth put her own fingers where mine were and drew in a sharp breath.

Next day a doctor confirmed our worry. The lump was most likely benign, he said, but it would have to be removed before we could know for sure. Thanks to the National Health Service, neither his examination nor the surgery would cost us anything, but Ruth would have to wait two months for the procedure. In the meantime, even a slim possibility of cancer in this precious woman loomed larger to me than the chance of my going to jail or my never finding a job in a university.

Before our letters announcing this latest worrisome news could reach our parents, stern letters arrived from both fathers, laying out reasons why I should serve my country by joining the armed forces. I wrote back to say that I *was* serving my country. Along with thousands of other young men, I was resisting a government that had betrayed our nation's highest ideals, a government that was slaughtering innocent people in our name. I wrote that the current administration in Washington, which I despised, shouldn't be confused with America, which I loved.

• • •

Ruth's surgery and my showdown with the draft board were both set for July. Our parents would gladly have paid my airfare to Lake Charles for the hearing, but I wasn't willing to ask them, so Ruth and I had to save every penny. No movies or plays, no restaurant meals, no trips out of town. I was just as glad to stay home, because I needed every spare minute, outside the hours devoted to research for my Ph.D., to make my case for refusing to fight. It was easy to call myself a conscientious objector but hard to explain the origins of conscience. Was it merely a product of my upbringing, as I'd told Mama on the phone? Was it a result of taking to heart the teachings of Jesus and the Hebrew prophets? Was it only cowardice in disguise? Or was conscience a spark of God's own light deep within me—whatever God might be?

The need to answer those questions bowed my head and set me praying, with a fervor I hadn't felt since childhood. As a boy I had hoped to woo favors from the Ruler of the universe, maybe stop Dad from drinking, make Mama happy, keep everyone I loved alive forever. Now I prayed for clear instruction. I wanted signposts showing me the path I should take, the way God marked the route to the Promised Land with a pillar of cloud by day and a pillar of fire by night. I wanted proof that the Creator loved life more than death. I wanted assurance that my sense of right and wrong was no mere private whim, but was rooted in the ground of being.

God did not oblige. No voice proclaimed the unambiguous message I longed to hear. Instead, I heard only the inner tumult of a feverish mind. So I took long, brooding rambles, which were another form of prayer. As in the most confusing times of my childhood, I craved contact with wildness, the original world, the one humans had not made. But in this long-settled town, wildness was hard to find. The fields were mowed for games of rugby or cricket. The trees were pruned. The flowers bloomed in gardens laid out in geometrical patterns. The river was hemmed in by stone walls.

Yet even on the placid river Cam, amidst punts jostling upstream and down, swallows cruised for insects. One day I happened to be watching as a swallow glided low over the water, dipped its bill, and took a sip on the fly. Overcome by the splendor of it, I bowed. I had witnessed such aerial drinking before, but until that instant, wrought up as I was about the war, I had never really *seen* it. As in boyhood, I disappeared into the seeing. I felt only the bird's thirst, its hunger, even a hint of its exuberant grace. And in that instant I realized whatever power brought such creatures into being must indeed love life more than death, and this was the power I wished to serve. Of course I knew that swallows live by devouring mosquitoes and midges, that life feeds on life, but I also realized that such killing was bounded by the limits of hunger and muscle. Swallows didn't invent machines to magnify their killing, didn't slaughter insects wholesale to enforce a change of ideology, didn't report body counts on the evening news.

This glimpse of careening beauty, there on the river Cam, confirmed me in my opposition to the war. I couldn't have justified by cool reasoning the way my heart moved. Certainly, I couldn't hope to persuade the draft board to see an argument for pacifism in the flight of a swallow.

So I sought advice from people I figured must be experts in pacifism. Over the course of a week, I talked with clergy in three churches where Ruth and I had worshiped off and on since moving to Cambridge. An Anglican priest asked me from above the white rim of his collar how I would have stopped Hitler, if I was opposed to war. I told him I had thought about Nazi Germany and the death camps and had decided I would have fought in World War II.

"Then you aren't a pacifist," he observed. "A pacifist won't go to war under any circumstances."

But circumstances make all the difference, I objected. America wasn't fighting Hitler in Vietnam. We were herding peasants into camps and burning their villages. Sometimes we didn't bother to remove the peasants but killed them outright before torching their homes.

"War is a dirty business," the priest conceded. "But if the government let every young man make up his own mind whether to fight, you'd soon have anarchy."

I asked him what he thought Jesus meant by saying "Blessed are the peacemakers, for they shall be called sons of God."

"His words could well apply to soldiers who make peace by waging war, as men of my generation did by fighting fascism."

I repeated my questions to the Methodist and Baptist ministers. What did Jesus mean when he said, "All those who live by the sword shall perish by the sword"? And how did that apply to napalm, Agent Orange, and nuclear weapons? Was Jesus serious when he said, "To him who strikes you on the cheek, offer the other also"? How about "Love your enemies, do good to those who hate you, bless those who curse you"?

"Ah," said the Methodist, "I suspect Jesus had in mind *personal* enemies, like a wife or a neighbor, not other nations."

As for the sixth commandment, "You shall not kill," the Baptist minister advised me this applied only in times of peace, not in times of war. "In war," he explained, "you may have to kill in order to prevent worse killing."

The more I talked with these servants of God, the less of a link I could see between the religion they professed and the movement of my conscience. To their credit, all three of them urged me to consult the Quakers, who took seriously the Bible's instructions about war and peace. "Maybe too seriously," the Anglican priest remarked.

One Sunday morning when Ruth stayed in bed with a cold, I bicycled across town to the Friends Meeting House. All I knew about Quakers, or thought I knew, was that they didn't use preachers and the men wore flat black hats. Nobody this morning wore such a hat, but the part about not using preachers proved to be true. I sat on one of the wooden benches and looked around at a sanctuary that was even plainer than the Brown chapel or the country churches I'd known as a boy, without altar or lectern, without stained glass in the windows, without so much as a cross on the bare walls. Since most of the forty or so other people on the benches had their eyes closed and their hands in their laps, I did the same. For a long while nobody spoke. The only sounds were the squeaking of floorboards as latecomers arrived and the shifting of bodies on the hard seats. The silence came to feel tangible, like a mist settling over all of us.

Then somebody stood up, and an old man's quavery voice told how recruiters had summoned George Fox to serve in Cromwell's army, back in the 1650s, when the Quakers were just beginning to gather in people's homes, and how Fox refused, saying that the spirit of Christ wouldn't allow him to take up weapons. I snuck a peek at the man who'd spoken, so I could go up to him after the meeting and ask whether George Fox had managed to persuade those recruiters.

We all sank back into silence. Then every few minutes another voice would break the stillness, each one adding some insight or memory or Bible verse having to do with making peace. As I listened, I felt a tingling along my spine, as if all these words were aimed at me.

Eventually there was a stirring in the room and I looked up to see everyone shaking hands. Before I could approach the man who'd spoken about George Fox, he approached me, extending a bony hand and giving his name as Harold Sims. From his great age and dignified bearing, I immediately thought of him as Mr. Sims. He was tall and thin, with a gaiety in his face I couldn't account for. He'd spotted me as a visitor, and I told him I was, and from my accent he guessed I was an American studying at the university, and I told him right again. Then he surprised me by asking, "What troubles you this morning?"

We talked for an hour over coffee, sitting on a bench in the meeting room, while the other worshipers milled about and gradually departed. Mr. Sims listened as I poured out my worries about Ruth, the draft, my studies, my prospects for work, my faltering faith.

"Faith in what?" he asked.

"In anything besides this," I said, rapping my knuckles on the wooden seat. "In some firm ground you can't measure with a ruler or a scale. Faith in something bigger and stronger and older than us and our appetites."

Since leaving home at seventeen, I hadn't spoken so openly with anyone except Ruth. Although I'd scarcely met this man, I trusted him.

He seemed tender and firm at the same time, sturdy in spite of his frail body, and joyful in spite of the world's miseries.

In response to my outpouring, Mr. Sims advised me to listen for God's voice in the silence—not just the silence of the meeting, but the silence at the heart of every moment. I told him I'd heard too many people call on God to justify segregation and greed and war. I didn't trust that name anymore.

"All the names are too small," he said. "That's why Friends often speak of the inner light, which isn't a name at all but a description of experience."

"Inner light," I repeated, thinking of the swallow sipping from the river.

"When it flares inside you, illuminating some dark place you've never glimpsed before, that's what Friends call an opening. Such an opening led George Fox to oppose war."

I asked if he knew what George Fox had told the recruiters when refusing to serve in Cromwell's army, and Mr. Sims quoted a line that I wrote down in my notebook: "I told them I lived in the virtue of that life and power that took away the occasion of all wars."

No light shines in Mother's silence. I wonder what keeps her alive, after she has lost memory and speech, after she has lost the use of her legs, control over her bladder, the ability to clean or dress or feed herself. Toughened by decades of dancing and hard work, her body simply will not quit.

Listing to one side in her wheelchair at a table in the dining hall, Mother doesn't see Ruth and me approaching because her eyes, though half open, are downcast. Nor does she hear me when I lean close and announce that we've come to wish her happy birthday. So I push a hank of white hair from her forehead and rub her shoulders. Still she doesn't respond, so I wrap my arms around her gingerly, press my cheek against hers, and repeat my name close to her ear. "It's Scott. Remember? Your rascally son?" Only then can she detect my presence through the veils that have fallen between her and the world, and she looses a throaty chuckle. I kiss her sunken cheek.

Today Mother completes her eighty-eighth year. I've just come from an afternoon of caring for Elizabeth, who will soon complete her sixteenth month. Feeding the baby is one of my delights. She eats avidly, lunging at the spoon. When the spoon is too slow, she grabs food in both hands and stuffs it into her mouth. I have to remind her to chew, with the seven new teeth that sparkle in her gums like gems. When I don't refill her dish fast enough, she waves her arm at what she wants and crows, "Dat! Dat!" Since birth, hunger has been her defining trait—first for Eva's milk and touch, then for Matt's voice, then for solid food and rain and music and play and every impression flowing into her.

In that eagerness, the baby takes after her great-grandmother, who until recently savored her senses more than anyone else I've known. Now Mother's hunger has abandoned her, leaving the husk of her body hunched in the wheelchair, like one of those cicada shells after the creature has flown. The aide trying to feed her must tickle her lip with a spoonful of food, then shovel it in quickly when Mother gapes. Although everything is pureed, as it was to begin with for Elizabeth, Mother struggles to swallow. Every bite, every sip of milk or juice, must be wheedled into her.

The aide is a woman of about fifty, the owner of uncommon patience, a booming laugh, and a swimming pool where her nine grandchildren gather on these hot August afternoons. She apologizes for Mother's loss of weight—twenty pounds in two months. This in spite of medicine aimed at enhancing appetite, puddings and shakes enriched with proteins, and heavy doses of vitamins.

"We get the food into her every way we know how," the aide says, "but we can't make her body use it. Mostly, it just passes through."

The aged pass through the rooms of this nursing home as well. Several have died since Mother moved here following hip surgery two months ago. When she arrived, a woman named Ruby was cruising up and down the hall in a wheelchair, sucking oxygen from a tank and pleading with everyone, "Help me, I'm dying!" On first hearing her, I rushed to fetch a nurse, who assured me that Ruby had been predicting her death around the clock for three or four years. Nonetheless, with good humor the nurse checked Ruby's oxygen, patted her hand, and pronounced everything in good order. No sooner did the nurse turn away than Ruby took up wailing again, "Help me, I'm dying!" And sure enough, within a week her prediction came true. No prediction is more certain to come true, sooner or later.

Mother eats no better for Ruth and me when we take over from the aide. If food touches her mouth before she sees it, she recoils as if from a snake. So I lift the spoon slowly, in clear view, again and again, but without any luck. I try every trick, and then Ruth does. Mother clamps her teeth shut. The teeth are her own rather than dentures, a fact she was vain about when still capable of vanity. Except for the cleaning crew, we're the last ones in the dining hall when Ruth and I give up, the meal scarcely touched.

We roll Mother outside, where we sit on either side of her under the shade of a gazebo, holding her dappled hands. Ruth reads aloud a sheaf of birthday cards. I brush against Mother's lips a spoonful of the vanilla ice cream we've brought as a token of festivity. At first she doesn't respond, but then her tongue tastes the cold sweetness and her mouth opens. I feed her three bites before the gate of her mouth firmly closes again.

"She still has a sweet tooth," Ruth says.

This craving for sugar may be the last of her appetites to go. She no longer looks at clouds, flowers, butterflies, or birds. We point and exclaim, but she won't raise her eyes. She no longer responds to photographs of her family. She won't look even at Ruth or me. I squat down until my face is directly in front of hers, but her gaze slants to one side, unfocused. Her eyelids keep sliding closed.

Ruth and I decide we should leave her in peace, birthday or no birthday. So we park her chair next to the aquarium just outside her room, where the nurses will collect her. I hug her again, kiss her, tell her I love her. She clears her throat but says nothing. Her arms jerk in her lap but do not lift. I push her limp hair back from her face, hold it a moment, let it fall. She doesn't look at me, or at anything. Ruth and I say our goodbyes.

Before we turn the corner of the hallway, I stop and glance back. From this distance, Mother seems like a doll who's lost her stuffing, slumped over, haggard, her eyes two dark slashes, her mouth a gash. She has always been feisty, tough, challenging anything that threatened her loved ones or curbed her will. Through the long ordeal of aging, she fought every inch of the way, insisting that doctors or exercise or her son ought to be able to pull her back to wholeness. But now she seems resigned to loss. If she knows anything, she knows there's no way back up the slope from oblivion. Painful as it was to ease her through those years when she fought her losses, it's even more painful now to see her give up. If we didn't trick her into eating, she would soon starve. Her will is broken.

Unless—it suddenly occurs to me—refusing to eat is her final spirited act. "What if starving is what she wants?" I say.

Ruth loops her arm through mine and leads me on beyond sight of Mother, considering before she speaks. "It may be," she answers.

"Eating is the last thing she controls. So isn't it cruel to spend every meal coaxing her to open her mouth?"

"It may be," Ruth says again. "We just can't know."

We must proceed by guesses for a woman who has lost her voice. And I'm guessing that the vibrant mother I've known my whole life wouldn't wish to be alive as she is now. She has no way of telling us what she wants, except by clamping shut those well-worn teeth.

Although Ruth's surgery was scheduled for a Sunday, the doctor put her in the hospital on the preceding Wednesday so medical students going their rounds could feel her breasts—the clinical term was *palpate*—and try to figure out what might be wrong. Ruth had given her permission, yet it made me uneasy to think of the woman I caressed becoming a mere specimen for strangers to study.

As recently as the summer before our wedding, I'd been unable to enter a hospital where one of our friends lay seriously ill. The sight of gurneys trundling by and the syrupy smells of antiseptic had made my head spin, as when I'd tried visiting Dad after his heart attack. Perhaps marriage had cured me of my ether nightmares, or I had simply outgrown them; for whatever reason, when I entered the Cambridge hospital I strode through the halls oblivious to everything except Ruth.

Visitors were allowed only between 7:00 and 9:00 p.m., so each evening I took flowers, chocolates, books of crossword puzzles, or newsmagazines to the hospital ward, where some twenty other women lay tucked under pale blue sheets. And each evening when I arrived, soon after the medical students had passed by on their rounds, I kissed Ruth so long and hard we both lost our breath. The students were sweet, she said, especially the men, who looked the other way as they touched her breasts, hardly ever probing deep enough to find the lump. Because this was a test for them, they sometimes asked her sly questions, to see if she would give away the secret. But she kept mum.

At 8:00 in the morning and again at noon, I stood on a spot we had agreed upon, under a NO PARKING sign across the street from the hospital. I waved up at the window of Ruth's ward, trying to hide my fear. I also tried to keep the fear out of my kiss when I visited her in the ward, but when I parted from her on Saturday night, shooed out by a nurse in a starched white hat, my face must have betrayed me, because Ruth said, "It will be all right, sweetheart," as if I were the one undergoing surgery the next day.

Unable to bear waiting in a smoke-filled lounge at the hospital with expectant fathers and peevish children, I returned that Sunday morning to the Quaker meeting, where the words offered in the silence had to do with famine in Asia, genocide in Africa, poverty in Central America, race riots in the United States. In a world brimful of suffering, was it selfish of me to ache with anxiety over one woman? Selfish or not, I could think of nothing else but Ruth. The stir at the end of meeting took me by surprise, for I had never settled into the silence.

Finding Mr. Sims, I returned an armful of books he'd loaned me to help in preparing my appeal to the draft board. With that curious mixture of dignity and gaiety, he showed me the spines of three more volumes he'd brought: Tolstoy's *On Civil Disobedience and Nonviolence*,

Gandhi's *Autobiography*, and Dr. King's *Letter from a Birmingham Jail*. "Would you care to read any of these?" he asked.

I accepted the books with thanks and tucked them into my satchel. Then I apologized for rushing off, explaining that my wife would be coming out of surgery any minute now.

"Oh, my," he asked with concern, "is she not well?"

"We'll find out soon."

Still breathing hard from bicycling across town and from rushing up three flights of stairs, I tried in vain to persuade the nurse on duty to let me enter Ruth's ward. The other patients might not be decent, she told me, and I replied that I had eyes for only one patient. Then I opened the door and barged in, figuring the nurse could call an orderly if she wanted to but I was going to see Ruth.

She lay asleep under the regulation pale blue sheet, her face smooth, her breathing shallow and slow. I reached under the sheet to hold her hand. I tried reading, but the words swam together, so I gave it up. The nurse who'd forbidden me to enter came round now and again to check the blood pressure gauge and heart monitor, giving me a scowl each time but saying nothing.

Ruth was just beginning to surface from the anesthetic, her legs stirring, her eyes fluttering, when the surgeon appeared. The lump was benign, he briskly assured us, a common type of cyst whose Latin name he gave, nothing to worry about. A white mask dangled beneath his chin, and for some reason I stared at this as I asked him to repeat what he'd said, which he did, more slowly this time, and I could feel Ruth's hand curling around to clutch mine.

During July, news stories about the upcoming moon shot crowded out stories about the war in Vietnam, while I armed myself for a grilling before the draft board with quotations from Jesus and the Buddha, Meister Eckhart and St. Francis, Tolstoy and Thoreau, Gandhi and Dr. King. On the wall above my typewriter I posted the line from George Fox—"I lived in the virtue of that life and power that took away the occasion of all wars." I pondered those words as I wrote answers to the questions I imagined coming from a panel of men who believed that the first duty of any red-blooded American male is to go overseas and kill strangers for his country. The question I thought about hardest was the only one they were sure to ask: "Do you solemnly swear, Mr. Sanders, that your objection to this war comes as a direct instruction from God?"

The truthful answer was that I had no inside word from the Creator. My convictions arose from observing and honoring the Creation. Why should I cherish my wife? Why should I tingle at the sound of dogs baying after a raccoon? Why should I marvel at a swallow sipping? Why should one moment shine forth with inner light while the surrounding moments remain dark and dim? I couldn't give a theological or a scientific argument for loathing war any more than I could explain my love for birds, trees, rivers, or the woman I married. I could only trust and obey the sympathy stirred in me by the creatures I met.

As it turned out, I was never given the chance to defend my conscience, because a few days before I was to fly back to Louisiana for my hearing, a letter arrived from the draft board reclassifying me, not as a conscientious objector but 4-F, a category for men who were blind or crazy or one-armed or otherwise unfit for military service. It was their way of dismissing me and my scruples. They would get someone else to fill my slot, someone who hadn't read a lot of books and consulted Quakers and written a thirty-page essay condemning the Vietnam War.

Instead of feeling relieved, I felt thwarted, as though I'd studied hard only to be expelled right before the final exam. I felt guilty knowing that the man they would send in my place had most likely had a rougher ride, with fewer years of schooling, maybe with darker skin, like one of those Cajuns I'd worked with at the Lake Charles factory. It didn't ease my guilt to remember that this other man was going into the army, and probably to Vietnam, not to save my neck or my principles but to help save face for a government bent on pursuing an immoral war. In refusing to fight in that war, I had learned to heed an authority higher than any government. I had come to understand conscience as a sympathetic vibration between my innermost fiber and the force that brings new creatures into being and lavishes so much beauty on the world.

Clouds parted long enough in the English skies to give us a view of the waxing crescent moon the night the American astronauts landed there. I had vowed not to watch the landing, for I understood the race to the moon as another battle in the Cold War, an excuse to build bigger rockets and more accurate guidance systems for delivering bombs. But Ruth wanted to go watch, and since I couldn't let her wander into the dark alone just a week after she'd come home from hospital, I walked with her down the road to a nearby residence hall, where twenty or thirty students in a lounge crowded around the flickering screen.

We found a spot on the floor close enough to see the grainy pictures and hear the crackling voices. The lunar module kicked up dust as it neared the chalky surface, then bumped at touchdown, and soon Neil Armstrong was announcing, "Houston, Tranquility Base here. The Eagle has landed." In spite of my misgivings I shivered with pleasure, for I had been dreaming of such a journey since first learning that the stars are other suns.

After touching down at 9:17 p.m. British time and before stepping onto the moon, the astronauts would need several hours to check their instruments. To fill the time, Mission Control broadcast images from earlier in the flight. One of them, taken from the lunar orbiter and showing the blue marble of Earth rising over the barren lip of the moon, made my eyes brim with tears. Another one, of the Saturn V lifting from the launchpad amidst a swirl of smoke and flame while voices from Houston shouted, "Go, baby, go!" made me queasy, for I knew how easily the same rocket could launch a warhead.

For the first time ever, the BBC would stay on the air all night, so Ruth and I decided to hang around long enough to see Armstrong and Buzz Aldrin walk on the moon. Eventually, most of the other students wandered off to bed. When a couch emptied, Ruth curled up on it and went to sleep. Adrenaline kept me awake, so I talked quietly with other die–hard moon gazers while studying the pictures beamed down from space. Shortly before 4:00 a.m., I kissed Ruth and she sat up to see Armstrong stamp the first human footprint into the lunar dust.

Cries of "Bravo!" and "Well done, lads!" from the lounge mixed with cheers from Mission Control on television.

"For a bunch of rebellious colonists," one of the students said to me in a stiff Oxbridge accent, "you Yanks are pretty clever."

I turned from the screen to the window, where I could see the un-televised moon sinking in the west. Maybe America had done something fine for a change. Maybe it was a hopeful sign that in the midst of a disgraceful war we could send ambassadors to the Sea of Tranquility. The moon seemed not diminished by this human intrusion, as many predicted it would be, but more alluring, for having called us across so many miles to meet her in the flesh.

23

WITHIN DAYS AFTER the astronauts returned safely from
the moon, our parents called us home across the ocean, saying
that two years was long enough to go without seeing our faces. The
ticket I'd bought for my draft board hearing, together with a ticket the
McClures bought for Ruth, carried us from London to New York,
with a stopover at Shannon airport in the west of Ireland, and from
New York to Indianapolis. We would stay six weeks, half the time with
each family.

In my eagerness to see loved ones, I didn't anticipate how much in
my homeland would trouble me. The trouble started during the layover
in Shannon, where the terminal overflowed with souvenirs priced in
dollars, leprechaun dolls and shamrock T-shirts and other trinkets that
nobody needed but that American travelers were snapping up left and
right. Ruth and I had often run into brash American tourists before,
had cringed at their loud voices, their insistence on speaking English regardless of the local language, their bellies bulging over the waistbands
of Bermuda shorts and polyester pants, their fists full of money. But
we'd never seen them in such concentration, nor so purely focused on
buying things, as in the Shannon airport.

Aboard the plane, a startling portion of the American passengers
were so fat they had to squeeze themselves into their seats. I tried with-
holding judgment about these swollen bodies, for I knew how my own
sister had fought obesity all her life, knew how cruel schoolchildren

could be toward plump classmates, knew how genes and glands could doom some people to put on weight. But what I saw on planes, in terminals, and in the smorgasbord where Mr. and Mrs. McClure took us for a meal after meeting us at the Indianapolis airport couldn't be accounted for simply by quirks of biology. The smorgasbord was advertised as "All You Can Eat," and many diners seemed to take this as a dare, returning time and again from the buffet with heaping plates. They ate as if they feared a coming famine, ate until they groaned. I lost my appetite watching them.

On our return to America, everything seemed bloated—not only waistlines but also cars, highways, billboards, office buildings, houses. The McClures' own house was modest by U.S. standards, but it seemed like a palace after our apartments in Cambridge. I didn't realize how thoroughly our time abroad had altered my view of what makes for a decent and becoming life. Without a car, telephone, television, refrigerator, or record player, without central heating or air-conditioning, without credit cards, without meat on the table more than once or twice a week, wearing clothes left over from college, Ruth and I had lived bountifully. Yet I sensed, in remarks dropped by Ruth's parents, that they feared their daughter had been dragged away into penury.

What I had in common with Earl and Dessa McClure was love for their daughter. Otherwise, we found little to talk about, since they didn't read books and I didn't follow sports, and religion and politics were taboo, especially my interest in the Quakers and my opposition to the war. The only time the Quakers arose in conversation, Ruth's mother observed, "They aren't Christian, are they?" I chose to ignore this challenge, as I ignored the most prominent photographs in the house, which were of Ruth's brother, Jim, in his army dress uniform. Then stationed in Alabama, where he belonged to a chemical, biological, and nuclear weapons team, Jim planned on a career in the military, and he was eager to rise in the ranks through service in Vietnam.

While Ruth caught up with her parents, I spent much time alone, reading for my dissertation or taking long walks. Block after block in every direction, I passed brick houses framed by tidy lawns, with roses blooming on trellises and late-model cars gleaming in the driveways. As a boy growing up in run-down farmhouses on buckled roads, I had longed to live in such a neighborhood, but now I found it oppressive. Everywhere the grass was fertilized and trimmed. The houses were variations on the same three or four patterns. The children all seemed to be indoors watching television, which I could see flickering through picture windows. The faces I glimpsed were all white, the voices I heard all midwestern, as if the residents, like their cars, had been turned out by the same few factories.

Returning on Sunday to the Methodist church where Ruth and I had been married two years earlier, I found the worshipers in the pews were likewise all white, and judging by their clothes they were all securely middle class. Nothing about my appearance or dress distinguished me from them; I realized how easy it would be for me to join this club and never look outside. On our wedding day, I had paid scant attention to anything but Ruth and my own racing heart. Now I noticed the exposed beams, rounded arches, white plastered ceiling, and paneled walls of the sanctuary, every detail faithfully imitating English churches from the era of Shakespeare. For the first time it struck me as odd how slavishly Americans mimicked the nation we had fought a revolution to escape. Were my own studies and travels in England merely another brand of mimicry?

The minister who spoke that morning was the one who had performed our wedding ceremony, a mild and generous man, and no doubt a convinced follower of Jesus. And yet he filled the hour without mentioning the war, assassinations, race riots, marches, or sit-ins, the millions of Americans living in poverty, or the homeless wanderers sleeping under bridges. He acknowledged no suffering at all except that of Jesus on the cross. Whatever meaning the service had for the other worshipers—all good and honest people, I felt sure—it had no meaning for me. Instead of opening us to the griefs of the world, these rituals enclosed us in a protective shell. Every song, every prayer, every line of the sermon assured us that we were loved by God, who required nothing from us except a belief in the saving power of Jesus, in exchange for which we would be granted prosperity in this life and pleasure in the life to come. I was relieved when the benediction sent us back outside to the open air.

Each Sunday of our visit, first in Indianapolis and then in Lake Charles, I sat through another service that left me cold. My parents' church in Lake Charles was Presbyterian, but the complexion and social class of the worshipers and the reassuring tone of the rituals hardly differed from those of the Methodist church, and except for the fancier clothes, neither differed much from the country churches that had roused such fervor in me during childhood. In these plush sanctuaries, I felt no hint of the awe that had set me searching the Bible and praying into the darkness for understanding. Christianity, at least as practiced by mild-mannered white Protestants in the heartland, didn't seem to have changed; I had changed. I could no longer embrace a religion that ignored the power pulsing through everything—the prostitute on the street corner, the civil rights marcher in jail, the starving child, the swallow, the river, the storm.

During our stay in Louisiana, Mama and I avoided quarreling about religion and what she called "those revolutionary students" by admiring the gardenias and salamanders in her backyard, by canning tomatoes, by going to art exhibits, and once only, by visiting Grandpa Solomon in the nursing home. Mama called it a rest home, as if he were merely tired rather than senile.

Mama was the one who deserved a rest. As far back as I could remember, she had always been on the go, fetching and doing for everybody, running Girl Scout troops and 4-H clubs, teaching art classes and Sunday school, looking after neighbors, nursing shut-ins, all this on top of cooking, cleaning, canning, sewing, gardening, and worrying for her family. She never sat down, and when she was in motion she ran at full speed. Dad wouldn't even try to keep up with her on a walk; he just waved her on to wherever she was headed and said he'd arrive by and by. When I still lived at home and she would take me to Cleveland or

Chicago or some other city for a look around, she'd run me ragged. She was a force of nature, curious about everything under the sun.

She turned fifty-three during our visit, while I was going on twenty-four, yet by the end of a day with her I could barely stand up and she was still going strong. It seemed the only thing that wore her out was looking after her father, who had recently moved to Lake Charles. Mama's brother and his wife up in Chicago had taken Grandpa Solomon into their house, and had cared for the tempestuous old man as long as they could bear it. But after a stroke put an end to his doctoring and swelled his bitterness into paranoia, they took away his revolver, took away his black bag, took away his Lincoln Continental with its grocery sack full of dollars in the trunk, and hauled him down to Louisiana, where he could torment Mama, Dad, and Glenn awhile. At first Mama made room for him in the house; but soon he began calling Glenn a thief and threatening him with a cane, whereupon Dad insisted on moving the old man into an apartment. Before long, Grandpa could no longer manage on his own in the apartment, even with almost daily help from Mama. So they moved him into a nursing home, a destination he feared more than death. Only tranquilizers kept him from raving continually. Although she was torn up by guilt, Mama herself wouldn't dream of taking tranquilizers, which were for crazy people, like those neurotic army wives back in the Arsenal.

On our visit to Grandpa Solomon, Mama had to point out where he lay curled in bed next to a window, for at first glance I'd seen only a twist of blankets. Although a short man, no taller than Mama, he had always been stout, and in his prime, when stopping with us in Tennessee and Ohio, he had radiated an uncanny strength, as if drawing on the ferocity of those ancient Assyrian warriors. His blunt fingers had delivered more than a thousand babies, cut out bullets, stitched skin, straightened broken bones, soothed patients thrashing in pain. Now he lay shriveled, beyond remedy by doctoring. Mama tried to rouse him by announcing that here was his grandson Scott. But it was clear from the filmy gaze he cast my way that he didn't recognize me.

I looked away, toward the light. On the windowsill, a row of pots bristled with thyme, oregano, basil, chives. The plants had made the move with him from Chicago, where he'd always grown his own spices, just as his mother had back in Persia. Now Mama tended them, pruning and watering, to preserve a living link to the man he'd once been.

"Tell Grandpa about your time in England," Mama urged.

I forced myself to look at the wizened man in the bed and rattled on about England, marriage, friends, and books until my voice petered out in the face of his vacant stare. I whispered to Mama, "Can he understand what I'm saying?"

"We can't tell, can we, Pappy?" she said loudly, running a hand over his forehead. Then to me she confided, "I keep thinking he's in there somewhere, behind all the drugs and craziness, hiding, like a dog that's been whipped."

Our visit was cut short by an outburst from a man in the neighboring bed, who began hollering "Help me! God in heaven, somebody help me!" Only *help* came out *hep*, reminding me of Dad, with his Mississippi accent, and the sudden image of my own father—or, even worse, my mother—lying broken in such a place choked me with sadness. I was grateful when Mama hustled us away.

In the car she said, "I'm ashamed he's there."

"Where else could he be?" I asked.

"In my house."

"Where he'd shout at Glenn and smack him with his cane and drive Dad to drink?"

Mama looked at me sharply then, for I had said a forbidden word. "Let's not talk about it anymore."

We didn't talk about it anymore, because we were a family more afraid of shame than of silence. We didn't talk about Glenn's angry adolescence or Sandra's string of miseries or our fear that Dad might find his way back to the bottle.

Dad and I avoided quarreling about the war by working in the woodshop and fishing in the bayous. So long as our hands were busy with tools, so long as we could study the grain in wood or the ripples on water, we enjoyed one another's company as much as ever.

The last week of our stay in Louisiana, Dad took a vacation so he and I could spend a few days floating on a cypress swamp. Because Glenn was already in school and Mama didn't trust him, at fifteen, to keep out of mischief, she stayed home, and Ruth chose to stay as well, having no taste for mucking about in the vicinity of alligators and cottonmouths.

Dad and I saw both in the bayou, cottonmouths sunning on logs or dangling from branches like oil-stained ropes, alligators winding among the trunks of cypresses and swamp tupelos. The trees were as wide at the base as the flying buttresses on English cathedrals, and their limbs were festooned with blooming orchids and the ashen tangles of Spanish moss. Snowy egrets took off and landed with a beating of wings like shaken bedsheets. Great blue herons and white ibises probed the shallows on their skinny legs. Dragonflies kept lighting on the bow of our aluminum boat, flexing their iridescent wings, then zipping away. Once we saw a fox and twice we saw bobcats on hummocks that rose above the swamp. We never saw a Louisiana black bear, although we might have, the place was wild enough. The water changed color with the movement of the sun, but mostly it was a faded khaki, like the old uniforms worn by the veterans whom Dad used to pick up hitchhiking after World War II.

The place reminded me that America was far bigger and finer than any gang of politicians or corporate executives. We had paved and pillaged much of the land, but much had so far escaped our machines, and this untamed country, like the bayou, innocent of hatred and greed, was reason enough to keep loving America. Our time on the bayou also reminded me of how much I loved my father, despite our differences over politics and religion. I could imagine he'd never drink again, never break Mama's heart or poison his own. We fished some, to give us an excuse for being there, but mainly we drifted. We didn't talk much; we never had. It wasn't Dad's way to speak of what was going on inside him, and when I was near him I fell silent as well.

Then, as we were hauling out the boat on our final day in the swamp, Dad looked around at the great bearded trees and said, "You ever wish you'd been born a couple hundred years ago?"

"I sure have."

"When the whole country was like this, the way God made it, before we'd fooled with it?"

"A lot of it's still like this."

"Only scraps. And even those won't last. Texaco's coming in here to drill in the next few months."

"Texaco? The ads say they're so careful they never disturb a single bird."

"They'll ruin it," he said with surprising vehemence. "They'll put in roads and spill oil and leave trash everywhere and then go ruin someplace else."

Now I looked around with new urgency at the mossy trees, the branches glimmering with orchids, the wading birds, the olive waters. I had taken such wild places for granted. America was large. Surely we could leave generous portions of it alone, to remind us of the original world, the one we had not made, the one we had not harnessed to our appetites. I thought of the smorgasbord, and I wondered if "All You Can Eat" had become the motto for our whole way of life.

On the flight back to London, I kept remembering a bumper sticker Ruth and I had seen everywhere during our visit home: AMERICA— LOVE IT OR LEAVE IT. Clearly aimed at young people like ourselves who questioned our government's actions, the slogan begged an enormous question: What is America? What in this land and its people invites our love? I could think of many reasons to love my country, from the bayous of Louisiana to the hardwood forests of Indiana, from the poems of Walt Whitman to the speeches of Dr. King. I could think of much to admire in my nation's history, from the Declaration of Independence to the Wilderness Act, from the building of free schools to the landing of men on the moon. Far from being protected by the mayhem in Vietnam, everything I treasured about America was endangered by that war.

Because I loved my country, I was more anxious than ever to complete a Ph.D. so I could return to America as a teacher and invest my life there. But first I had to write a dissertation. I spent the winter struggling to find something worth saying about the novels of D. H. Lawrence—or about any work of literature, for that matter. What was the point of translating into abstract language a vision of life that some talented writer had already rendered more vividly?

Some of Lawrence's views, especially about sexual politics and race, appalled me, but they were plain enough on the page, so I trusted readers to make up their own minds about what was repulsive and what was attractive in his work. What attracted me, aside from his bred-in-the-bone sympathy for people who worked with their hands, was his way of portraying the whole earth as alive, every pebble and grass blade, the desert tortoises and blue gentians, the lordly snakes and deep-rooted trees, the dirt itself, all glowing with a single holy fire, and our own two-legged kind shining along with the rest. Lawrence, too, had been a Bible-reading, hymn-singing boy, and he, too, had come to feel as an adult that churches had lost touch with the sacred, which flamed up everywhere, if only we had eyes to see. He gave me language for speaking about the first great truth I'd ever grasped.

I longed to write of this animating power directly, instead of at secondhand through commentary on someone else's books. If I hadn't set my heart on teaching at a university, if I hadn't felt responsible for supporting Ruth and our dreamed-of children, I might have quit graduate school and tried making my way as a writer, as Lawrence, Orwell, Faulkner, and some of my other literary heroes had done. I had already begun freelance editing and reviewing for British magazines, but the amount I earned from those jobs wouldn't have paid to keep our gas fire burning through the winter. I didn't see how to leave the safe academic path without risking Ruth's happiness and alarming our parents. Maybe I was more afraid of failing than of starving.

So I devoted my days to the dissertation, my evenings and weekends to antiwar work and conversations with friends about the state of the world. That left early mornings for my own writing. I rose before daylight, stole away from bed, put on a jacket and cap and a pair of knit gloves with the fingertips cut away, and then hunched over the type-writer at our kitchen table and tried capturing on paper the voices, faces, places, and events that had left the deepest impressions on me. The words hardly ever lived up to what I remembered or imagined, but every now and again they did, for a line or two, and those rare successes kept me trying.

I had trouble believing any sort of writing—dutiful dissertations or in-ept stories—mattered as the war in Southeast Asia spread from Vietnam to engulf Laos, Thailand, and Cambodia. By the spring of 1970, news-papers were estimating that half a million Cambodians, the vast major-ity of them civilians, had died under U.S. bombing. Every week hundreds of GIs were shipped back home in body bags. A few of them were boys I had known in school. Each one of those lives had been as precious to the person who lost it as mine was to me; each one was as cherished by family and friends.

On Easter Sunday, which fell that spring near the end of March, Ruth and I traveled to London for a peace rally sponsored by the Cam-paign for Nuclear Disarmament. Joining a crowd of some ten thousand, according to police estimates, or thirty thousand, according to the or-ganizers, we stood in a cold rain before the entrance of St. Paul's Cathe-dral as worshipers filed in for the midmorning service. Dressed in boots and jeans and mackintoshes, sheltering under umbrellas, holding up signs denouncing war, singing "We Shall Overcome" and "Down by the Riverside" and other standards made famous by the American civil rights movement, the peaceniks opened a path for the churchgoers, who were dressed as though for the opera, from polished shoes to fur stoles and top hats.

Organ music rolled from the open doorway of the cathedral, fol-lowed by a loudspeaker voice proclaiming "Christ is risen!" I felt an old hankering to go inside and wrap myself in that story. But I had come to believe that comfort was not the point of the story—the point was awe, a fearful wonder in the face of life's triumphant arising out of a dead universe. The point of the story was not to dress up in fancy clothes and gather at a set hour in a special building and recite creeds and hear promises of one's personal salvation but to seek the divine spirit in every place and every moment, in rags or rain. I didn't begrudge those worshipers their comfort, but I knew I belonged out here in this scruffy crowd, striving toward the peaceable kingdom. If Jesus rose from the grave as a sign that life is too precious ever to be extinguished, then wars and the weapons of war, especially nuclear weapons, are abominations. And if Jesus did not rise from the grave, if death had the last word, that was all the more reason to work for peace.

Just over a month after Easter, on the first of May, American troops invaded Cambodia. As soon as the news broke, students began protesting on campuses from Berkeley to Brown. On May 4, troops from the Ohio National Guard fired into a crowd of demonstrators at Kent State University, wounding nine and killing four. A photograph carried in the British papers showed one of the dead students lying facedown on pavement, while a young woman knelt beside him with her mouth agape and arms outstretched in woe. I knew that patch of concrete, knew the campus, for it was only a half hour's drive from the Arsenal and our farm on Esworthy Road. I had gone there often during my school years to watch plays, to compete in basketball tournaments or science fairs, and to visit Sandra while she was earning her degree in art. Less than two weeks after the shootings in Ohio, police opened fire on demonstrators at Jackson State in Mississippi, killing two students and wounding a dozen. I didn't know this black college, but I knew the town, for one of my aunts lived there, and Dad himself had grown up not far away. These killings felt personal; they stunned me. I knew that in my country protesters might be clubbed, teargassed, fire-hosed, tailed by the FBI, or set upon by police dogs, but I hadn't imagined they would be shot.

The *International Herald Tribune* began printing a daily box score showing the number of strikes, sit-ins, and other incidents on campuses across America. The most violent episode, after the shootings at Kent State and Jackson State, was the bombing of the Army Math Research Center at the University of Wisconsin in August of 1970. The explosion was produced by a combination of ammonium nitrate fertilizer and fuel oil. In Ohio, we had heated our farmhouse with such oil, and we had spread such fertilizer on our fields. I could have made the bomb myself, knowing only the chemistry I'd learned from launching model rockets. Dozens of buildings on the Madison campus were damaged, bystanders were injured, and one person—a physics graduate student who'd stayed late in the lab to work—died. I could have been that student, had I stuck with physics and accepted handouts from the Pentagon. Again the murder felt personal, only this time the violence had come from the protesters, four men about my age who later testified, in court, that they wanted to break the military's stranglehold on the university.

Following this turmoil in my homeland from across the ocean, I felt more and more guilty over enjoying the serenity of Cambridge. True, Ruth and I joined rallies against the war, circulated GI newspapers, exposed ourselves to surveillance and minor harassment from U.S. and British agents, but all of that seemed like child's play compared to what was happening back home.

Although my scholarship would have allowed us to stay in England for a fifth year, I pushed to complete the Ph.D. a year early, so I could begin teaching back in the States in the fall of 1971. Setting aside my qualms about the relevance of reading and writing books amidst so much violence, I hammered out page after page of the dissertation. I argued that Lawrence showed us the whole universe pulsing with a single magnificent energy; he regarded this energy as holy, and sex as our most direct way of participating in it; he celebrated wildness as an antidote to a corrupt civilization; he saw war as the inevitable outcome of the scramble for money; he honored the lives of laborers, peasants, indigenous people, and the poor, all of whom suffered under the industrial regime that was devouring the planet. That is to say, I described Lawrence as a writer who saw the world much as I had come to see it.

In late December of 1970, I carried a draft of the dissertation with me to the Modern Language Association meeting in New York City, where I interviewed for teaching jobs. By my return to Cambridge in

January, offers had arrived from several colleges, including ones in Pennsylvania, California, Illinois, and Ohio, along with Ruth's alma mater in Indiana. Ruth put in her bid for Indiana. Even apart from our romantic ties to Bloomington, I was inclined to agree, for Indiana University was a midwestern school set down in hardwood hill country, out there in the largely unstoried heartland, where a writer might do some useful work; it was a big school, with room for every sort of artist and thinker; and it was a public school, which meant I could work with students who'd grown up in circumstances not so different from those I'd known as a boy.

That night, however, the gaggle of friends who came over to celebrate my prospects for gainful employment urged me to accept one of the jobs near the coasts, in Philadelphia or Berkeley. The friend with whom I'd had the most intense literary conversations, an American scholar who'd chosen to make his career in England, asked me to name one writer of the first rank from the Midwest. When I listed Mark Twain, Ernest Hemingway, F. Scott Fitzgerald, Willa Cather, and T. S. Eliot, my friend pointed out that they had all *left* the Midwest, moving to New York or Paris or London or some other center of culture where people actually cared about books. The only writers of note from Indiana, he claimed, were Theodore Dreiser, who'd been drummed out of the state for being a socialist, and Kurt Vonnegut, Jr., who'd moved away and then made a practice of mocking the rubes back in his birthplace.

All evening I tried to think of a great writer who had stayed in Indiana or anywhere else in the Midwest, the way Thoreau had stayed in Massachusetts or Faulkner in Mississippi or O'Connor in Georgia, and I couldn't come up with a single one.

After the last of our guests had left, Ruth asked, "Did they change your mind, rhapsodizing about the coasts and name-brand schools?"

"Did they change yours?"

"No. I want to go home to Indiana."

In truth I was tempted by the name-brand schools, which were offering to fly me back to the States for campus visits. But Ruth had given up Harvard and her own graduate fellowship to join me in Cambridge; I couldn't ask her to give up Indiana to follow me someplace else. "Then that's where we'll go," I said.

"Oh," she cried, "think how handy it will be to have my parents nearby when our children come along."

We'd been talking for months about starting a family—or Ruth had been talking and I had been giving one reason after another to wait. Not until I finish my thesis, I said; not until I have a job lined up; not until we know when our health insurance will kick in. As of tonight I had run out of reasons for delay, except the deepest one, which was my unease over bringing a child into a world so full of suffering. Time and again Ruth had countered my worry by saying the world had always been a scary place. If couples had postponed having children until the world seemed safe, she insisted, the human race would have died out long ago. I knew she was right, and so tonight I didn't confess my fear. If she was ready to become a mother, I was ready to become a father.

"Where are these children coming from?" I asked.

"You don't know? Did you skip the juicy parts in Lawrence's novels?"

"I had my mind on higher things."

"Then I'll have to explain what you missed," she said, loosening the buttons on my shirt.

After making love, suffused with joy because we knew we were going home, knew where we'd be living, knew how we'd earn a paycheck, we lay under piles of covers in our chilly bedroom and listened to bells ringing midnight. Ruth's body next to mine seemed a miraculous gift, unearned, unaccountable. I could feel her breath gentling down like a river below a rapid. My own body was still synchronized with the New World, where it was too early for sleep. When Ruth drowsed off, I slid out of bed, pulled a quilt around my shoulders, and stood at the window, watching the bare trees gather moonlight, imagining inside my wife the spark of a child.

24

B Y T H E T I M E Cambridge broke out in daffodil gold that March, Ruth felt certain she was pregnant. On the first day warm enough for open windows, she went to see if the doctor agreed. To fill the nervous time until her return, I laid out on my desk the books and papers I needed to review for my thesis defense. Instead of reading, however, I went outside to pace around the yard, hunting for new blossoms, poking my head into the bomb shelter, listening for birds. When boys at the choir school behind our place began trilling their scales, their voices brought me to a standstill in the grass. How could their parents bear to part with them, sending them here to live away from home, so young? So young, and yet these boys had already been looked after, doted on, and guided, night and day, for years and years. It flashed on me that becoming a father was even more grave a responsibility than becoming a husband, for a wife entered marriage on her own two feet and could walk away if she chose, but a child was born helpless and raw.

Intent on the choirboys, I didn't hear Ruth steal up behind me until she slipped her arms around my waist and said, "Hello, Papa!"

I turned and lifted her, laughing, into the blessed air.

Our flat soon filled with exercise charts, vitamin supplements, sewing patterns for impossibly tiny clothes, knitting patterns for booties and caps, postcards from friends welcoming the news, and books on pregnancy. Ruth began her reading with *Baby and Child Care* by Dr. Benjamin Spock, whom we'd heard speak in Cambridge the previous fall, when he delivered a passionate speech against the Vietnam War. On leaving the hall after his talk, we found him waiting for a cab in the rain. So Ruth and I approached him and shared our umbrella. This was not an easy feat, for he was a big man, tall and broad, with a booming voice to match. After thanking us for the shelter, Dr. Spock asked if we had any children, and when we answered no, he said, "Well, if you ever do, you'll wonder how you filled your life before they came along. They're loads of work and loads of fun."

I wished we could huddle beneath that umbrella with Dr. Spock now, so we could say, Yes, yes, we're going to have a child! Ruth and I talked incessantly of the baby, which was due in November. We called the fetus Lee, to avoid saying "it," and to avoid fixing our hopes on either a boy or a girl. We would love whatever child arrived.

I much preferred dreaming about Lee to cramming for my thesis defense, which at Cambridge was called the *viva*, short for *viva voce*. In Latin the phrase means "with living voice," but it recalled for me the Italian and Spanish *viva!*—a cheer cast up for an honored person or a treasured gift. So I came to think of *viva* as a celebratory holler, like a baby's or a lover's joyous cry, meaning something like "Hooray!" The oral exam was a holdover from the Middle Ages, when the doctoral candidate had to prove his mettle by answering questions, in person, from the whole assembly of scholars. Now only two scholars put the questions, but neither examiner was the thesis director, whom one might count on to be friendly, and either one could force the candidate to rewrite the thesis, condemn the candidate to receive a master's degree instead of a doctorate, or fail the candidate outright. I knew graduate students who had suffered each of those fates. In spite of the high stakes, I couldn't focus on the *viva* for thinking about what lay beyond.

The defense was scheduled for the middle of April. Our lease would run out two weeks later, and we planned to begin in May a long European trip, a last fling before we settled down in Indiana. While Ruth pored over baby books, I pored over maps, laying out our itinerary. I might say "Florence," and she would answer dreamily, "No, that's too old-fashioned," and I would explain that I wasn't thinking of names for girls but of cities to revisit. Or she might remark, "We need to eat liver," and I would point out that *she* needed to eat liver, because she was the only one pregnant; then both of us would laugh.

The first week of April, Ruth began to bleed. She went to see the obstetrician, who told her she was in danger of having a miscarriage, for the fetus was not securely implanted in the womb. She must not travel, must not ride a bicycle, must not even walk more than necessary, must keep quiet at home.

"You mean, Lee—" I began.

"Don't," Ruth broke in. "The name makes it harder."

The news threw all our plans into disarray. We couldn't go on our European tour, yet we couldn't simply fly back to the States either, so we had to find a place to live here in Cambridge beginning the first of May. Ruth might have to remain in England at least through the birth in November, if she managed to carry the baby that long, while I would have to report for work in Indiana by August. In order to keep that job, or to secure one anywhere else, I had to pass my *viva* this coming week.

"We'll manage just fine," I kept assuring Ruth as she lay in bed or sat on the couch in her robe, staring at a book or a crossword puzzle, brooding.

To amuse her as well as feed her, I baked every sort of cookie and cake in my repertoire. She nibbled politely, but her mind was not on food. I quizzed her for recipes while I prepared elaborate suppers, which neither of us had the appetite to finish. I carried our few possessions, item by item, to the bedside or couch, where she could declare what should be packed, what kept out for use, and what given away. Since we would be sailing home to America, with lots of room for baggage, we decided to take our faithful old bicycles, so I oiled and tuned them. All of my books, except the few I should have been reviewing for the *viva*, I packed into plywood tea chests, which I'd found at an import shop in town. I cleaned the apartment and patched holes in the walls in preparation for ending our lease. I tried not to run errands unless a friend was there to keep Ruth company, because the few times I left her alone I returned to find her weeping.

• • •

Before dawn on the day of my exam, I woke to the sound of sobbing, like the hushed, liquid sound of water purling over rocks. "What is it?" I said, sitting up in a panic.

Ruth perched on the edge of the bed next to me, hands in her lap, staring at the black window. "I lost the baby," she said quietly.

"You lost—"

"It bled away."

"When?"

"I don't know. Two hours ago. Maybe three."

"Why didn't you wake me?"

"You needed your sleep before the defense."

"Oh, sweetheart," I said, drawing her to me.

"I wouldn't have wakened you now, but the bleeding won't stop."

I rose then and threw on my clothes, ran down the street to a phone booth, and called the maternity hospital. Soon the ambulance arrived with lights flashing. The commotion of orderlies carrying Ruth outside on a gurney was enough to rouse our neighbors in St. Chad's. Windows opened and voices called out questions, and I kept saying we'd lost the baby, lost the baby, as if we could have misplaced something so precious. No, the attendant insisted, regulations wouldn't allow anyone but the patient to ride in the back of the ambulance. I told him to hell with regulations and climbed in and knelt down beside Ruth. The attendant shrugged and climbed in after me. He was an Irishman of about my father's age and with the same sandy hair, and on the way he told us how happy he was to be going to the maternity hospital, where his own daughter had given birth to a bonny girl three nights before, and don't you know he'd been rattling about in this ambulance during visiting hours ever since, without a chance to see the lass or the first grandchild, and now here he was riding straight to them, praise God.

I told him we'd rather not hear about his granddaughter just now, but Ruth said, "No, please, keep talking. You should be happy. Someone needs to be happy."

Placed in a ward with five other women who'd just given birth, their babies mewling and wriggling at their sides, Ruth soon had her fill of others' happiness. After examining her, the doctor said she would be able to go home that night. I stayed with her until noon, when I needed to leave for the exam.

"Go on," she said. "I'm not afraid anymore."

"Don't you worry. We'll have babies."

Instead of answering, she rolled on her side and watched a mother in the next bed suckling a newborn. When I hesitated, Ruth said, "Go on. Don't throw away all your work."

Riding a bus to the university, I kept looking at the schoolchildren who were on their way home for lunch, their uniforms rumpled or grass-stained, their faces clear, eyes bright, mouths rounded by laughter as they teased and shoved one another. Their twitchy bodies and screechy voices proclaimed *Viva!*

The examiners, two scholars who'd written notable studies of Lawrence, began by asking stern questions, implying that I had taken the wrong approach in my dissertation. Shaken by one loss, I wasn't about to suffer another if I could help it, so I fought back, drawing on everything I'd learned or thought or imagined to argue my case. Evidently the examiners had meant only to provoke me, in the classic British way, to see how I would respond under pressure, for they soon relented. By the end of two hours, their cordial manner and congratulatory handshakes revealed, though they couldn't officially tell me so, that I had passed.

Back from the hospital that evening, Ruth sat propped in bed while waves of friends arrived bearing flowers, casseroles, chocolates, and wine. They hugged her first and bemoaned the miscarriage, then hugged me and cheered the completion of my degree, their faces betraying the same tussle of emotions that bewildered Ruth and me. For a long while, nobody knew what tone to set. Then a woman with whom Ruth had taught at the school for handicapped children said to her, "The baby's in heaven."

"There wasn't a baby," Ruth said firmly. "There was a mass of cells, loosely attached and starved for nutrients. The miscarriage was nature's way of avoiding a mistake."

The eight or ten friends encircling the bed relaxed then, and so did I. A platter of cake and a carafe of wine began to pass from hand to hand. Here and there conversations bubbled up into laughter. For the first time since she'd wakened me before dawn, I saw Ruth smile. She wasn't merely trying to cheer us up; she was accepting what the study of biology had taught her. Life is precarious and improbable, a flame in matter, easily snuffed out. Nature shows no regard for the individual spark, in this creature or that, but only for the spreading of the fire, like an ember passed from cell to cell. I still didn't know how to feel at the end of this bewildering day, except to give thanks for feeling itself, for breath, for being able to say *Viva!* Here I am, for this brief moment, alongside my wife and friends, alongside daffodils and robins and pines. What could any of us ever say that was more astonishing?

When Elizabeth spies me coming up the steps at noon for my weekly babysitting stint, she lights up with a grin, wags her arms excitedly, and cries out "Dee! Dee!"—as much of the name "Granddaddy" as she can manage. For the next four or five hours, unless she has skipped her morning nap, she climbs all over me, over the furniture, up onto the cats' carpeted tower, up and down stairs. She dances, babbles, sings, smacks a tambourine or drum, digs through her toys, works wooden puzzles, flips through books, crawls in and out of her cardboard-box playhouse, pausing only to eat and drink. The drinking she does on the fly, sucking from a water bottle. For meals I buckle her into the high chair, but even there, as she gobbles everything I put before her, she's never still, feet thumping, hands waving, mouth going a mile a minute.

The language that comes out of her, at a year and a half, still bears little resemblance to English. Yet between the vivid expressions on her face and the signs she makes with her hands, I'm rarely in doubt about what she's trying to say. Lately, some of what she says has become devious, as full of guile as the serpent's sales pitch to Eve in the garden.

Today, for example, I roll a toy car from my feet up onto my head, leaving it balanced there, and I ask her, "Now where *is* that purple car?" Elizabeth gives me a serious look, then points into the next room, saying, "Dere!" When I rise to go look for it, the car tumbles to the floor and she squeals with laughter, pointing at my bare scalp. We repeat the skit five or six times, and each time she gives me false directions.

No longer the innocent newborn, Elizabeth can tease, joke, and play make-believe because a gap has opened between what she knows to be so and what she pretends or imagines. More than any other quality, this gap is what distinguishes our species, enabling us to deceive one another and ourselves, but also enabling us to see beyond the way things happen to be, to envision alternatives, to make art and science and revolution, to invent things new under the sun.

Today, as it happens, Elizabeth has skipped her morning nap, so eventually she winds down, and after a few songs she allows me to put her in the crib. Then she sleeps with an utter abandon I can remember from my own early years, a sleep unruffled by plans or frets. When she awakes and calls out to be rescued from the crib, I find her standing at the rail, flexing her legs like a ballerina at the barre. I lift her from the warm bed, and she cuddles against me for a few minutes in a drowsy limbo. Then she lies still just long enough for me to change her diaper before she squirms to get down. I set her on the bathroom floor and she dashes away. In the time it takes me to put the wet diaper in the hamper, she scuttles into her parents' bedroom, pulls the phone off the hook, and begins punching numbers, as she has seen grownups do.

At the playground in the park, she clambers up ladders and down slides, pushes the merry-go-round, scoots in and out of swings, monkeys around the climbing frame. She halts her whirl of activity only to watch other children or to gape at the big boys who leap and shout on the basketball court, staring at them as if memorizing their moves; then off she goes again. I follow her from slide to monkey bars to swing, like a circus clown roaming beneath the high-wire queen, ready to catch her if she falls.

Unlike Elizabeth, I've not had a nap, so after chasing her awhile I suggest we mosey downtown to the library. She consents to ride in the stroller so long as we keep moving. No stops to chat with neighbors. As we roll, she cranes around to look at everything. She asks for graham crackers, for water, for a scarlet maple leaf. We collect stones from a

driveway and she examines them as if they were jewels. Despite the
ruckus she's making, she notices every sound, touching a finger to her
ear and spinning around to make sure I've heard the motorcycle or siren
or bird. Time and again as we near the library, she rears back in her
stroller hard enough to lift the front wheels off the sidewalk, tossing her
head until the blond curls fly.

Seeing one of these lurches, a young woman calls from the doorway
of a shop, "Yahoo! Ride that bronco, cowgirl!"

The only grown person I've ever known with gusto rivaling that of
Elizabeth at eighteen months was Mother in her prime. After the miscarriage, Ruth and I resurrected plans for our ten-week tour of the
Continent, which included a month of traveling with Mother. She met
us in Paris and left us in Rome. In between, she walked us into the pave-
ments of Heidelberg, Nuremberg, Munich, Venice, and Florence. She
wanted to see everything. She wanted to taste and touch and smell everything. No marathon of museums, markets, gardens, fairs, churches,
glassblowing studios, antiques shops, gondola rides, or ruins could wear
her out. She stayed without complaint in the cheap hotels that were all
Ruth and I could afford, washing her clothes and taking spit baths with
cold water in sinks, smuggling food into our room past hawkeyed
concierges who fumed because we wouldn't dine in their salons.
Mother ate as we did, making meals from a loaf of bread, a slab of
cheese, a handful of strawberries or plums.

In the evenings, when Ruth and I sank into a dazed stupor, overloaded with impressions, Mother goaded us back outside to see what
was happening in the piazza. In Italy, what was happening in the piazza
often boiled down to a bevy of women parading past a gallery of men,
the men gazing lecherously and calling out their appraisals, the women
feigning nonchalance but never ceasing to parade.

"It's disgusting," Mother declared. "It's like a livestock auction!"

Her disgust didn't keep her from dragging us out to watch the spec-
tacle night after night, on the chance that something more uplifting
might occur. Nor did her wariness of wine keep her from sampling the

bottle we refilled every few nights from the nearest and cheapest cantina. Usually she stopped at half a glass, but in Florence, after a rapturous day of Michelangelos, Leonardos, Raphaels, and Cellinis, she allowed herself a full glass, and with gay eyes she proposed a toast: "To Daddy! May he never touch a drop of this!"

In Rome, she worried aloud that the Colosseum would soon fall down if the authorities didn't take better care of it. To demonstrate the danger, she pried loose a small chunk of stone with her fingers. Rather than waste such a relic, she placed the stone in her tote bag, where it joined the bits of pottery and glass and tile she kept picking up from the ground at all the old Roman sites. Nothing I said about rules or propriety could discourage her. When she returned home, she was going to have Dad build her a fountain for the backyard out of concrete, in which she would embed these fragments of the Old World as mementos of our trip.

When I escorted her to the Rome airport, I had to keep switching the tote bag from one hand to the other to ease the ache in my arm. Aside from the Roman shards, it held onyx eggs, glass birds, plaster angels, porcelain clowns, silver spoons, a clutch of art books, and sundry other items she referred to as "my pretties." As I watched her board the plane, I felt relieved that Ruth and I would now be able to slow down to our own pace, and I felt regret that I might never again spend so much time so close to my mother's whirlwind energy.

I try to keep such scenes in mind when I visit Mother in the nursing home, lest the shriveled woman I see now efface entirely the dynamic woman she used to be. Today I'm waiting outside her room when two aides, having lifted her out of bed into her wheelchair, push her into the hall. On seeing me, Mother breaks into a radiant smile. "My darling!" she cries. "Oh, my darling, my darling!"

I'm startled. These are the first comprehensible words I've heard from her in weeks.

"You've made her day," says one of the aides as she strips off the latex gloves.

Law and common sense dictate the use of these gloves, yet they chill me, as if age had rendered Mother untouchable. To compensate, I stroke her cheeks, hold her hands, rub her shoulders, brush her lank white hair. I long to lift her out of the metal chair and cradle her against me, as I do baby Elizabeth. But I dare not move her, for fear one of those brittle bones might snap.

After that burst of recognition, Mother lapses into silence, eyes lowered, lips drawn into a grim line. I want to do something for her, yet there's little I can do. Even my attempts at brushing her hair leave it looking bedraggled. I ask if she is cold, if she hurts anywhere. Nothing, nothing. I ask three times if she is thirsty, and after the third time she appears to dip her chin ever so slightly. Maybe she's only trembling or maybe she's saying yes. She can no longer suck from a straw, so I try giving her a drink from a cup, but she leans so far to one side that water dribbles from the corner of her mouth. When I try tugging her upright, she whimpers, so I gently let her back down.

I would like to imagine that Mother has wandered into a twilit landscape, all blurred shapes and shadows, the sounds muffled by mist. But she hasn't wandered anywhere; she has been dragged, cell by cell, nerve by nerve, and the place where she is trapped may be shadowed, yet it is shot through by flashes of pain. Every now and again the pain shakes her body and squeezes a cry through her clenched teeth. If I made her happy for an instant when I first arrived, for the rest of my hour-long visit I can rouse no other response from her, not a sound, not a glance, not so much as a lifted hand. It's as though the sight of me sent a charge through her brain, enough to pierce the fog for a moment—but only for a moment. If I were to return every day, two times, three times a day, would each arrival give her that fleeting joy? And if I cleared out my days so as to make such visits possible—no more afternoons with Elizabeth, no more evening walks with Ruth—how often could I meet this gaunt face without wearing a callus on my heart?

Our final gift from the British people, by way of the Marshall Scholarship, was a pair of tickets aboard the *France*, which sailed from Liverpool to New York in late July 1971. Early on the fourth morning at sea, Ruth and I stood near the bow to keep watch for land. When at last we saw the towers of Manhattan, the bold bridges, and Lady Liberty holding her torch aloft, I felt not the unmixed surge of joy I had felt four years earlier on spying Land's End but rather a compound of yearning and dread.

After we docked, Ruth was eager to go ashore, but I made excuses to delay, for I was reluctant to commit myself once more to this magnificent and maddening country. I still loved the land itself, and I admired much of what humans had accomplished here. But during my time abroad I had come to see how sorely we had abused the land and its creatures, from butchering bison to poisoning rivers. I had come to view with dismay the violent strain in our history, from the enslavement of Africans through the slaughter of Indians to the napalming of Vietnamese. And I had come to lament the arrogance and greed that were too often the aspects of America most visible to the rest of the world. Estranged from so much in my homeland, I wondered if I would be able to make a life here without constantly feeling vexed.

When at last we stepped ashore, Ruth breezed through the passport check without a hitch, but I was held up by an official who'd evidently found my name on his list of suspicious characters, for he took me aside into a small room and examined my papers with care. He asked me the reasons for every trip inscribed in the green pages of my passport, especially those to Prague and East Berlin. What business did you have in those Communist cities? Only tourism, I replied. Did you meet with anyone during your stay? Did you bring back any literature? Are you in contact with anyone there? No, no, and no.

Eventually I was allowed to rejoin Ruth and proceed to customs, where another gruff officer quizzed us about our baggage. He began by asking why we had shipped across the ocean two battered old bicycles. Because we were fond of them, I told him, because they had carried us on many journeys, because we planned to use them instead of a car for getting around in our new hometown. Our preferring bicycles to cars seemed to renew his suspicion, for then he asked whether anything was hidden inside the frames. Any drugs, for example? No, I assured him.

Laying his hand on one of our plywood tea chests, the officer demanded, "What's in this crate?"

"Books," I answered.

"And this one?"

"More books."

"All of them?"

"All of them."

"Why so many books, Mr. Sanders? Do you sell them?"

"No, I read them."

When at length these guardians of America's shores let us enter and we pushed our laden cart toward the street, Ruth asked, "What was that all about?"

"Most likely a greeting from the FBI, reminding me they've got my name in their files."

"Just for protesting the war?"

"For helping GIs protest the war. For threatening the military machine by encouraging soldiers to think before they follow orders."

We had planned for Ruth to stay at the curbside with our baggage while I went off to rent a truck, but after a look at the seedy neighborhood near the dock, she was afraid to stay alone, and I didn't blame her. So we chained our bikes together and left the trunks and tea chests on the cart, hoping they would be there when we came back. Then we picked up our suitcases and walked several blocks past huddled figures slumped in doorways or lying in tattered heaps near subway grates, through the smell of urine, vomit, wine, and unwashed bodies, until we came to the address we'd been seeking.

A steel screen covered the window of the rental office, but even with that precaution the glass had been cracked and now it was held together by a silvery length of duct tape. Inside, the clerk dealt with us grudgingly from a booth protected by thick bars, while a Doberman paced behind him, its tongue hanging out. You gotta be twenty-five to rent, the clerk told me. I answered that I was twenty-five. He said I didn't look it. So I showed him my passport, which he held up to the light and studied skeptically. And how old is the lady? he wanted to know. Twenty-four, I said, but she wouldn't drive. Then he demanded to see the credit card we planned to use in renting the truck, and I explained that we didn't own any credit cards and would be paying in cash, and this set him grumbling about the risk, the nuisance, the crap he had to put up with. As he raised his voice, the Doberman stopped pacing and stared at me through the bars, lips pulled back, teeth gleaming. I would have walked out then if I had known anyplace else to go. So I stood there, and finally the clerk filled out the papers and handed me the keys. When I asked him the best way of leaving the city headed west, he grunted and said there wasn't any good way of leaving the city headed anywhere.

I drove our panel truck warily past the slumped figures to the dock, where we found two men in ragged clothes prying at our tea chests with sticks. I parked by the curb and leapt out and ran at them, shouting, and they scurried away. Although the trunks and chests and bicycles had been moved about, nothing appeared to be missing. Yet when Ruth and I had loaded our possessions into the back of the truck, they formed such a small pile I could hardly believe we had accumulated so little in four years of marriage.

After several wrong turns and hours of dense traffic, we finally reached a clear stretch of highway in Pennsylvania and I let out a great breath. "Land of the free and home of the brave," I muttered.

"Things will get better," Ruth said.

"I keep wondering if we should have stayed in England."

"We belong here," Ruth insisted. "We're going home."

Nothing I had seen since the *France* glided into port that morning had looked or felt like home. But as we drove west, we skirted small towns bristling with steeples, we passed well-kept farms and new-mown hayfields and shaggy woods, we snaked along beside big rivers and crossed the Allegheny Mountains and rolled down onto the glacial plain in Ohio, and mile by mile I felt a growing sense of recognition, as if I had come back into the presence of long-missed kin, as if I were being lifted up and embraced.

25

AMONG THE STUDENTS who filled my classes at Indiana University that fall of 1971, a few were disillusioned vets recently back from Vietnam, a few had burned their draft cards, a few had helped occupy the administration building on campus or tussled with police or smarted from tear gas, and a fair number had decided that all whites or all males or all teachers or everyone over the age of thirty was an oppressor. At twenty-five, I was suspect on all grounds except age. And even that qualification was temporary, as the clock ticked on.

I couldn't undo my pale skin or male sex, but I could try to shrug off the teacher's mantle of authority. I didn't feel like much of an authority, never having taught before, at Cambridge or anywhere else. Instead of wearing a coat and tie, I dressed in the same discount-store shirts and trousers I'd worn in England. Instead of sitting behind the desk in our classroom, I sat in a chair alongside the students, pretending to be just another voice in the circle. Instead of lecturing, I asked questions. But the students weren't fooled. They knew I would assign the grades. They knew I had drawn up the syllabus and picked out the books. They knew I had chosen to make the reading and writing of literature my life's work. Besides, if I didn't possess any knowledge worth delivering to them, why was I collecting a salary while they paid tuition?

Like it or not, I had to admit I wasn't just another voice in the classroom. I was now an "assistant professor," according to the tag on my office door, which meant I ought to have something worth professing, some insights and skills I believed in strongly enough to shape my life by them and to share them with others. No matter what clothes I wore, no matter where I sat, I was no longer merely cultivating my own mind. In becoming a teacher, I had taken on a responsibility for nurturing other minds. This meant I needed to understand my students, to learn what they'd gone through, where they hoped to go. All along, the study of literature had been preparing me to do just this, to imagine and care about lives other than my own.

My students, by contrast, weren't obliged to understand or nurture me. In this respect, the teacher's role was like that of a parent who helps a child to flourish, while the child is slow to recognize the parent's needs. I began to puzzle about my father and mother only when their fights over booze and money broke into my blithe self-concern. During my first months as a teacher, I thought back over my own teachers, those outside as well as those inside of school, and I realized how eagerly I had received all they had to give, and how rarely I had considered the cost of their giving. I had felt respect for nearly all of them; I had loved a few. But I had taken their generosity for granted, as if it were the quickening sunshine or nourishing rain.

In the evenings that fall, I wrote letters to all of my former teachers whose addresses I could track down, belatedly thanking them for their gifts. I also wrote letters of gratitude to my parents, saying carefully on paper what I could only say awkwardly on the phone. And I wrote letters to my literary and peacemaking friends from graduate school, trying to keep alight the flame of our conversations. Those letters, along with comments on student manuscripts and hasty entries in my journal, were the only writing I found time to do in my first year as a so-called professor. Figuring out what and how to profess, striving to become a good teacher, absorbed nearly all my waking hours.

What little energy I had left over I spent helping Ruth fix up our apartment, which occupied the second floor of a house owned by the university. We scavenged cast-off furniture from her parents' basement in

Indianapolis and from yard sales in Bloomington. We hung curtains and prints. I made bookshelves and picture frames, thinking of my father amidst the fragrance of freshly cut pine. I mended broken tables, chairs, and lamps retrieved from the Dumpster of the fraternity house behind our place, thinking of my mother's eye for bargains. Although we lay down at night bone weary, Ruth and I often woke to raucous music and drunken shouts from the fraternity out back or to the wail of sirens racing by on the crosstown street out front.

Ruth's mother had rented the apartment for us before we left England so we wouldn't have to hunt for a place after we arrived. Mrs. McClure evidently hadn't considered our need for quiet, but she'd made sure the location was within walking distance of the university and within bicycling distance of libraries and stores, since we stubbornly refused to buy a car. She also made sure the apartment had two large bedrooms. "Enough space for a study," I remarked when we stopped through Indianapolis. "Enough space for a baby," she replied.

After four years of living abroad, Ruth had moved away from her parents' views on religion, the role of women in society, the respect due men in suits, and the virtues of conspicuous consumption. She had rebelled against their midwestern, Protestant, Republican verities on matters large and small, from the way she voted to the way she wore her hair. But on the subject of babies, Ruth shared her mother's enthusiasm. She thought it was high time we tried again to start a family. We had a second bedroom. We had health insurance. We had a salary coming in from an enterprise that wasn't likely to go out of business or to ship my job overseas. As if those weren't reasons enough, we discovered in the attic of our house a walnut cradle, left there by some previous occupants, and that clinched the decision.

To the usual pleasures of our lovemaking was added once again the tingle of expectation, as when we'd first set our hearts on conceiving a baby in England. On my part, at least, there was also added a tinge of anxiety. I thought not only of the miscarriage, with its dashing of hopes, but of the torment my parents had suffered over my stance on the Vietnam War, over Sandra's persistent gloom, and especially over my brother Glenn's rebellion this past year.

At sixteen and seventeen, Glenn had defied our parents on school-work, smoking, curfews, cars, and girls, landing in a series of troubles from which they had patiently rescued him, only to have him run away from home the month of our return to America. They thought at first he had hitchhiked to California, that nirvana of free love, as he had been threatening to do. After weeks of worry, they learned he had rented a room in a college town not far from Oklahoma City, where they had recently moved at the behest of my father's company. Glenn returned to our parents' house only long enough to grab his things, which he hauled away without explanation or apology. How he would feed or clothe himself or pay his rent, they couldn't say, nor did they know how to contact him.

Mother broke down weeping before she could relay this news to me over the phone, so Dad told the story in a pinched voice that I'd heard from him only two or three times before, when someone he loved had died. Even if I had known how to reach Glenn, I wouldn't have known what to say. I had missed his growing up. When I left home for college, he was nine, a curious and playful kid, and now he was a teenager on the verge of college himself, filled with a mystifying contempt for our mother and father, who had given him, so far as I knew, the same loving care they had given Sandra and me.

As I tried to envision becoming a father myself, I kept thinking of the heartache my parents were feeling. When I confessed my disquiet to Ruth, she responded in her unflappable way, by saying that no doubt heartache would be part of the mix, along with exaltation and joy.

"Glenn will grow out of it," she predicted.

"But at what cost to Mom and Dad?"

"They're tougher than you think."

Hoping she was right, I cleaned up the walnut cradle, reglued the spindles, and pasted felt on the bottoms of the rockers to keep them from scratching the hardwood floor. Ruth fitted the cradle with a mattress and bumper pads, all covered in a fabric the watery blue of robins' eggs.

•   •   •

The following spring, in March of 1972, the songs of robins began pouring in through our open windows well before dawn, a few inquisitive notes at first, as if the birds were tuning up, and then a lilting, full-throated chorus that continued until bright day. I thrilled to hear it, as I would thrill later on, in summer, to the susurrus of crickets and cicadas, the rumble and flash of thunderstorms, and the glimmer of fireflies, sights and sounds I knew in my bones but had sorely missed during our time abroad.

Going outside to fetch the newspaper one morning, I found the empty halves of a robin's egg on the grass beneath a spruce tree in the yard of our house. I stared up into the branches, looking for a nest, but could hear only the persistent chirp of a begging chick. I gathered the pieces of shell to show Ruth, who'd grown discouraged as her menstrual cycle rolled on without interruption, month after month, through winter and into spring. Cupping the shell in her palm, she mused, "Just think, all that singing comes out of such a small container."

The morning's newspaper announced that President Nixon, claiming the North Vietnamese weren't negotiating in good faith, had pulled the U.S. delegation out of the Paris peace talks. A week later the North Vietnamese sent 200,000 troops across the border into South Vietnam, in the largest offensive of the war. The United States responded with air and naval bombardment, aimed not only at enemy troops but at North Vietnamese harbors and cities, from Haiphong to Hanoi, including carpet bombing by B-52s. Protests immediately broke out on streets and campuses across the nation and in countries around the world. Unease crept even into the halls of Congress. A few politicians had spoken out against the war from the beginning, but most had quietly or vociferously gone along, first with Lyndon Johnson's administration and then with Richard Nixon's, voting ever more funds, passing patriotic resolutions, as if, once bodies began arriving home in bags, to question the purpose of this mayhem was an act of treason.

By that point in the war, more than fifty thousand U.S. soldiers had been killed, three times that many had been seriously wounded, and hundreds of thousands of Vietnamese, Cambodians, Laotians, and

Thais, most of them civilians, had died in the maelstrom. Much of the goodwill and respect that earlier generations had earned for our country from other nations had been squandered. The current generation of young people—including my brother and, so far as I could tell, most of my students—had come to mistrust nearly everyone in authority, from parents and preachers to presidents. Now a minor authority myself, I felt a mixture of outrage and grief whenever I thought of the war, and I thought of it every time a siren went screaming past our house or a student asked me whether I saw any hope for America.

As the bombing intensified and television filled with images of gutted buildings, torched villages, GIs writhing on stretchers, and mutilated children, more and more students confessed to me the despair they felt about the future. The more lively their intelligence, the more likely they were to express fear, not merely for their own prospects here in America but for the prospects of life everywhere. Students nearing graduation asked me how I thought they could earn a living without selling out to the "Establishment," a word that summed up for them a conspiracy of the rich, who would stop at nothing, including the sacrifice of American soldiers and the devastation of foreign lands, to preserve their privileges. Find some real human need, I suggested—the need for shelter, say, or food, health care, education, community, art—and learn the skills necessary for meeting that need; or consider what gives you the deepest joy—beauty, say, or conviviality, kindness, laughter—and then devote yourself to bringing more of that richness into the world.

All the while I was talking to myself as well, trying to fend off my own fears about the state of America and the fate of Earth. As I watched my students teeter on the brink of despair, it occurred to me that the hope of young people was like seed corn, a potent reserve we would need to draw on in the future. We needed the young to believe that the world can be made better—more peaceful, more generous, more just. Yet most of them had been raised in a religion whose founder was crucified for challenging tyrants, and whose ministers, by and large, had avoided a similar fate for two thousand years by ignoring injustices or by collaborating with the powers that be. My students knew how risky it was to speak up against hatred, for the assassination of Dr. King was still fresh in their memory, as were the murders of war protesters at Kent State and Jackson State. On top of this discouraging history, many of the TV shows they watched and lyrics they heard and books they read treated life as absurd. No wonder they slid toward despair.

What happened to a nation that devoured its seed corn? What happened to a nation that turned its young into nihilists? I thought of Glenn, holed up in his rented room, scorning our parents. I thought of the honors student who had leapt to his death from the ninth floor of the building where I taught, the note he left behind proclaiming his disgust with the pirates running our ship of state. I thought of the kids too strung out on dope to read a book, too bitter to call home. I thought of those graduates, equally bitter, who saw no alternative but to dress up in suits and join the pirates and grab whatever they could get.

Many thousands of young people emerged from college during the Vietnam War determined, as I was, to help create a more just and peaceful society. But the worshipers of money had a stranglehold on our country, and I didn't see how, even in our thousands, we could break their grip. How could we halt the arms race or the wars of empire? How could we win back respect for America from the rest of the world? I would spend my life searching for answers to those questions. In the meantime, maybe I could help keep my students from sliding into cynicism. Maybe I could help them find voice for the feelings that lay clenched and confused inside them. Maybe I could put into their hands a story or a poem or a play that would lift their hearts, open their minds to the world's wonders, and renew their yearning for a life devoted to high ideals. The promise of doing such work, though modest and chancy, kept my own hopes alive.

In June, when the robin hatchlings had fledged and the parents were resting up before starting their next brood, Ruth felt certain once again that she was pregnant. She confirmed the hunch with her doctor before saying a word to me, and the word she did finally say, over supper one firefly evening, was the same one she had uttered joyously in our garden in Cambridge. Only this time she said it cautiously: "Papa."

With the same restraint, I asked, "Are you going to be a mama?"

"I'm working on it." She allowed herself a careful smile.

I slid a hand across the table and held one of hers. "How far along?"

"Two months. I'm due in January."

"January," I repeated, as if it were the name of a country.

"But that's a long way off."

A long way off, and much could happen between now and then. The miscarriage in England had taught us the danger of counting a baby before it was born. So this time we refrained from naming the fetus. For weeks, we told the news to no one, not even our families. We stored the cradle in a back room, out of sight, and we put off buying or borrowing the diapers, miniature clothes, playpen, and other paraphernalia we'd need. For the next month we rarely spoke of the baby. It wasn't superstition that held us back; we didn't fear we'd change the course of the pregnancy by uttering a careless word. We merely wished to avoid looking too far ahead, lest our hopes be crushed again.

Trying not to look ahead, I savored this burgeoning life day by day. Ruth never suffered morning sickness, yet her skin was flushed, and every glimpse of her set me thinking of the cells proliferating in her womb. When I stroked her belly, the heat under my hand seemed like the furnace of creation, as if she were a star fusing new elements in her depths.

The obstetrician told Ruth she was wonderfully healthy; the heart murmur from rheumatic fever had all but disappeared, and the fetus, he kept assuring her, was doing just fine. So at last we decided to announce the pregnancy to our parents, because we knew they'd be upset if we waited any longer. But we also knew that once the announcement was made, we'd be talking about the child from now on. There was no way of preparing for birth without risking the agony of another miscarriage.

We could telephone my parents in Oklahoma City, but Ruth wanted to deliver the news to her parents in person. Since we had no way of driving to Indianapolis, we invited the McClures to our place for a Sunday meal. Ruth's belly had begun to swell, but not enough to show under the loose blouse she wore as we opened the door to her parents. Before either of us could say a word, Mrs. McClure took one look at Ruth and said, "Oh, honey, you're pregnant!"

"Is that so?" Mr. McClure asked, raising his eyebrows.

For answer, Ruth threw her arms around her mother's neck, and the two of them swayed side to side.

Mr. McClure gave them a bemused look. "No one told *me*."

"She didn't tell me, either," said Mrs. McClure. "I could see it in her face."

For the rest of the visit, Ruth and her mother made plans for gathering the necessary baby gear, while her father asked me questions about life insurance, savings accounts, and cars. I told him we felt in good shape on the first two items, but we were holding off on buying a car.

"I see," Mr. McClure said. "Then how does Ruth Ann go to the doctor?"

"On her bike," I said. "The way she did in England."

"And in winter, when it's snowing?"

"We'll call a taxi."

Mr. McClure was never one to push, yet he could make his point through low-key persistence, as he could make everyone at the supper table aware of the dish he wanted merely by staring at it.

"What if the baby comes in the middle of the night?" he asked.

"Taxis run all night."

"I suppose they do." He paused, then delicately added, "If it's a question of money—"

I assured him we could afford a car. It was a matter not of money, but of principle. If everyone bought a car we'd never get decent buses or trains, we'd keep on building roads and malls, we'd cut ourselves off from neighbors and retreat into suburban castles, we'd burn up the world's dwindling petroleum, and we'd pour ever more filth into the air.

"That may well be," said Mr. McClure, who never seemed fazed by my tirades, "but if you change your mind, you might look at Buicks. We've always been pleased with ours."

When we flew to Oklahoma City to visit my parents a few weeks later, I tried the same arguments on my father, but he gruffly swept them aside. He told me he wasn't going to have his sweet daughter-in-law and his future grandbaby riding around on a bicycle or waiting around for a taxi. So the question wasn't whether to buy a car but what kind to buy. He favored Pontiacs, although he'd had a couple of good Fords.

When Ruth admitted she would feel safer with a car, I gave in, and asked Dad if he'd go along with me to dicker over prices with the dealers. But I refused even to consider any of the bloated, chrome-bedecked gas guzzlers from Detroit. I wanted a sensible car with high gas mileage and enough room in the back to haul a folded-up baby carriage. That's how Ruth and I wound up buying a little Fiat station wagon, which was the same ethereal blue as the Renaissance paintings of heaven we'd seen in Italy. As I signed the check, I felt I was taking another bite out of the apple from the tree of good and evil.

On our drive home to Indiana, I stopped every couple of hundred miles to check the oil and let the engine cool. Dad would have laughed at my precautions, for he believed in pushing cars to their limits. Yet I felt so guilty for owning a car at all, I wanted to make sure this one held up as long as possible. During one of those stops, Ruth recounted conversations she'd had with Mother, who'd given her enough advice during the few days of our visit to last until the baby was grown and out of college and ready to have a baby of her own.

"How does she know it's going to be a girl?" I asked.

"Because I told her," Ruth said.

"And how do you know? Did the doctor say?"

"No, no. It's how she moves." A faraway look came into Ruth's eyes. "Like right now. Here—feel." She laid my hand on her belly, choosing the spot carefully. At first I sensed only the familiar resilience and warmth, and then my fingers caught the faintest nudge, followed by two firm thumps, and I gave a loud whoop and Ruth jumped and I jumped and we both laughed and the baby kicked.

When I caught my breath, I asked, "So what tells you that's a girl?"

"I just know," Ruth said.

Given her certainty, there seemed little point in mulling over boys' names along with those for girls, but we did so anyway, just for the fun of it. And who knew, even if the baby was a girl, maybe we'd have a second child someday, and we might need a boy's name after all. I felt nervous even dreaming of a second child while the first one kicked in Ruth's womb, yet I got caught up in the glee of naming, as if I were tasting the wonder our legendary first parents might have felt while naming animals in the Garden of Eden. The wonder was not in the power of language but in the *need* for it, as new creatures kept pouring into the world, each one awaiting its name.

By the time we reached Indiana in our heavenly blue Fiat, we had a short list of names for boys, with Jesse in first place, and a longer list for girls, with Eva at the top and Rachel just behind. One of Ruth's best friends in Cambridge was an Eva, and so of course was that primordial mother in the Bible, whose name in Hebrew meant "life" or "being," as if she were the very mystery itself, the ceaseless outpouring that fills cradles and flings out constellations. Until we had spoken the name over and over in the car, listening to the music it made when combined with Rachel, neither of us mentioned that my mother was also an Eva. Then I recalled a song my father liked to sing when he was plumb happy, a song he'd made up while courting the Solomon girl in Chicago, with a refrain that went "She hits my heart like a shovel, and her name is Eva Mary." I sang it then, lifting my voice above the rattling four-cylinder engine and slipping the name of our hoped-for daughter into the refrain: "And her name is Eva Rachel."

In September of 1972, midway through her pregnancy, Ruth began taking classes that would lead to a master's degree in special education and I resumed teaching classes of my own. While choosing the books my students and I would read, I had searched for stories in which a husband and wife love one another deeply, feel grateful toward their parents, look forward to becoming parents themselves, and then welcome into their marriage a child who arrives like an emissary straight from glory land.

In my haphazard search I couldn't find any such books, at least none written well enough to deserve my students' dollars and time, although I found shelves of celebrated novels chronicling the failure of love, the betrayal and breakup of marriages, the spurning of parents, along with a litany of violent deaths. If pregnancy occurred in such fiction, it was usually a catastrophe rather than a blessing, and if children appeared at all, they were either walking reminders of guilt or pawns in grownup feuds. The keynote for all that literary misery was sounded in the first line of *Anna Karenina*: "Happy families are all alike; every unhappy family is unhappy in its own way."

If you wish to make significant art, I heard Tolstoy saying, you must delve into suffering, and I agreed with him, but surely there was plenty of pain to write about beyond that of star-crossed lovers or shattered families. Maybe with good parents behind you, a solid marriage to steady you, and children to bind your heart to the future, you would never think of yourself as a victim, indeed would think less and less about yourself at all, and you could bear witness to the suffering of those who really *are* victims, whether of prejudice, poverty, tyranny, or war. And in proportion as you thought less about your own small self, you could think more about the universe, every atom of it a gift from an inscrutable source, the whole whirl of bodies and beings caught up in a wild, breathtaking dance.

In the end, I found no great novels about happy families, so I settled for books whose authors clearly loved the world in spite of its darkness, and who held out hope for humankind in spite of our faults. During those anxious months leading up to the birth, I kept circling back to the need for hope, like a deer returning to a salt lick. Hope, this compound of courage and imagination, now seemed to me the essential ingredient not merely for a teacher or a writer but also for a father.

Ruth was determined to hold on to this baby until the due date in January, for on the first of that month Bloomington Hospital would begin allowing fathers into the delivery room, and she wanted me beside her to share in the birth. But as the semester wore on, and Ruth swelled like the waxing moon, her professors asked if she felt confident of sticking with classes through final exams in December. She told them not to worry, she'd finish just fine, and I believed her, for I'd never seen anyone more confident than Ruth was in those last weeks before the birth. She moved with unwavering purpose through the day, attending classes, writing papers, cooking, sewing, cleaning, turning the apartment into a nest. In the evenings, while I marked student essays, Ruth sat with one hand balancing a textbook and the other hand rubbing the mound of her stomach in leisurely circles, as if she were polishing a bowl, the corners of her lips turned up in the sly smile of a woman contemplating a secret.

Whatever confidence I felt, I picked up from Ruth or from the childbirth classes we attended on Saturday mornings in a church hall. There were nine couples in the class, all paired up in the approved Adam and Eve fashion, which made me wonder where single mothers and lesbians went to learn about bearing babies. Each woman sat on the floor atop her own blanket or mat, and each man knelt beside his rounded mate, while our ponytailed instructor, who looked too lean and spry to have borne three children, taught us exercises to protect the mother's body and strategies to ease her pain.

"Your wife is the athlete," she told the husbands, "and you're the coach. When she goes into her body, you must keep a clear head."

I seized on the instructor's words as if she were giving me directions for a perilous journey, even though she kept reminding us that nothing was more natural than childbirth. I made notes about the rhythmic breathing, the ambling walk, the back rubs, the chipped ice, the postcard showing a serene view, and everything else I would need to remember when Ruth was gripped by contractions.

Ruth had been gripped by a current from the moment of conception last April, or maybe even from the moment of her own birth, when eggs formed inside her like infinitesimal seeds, and now she was carried as if by a great river, while I paddled along trying to keep up. Her body itself was the boat, and the river was the one life that flowed through everything, so I rode the current as well, although I felt myself floundering in the eddies near shore, fighting through snags, looking for landmarks, while Ruth sailed on down the main channel.

By promising to achieve peace with honor in Vietnam, Richard Nixon won a second term as president that November, defeating George McGovern, the outspokenly antiwar candidate put up by the Democrats. The percentage of Americans who voted in the 1972 election was the lowest since 1948, and a significant majority of those who did vote seemed to endorse the relentless bombing of cities, the spraying of Agent Orange on forests, the dropping of napalm on civilians, and the fashioning of ever more powerful weapons. The complacency or complicity of so many fellow citizens disheartened me, even as the prospect of our coming child elated me. And this seemed to be the way of life, blessings coming to us against a background of sorrow.

In December, Ruth finished her classes, her term papers, and her final exams, just as she had predicted. While I was grading my own students' exams, the seventeenth and last Apollo mission took off for the moon. Since the first moon landing in 1969, these trips had become so routine, and Luna herself had proven to be so dull compared to Earth, that the launch of *Apollo 17* scarcely made a ripple in the news. But magazines did print a photograph taken from the ship soon after liftoff, showing the full earth luminous with reflected sunlight, a ball colored ocean blue, desert tan, forest green, and snow white, a bright globe wreathed in scarves of cloud and quietly shining against the black void of space. Pundits remarked that it looked like a blue marble. To me, this metaphor seemed too cold and hard. Our home planet looked more like an eye, alert and gleaming, or like an egg, brimming with life.

Ruth and I drove to Indianapolis the day before Christmas in order to spend the holiday with her parents, her brother and his family, two grandmothers, a great-aunt, and assorted in-laws. By then Ruth's brother was following in Mr. McClure's footsteps by pursuing a degree in accounting, having given up plans for a career in the Army, but I still couldn't talk with him or with anyone else in the family about the war.

We all pretended that people weren't dying under American bombs as we drank our eggnog, munched our cookies, and watched lights blink on the tree. We pretended that untold numbers of babies weren't starving in shantytowns and refugee camps around the world while we celebrated Ruth's pregnancy and the birth of Jesus. At the Christmas Eve service in the church where Ruth and I had been married, we all sang hymns and joined in prayers and celebrated God's gift of new life.

I could sing all the verses without looking at the hymnal, could recite the Gospel passages without looking at the Bible. These words and songs and rituals ran deep in me, deeper than the multiplication table, deeper than any physics equation, deeper than any poem or novel I had ever read, so deep that I could not have unlearned the elements of my childhood religion even if I had wanted to; and I did not want to. What I wanted was a larger view of life, a view more tender, more curious, more open to awe. I longed for a religion grand enough to hold the universe revealed by science. I wanted a religion generous enough to embrace all of the world's young, not merely the Christ child, not merely our own children, and not merely the offspring of our species, a religion that would keep a man from worshiping in the White House chapel and then going downstairs to order bombing raids on cities filled with strangers.

One Sunday afternoon in the third week of January, Ruth was knitting a pair of booties—not pink, not blue, but meadow green—while I read about the latest sorrows in the newspaper. Every now and again her fingers grew still, her breathing sped up, and I knew she was feeling a contraction. I would glance at my watch, and then glance again the next time she paused in her knitting. Twelve minutes apart. Ten minutes. Eight. No need to call the doctor until they began arriving every five minutes or less. She'd been feeling contractions off and on for the past week, so neither of us spoke of them now, didn't need to speak, our bodies were so attuned.

She had no appetite for the supper I cooked, and therefore neither did I, not because the supper was my usual amateur fare but because

Ruth had completely filled her skin, and could take in nothing more until this new child swam out of her. She kept shifting her weight in the chair, trying to find a point of comfort, and I kept looking at her as I put our nearly untouched food in the refrigerator, washed the dishes, watered plants on the windowsill, and swept the floor. When she grabbed the edge of the table, I said, "Remember to breathe, sweetheart."

Ruth nodded and then fell into the shallow panting we had practiced. After the pain eased, she tried smiling at me, but her lips wouldn't cooperate.

"Is this it?" I asked.

"I think so. I hope so."

"Let's walk."

She stood and looped an arm around my waist and leaned against me, and as we paced in slow circles through the apartment, I rubbed her lower back. Every time we passed the cradle, she reached out and set it rocking. Whenever a contraction made her stop, I stopped with her, and then I moved again when she lifted her foot, as if she were leading me in a dance. When the pains began coming five minutes apart, regular and hard, I called the doctor, who was already at the hospital delivering another baby; by the time he returned my call the interval between contractions was down to three minutes, and the doctor told me not to break the speed limit but also not to dawdle in getting to the hospital.

As I drove, I kept glancing at the rearview mirror, where I could see the moon, perhaps two or three days past full, rising into a clear night sky. Trying to imagine our child—an astounding phrase, "our child"—I thought of the full earth photographed from *Apollo 17*, this drop of life shining against the lifeless dark. I remembered watching the screen in Cambridge as a human stepped for the first time onto the moon's cold, dusty surface, and then seeing through a window the untelevised moon setting in the west. I remembered the night during science camp when I stood in line at the observatory behind a girl named Ruth, breathing in her scent, my heart pounding, and then took my turn gazing through the telescope at unimaginably ancient and distant galaxies. I remembered yearning to understand the forces that shaped the universe, yearning to build a spaceship and venture out there myself, a longing that stretched back through my childhood, back to a time before I learned of bibles or bombs, before I could read, before I had acquired much past or dreamed up any future, perhaps as far back as the instant when lightning shattered the oak while my father held me tight in his arms.

In the delivery room, Ruth's hand squeezed mine as she pushed. I was amazed by her grip, as I'd been amazed in childhood by my father's giant strength. How he would have loved to witness the birth of his children! Why had fathers been kept out of the delivery room in our hospital until this very month, and why were they still kept out of most delivery rooms? I was grateful to be here with Ruth, feeling the pressure of her hand, hearing her fierce breath. The effects of her pushing were visible in a mirror mounted at the foot of the birthing couch, the mouth of her womb gradually opening. I sat on a stool beside her, and with my free hand I wiped a damp cloth over her forehead, fed her chips of ice, rubbed salve on her lips. The hard labor lasted from one in the morning until nearly four, and all the while I bent down and murmured in Ruth's ear, the words rising from a place I hadn't known was inside me.

Ruth called back to me from a place I hadn't known was inside her, a run of grunts and laughter and shouts, culminating in an exultant roar when the baby's head emerged, with eyes blinking at the lit-up world, gray eyes in a red face, and with a tiny mouth that sucked in air before letting out a roar of her own, and then both shoulders emerged, then the arms, wildly waving, and then quickly the whole child, torso and legs and wriggling feet, a dancing girl, bound by her umbilical cord all the way back to the source of life, and then Ruth was holding Eva Rachel on her chest and bellowing right along with the baby, mother and child singing the oldest song.

EPILOGUE

ORN IN THE DEPTHS of winter, Eva met snow before she
met rain. As spring flamed up in our neighborhood, I took her
outside to meet the fresh grass, the flowers, the birds, the wind. Here is
the sun, I told her, and here is the moon. From the window of her bedroom at night I showed her the stars.

Then in April I bundled her in a blanket and carried her onto our
porch to meet a thunderstorm, as my father had carried me when I was
still small enough to ride in his arms. I sang to her as my mother had
sung to me, and between lullabies I named the blooms we could see
nodding in the rain—azaleas, bluebells, dogwood, forsythia, redbud—
names my mother had given to me. I was simultaneously a child, remembering my parents, and a man, holding my own child. The baby
shivered and I shivered with her as rain thrummed on the roof above us,
mist blew on our faces, lightning cracked the sky. This is what you are
made of, I told Eva, this water, air, earth, and fire. You are a sprout
from this astonishing ground. May you live long and well, with a heart
full of awe.

Ruth watched these maneuvers from indoors, wearing an indulgent
smile, never asking what I murmured to our child, trusting me to protect Eva from harm.

Thirty Aprils later, Eva was the one who showed trust in me as I
carried her newborn Elizabeth Rachel, only a few days old, onto the
porch of Eva and Matt's house to meet thunder and lightning and siz-

zling rain. Wrapped in a baby quilt that Ruth had made, Elizabeth dozed through most of the storm while I sang lullabies. Then a nearby flash and boom opened her eyes for a few seconds, long enough for me to tell her what I had told Eva all those years before. This is what you are made of, little one. Fire, air, water, earth. This is your marvelous home.

Notes

EPIGRAPHS

The passage from Walt Whitman appears in section 46 of "Song of My-self," which may be found in any standard edition of *Leaves of Grass*. Thomas Merton's remark originally appeared in his *Conjectures of a Guilty Bystander* (1966); I found it quoted in Patrick Hart and Jonathan Montaldo, eds., *The Intimate Merton: His Life from His Journals* (San Francisco: HarperSanFrancisco, 1999), p. 103.

50   Psalm 24:1–2, King James Version (KJV).

50–51   Amos 4:13; Isaiah 40:6–8, both KJV.

52   Isaiah 1:19–20; Jeremiah 4:25–26; Amos 5:18–19, all KJV.

52   Psalm 22:1–2, KJV.

56   The parable of the Good Samaritan is told in Luke 10. The line quoted is Luke 10:36, KJV.

77   Psalm 23:4, KJV.

97   Matthew 13:31–32, KJV.

100   Psalm 8:3–5, KJV.

103   William Blake, "The Marriage of Heaven and Hell" (1793), Plate 14.

118   Song of Solomon 7:1–3, KJV.

119   2 Timothy 2:22; Galatians 5:17, 24, both KJV.

153–54   Psalm 8:3–4, KJV.

161   John 1:1, Revised Standard Version (RSV).

162   John 1:2–5, RSV.

164 John 1:14, RSV.

165 John 3:16–18, RSV.

166 John 1:18, RSV.

166 Luke 17:20–21, RSV.

173 Psalm 68:20–23; Psalm 69:24–25, 27–28, RSV.

174 1 Corinthians 15:24–26, RSV.

179–80 The quotations from Martin Luther King, Jr.'s "I Have a Dream" may be found in James M. Washington, ed., *I Have a Dream: Writings and Speeches That Changed the World* (San Francisco: HarperCollins, 1992), on pp. 104–105.

183 Job 10:1, RSV.

184 Martin Luther King, Jr., in Washington, ed., *I Have a Dream*, p. 103.

202 Ralph Waldo Emerson, *Nature* (1836), in Joel Porte, ed., *Ralph Waldo Emerson: Essays and Lectures* (New York: Library of America, 1983), p. 10.

203 Henry David Thoreau, *Walden*, ed. J. Lyndon Shanley (Princeton: Princeton University Press, 1973): "Shams and delusions," p. 95; "Nearest to all things," p. 134 (italics in original); "This is a delicious evening," p. 129; "There are probably words," p. 107.

209 William Wordsworth, "Lines Composed a Few Miles Above Tintern Abbey" (1798), lines 93–102; available in any standard edition.

210 Amos 4:13, RSV.

214 "I Sing the Body Electric," section 2, lines 1–2, from *Leaves of Grass* (1891–92).

215 *The Journal of John Woolman* (Secaucus, N.J.: Citadel Press, 1972), p. 142.

220 Martin Luther King, Jr., "A Time to Break Silence," in Washington, ed., *I Have a Dream*, p. 150.

Thanks

As a child, I was blessed by the company of adults who honored my sense that the world is astonishing and that our brief transit here, alive and alert, is even more astonishing. Chief among those adults were my parents, as I have tried to show in these pages. But I also count as guides the librarians who placed in my hand just the books I needed to read, and the authors of those books, and the ministers who patiently answered my questions, and the teachers who shared with me their passion for learning. I name in this memoir only a sampling of my benefactors; I am grateful to them all.

Since leaving childhood, I have been blessed by the company of friends who've wondered aloud with me about the mystery at the heart of things. With apologies to the many I leave out, I list here a few of these inspiring companions: Jan and Harold Attridge, Charles Baldwin, Albert Barden III, H. Emerson Blake, Carol Bly, Julien Colvin, Malcolm Dalglish, Alison Deming, John Elder, Peter Forbes, Marion Gilliam, John Grim, Judith Klein, Kyle Kramer, Ursula K. Le Guin, Hank Lentfer, Guy Fitch Lytle III, Bill McKibben, Dorik Mechau, Christopher Merrill, Kathleen Dean Moore, Barbara and George Morgan, Carrie Newcomer, William Nichols, David Owen, Chet Raymo, Pattiann Rogers, Alvin Rosenfeld, George Russell, Carolyn Servid, James Alexander Thom, Mary Evelyn Tucker, and Helen Whybrow.

The writing of this book would have been delayed for years without the double gift of a sabbatical leave from Indiana University and a fellowship from the National Endowment for the Arts. I am grateful to the legislators and taxpayers who support the vital work of the endowment and the university. And I am grateful to my colleagues and students, who challenge me to keep thinking about literature, language, and life.

I warmly thank the editors of the following publications, in which portions of this book first appeared: *Image*, *Maize*, *The Missouri Review*, *Orion*, and *Witness*.

I offer thanks to Jonathan Galassi, for seeing promise in this book when it was only an idea, as small as a mustard seed; to my editor, Paul Elie, for helping the book find its proper shape; and to my agent, John Wright, for wise counsel throughout the long labor.

Finally, I thank my family—my late father, my mother, my sister and brother, my wife and children, my children's spouses, and my granddaughter—none of whom asked to become part of this book. I hope they will feel that I have represented them lovingly.